Sinead



# THE CONSTITUTION OF NORTHERN IRELAND

**Servicing the Legal System**

*The Servicing the Legal System Programme was inaugurated in August 1980 in the Faculty of Law of the Queen's University of Belfast to promote the publication of commentaries on various aspects of the law and legal system of Northern Ireland. Generous financial and other support for the programme has been provided by the Northern Ireland Court Service, the Inn of Court of Northern Ireland, the Bar Council of Northern Ireland, the Law Society of Northern Ireland, the Northern Ireland Bankers' Association, TSB Northern Ireland plc, and Queen's University. Details of all SLS publications may be obtained from the SLS Office, Faculty of Law, Queen's University, Belfast BT7 1NN, Northern Ireland.*

# THE CONSTITUTION OF NORTHERN IRELAND

**Brigid Hadfield**

*LLB, LLM,*

*Senior Lecturer in Law, The Queen's University of Belfast*

**Belfast**

**1989**

*First published in 1989 by SLS Legal Publications (NI) Ltd, Faculty of Law, Queen's University, Belfast BT7 1NN.*



ISBN 0 85389 330 6

Typeset by SLS Legal Publications (NI) Ltd
Printed by Express Litho Ltd, Belfast

*To my mother and father*

# PREFACE

However obvious the title of this book may seem, it has been carefully chosen. Let the disclaimer be made first. The book is not about the substantive constitutional laws of Northern Ireland. Those areas which have become virtually synonymous with Northern Ireland—special powers and emergency powers, police powers and army powers, fair employment and public order law, extradition and the prevention of terrorism—however vitally important (literally) they are, are not covered here. This book rather is concerned with forms and structures. It attempts to provide an account of the constitutional framework within which the constitutional laws operate. This book, therefore, is about the legislative and executive institutions of government in and for Northern Ireland and their powers. The main aim of the book has been to describe proposals, made over a period of one hundred years by successive United Kingdom Governments, for the governance of what is now Northern Ireland. An attempt has been made to bring to bear on this descriptive role whatever detachment is possible from one who is English, has a degree from a Scottish University and has taught Public Law at Queen's University for the last fifteen years. In an area where detachment is either not easy or not possible, I have tried to be fair in the presentation and consideration of the developments which have taken place. Where analysis may have led into an articulation of political preferences, the analytical role has been eschewed. The book, therefore, has a narrow but often neglected focus and so it has been written in the hope that it will be of some interest—and perhaps of some use—to those who care about Northern Ireland.

There are several people to whom I am particularly grateful for their assistance in the preparation of this book. My thanks go to Professor Herbert Wallace, formerly Director of SLS, to Mrs Sara Gamble, Miss Patricia McCann and Mrs Pauline Rainey of SLS, to Miss Elizabeth Madill of the Law Library at Queen's University, and to Mr J. A. D. Kennedy, Clerk to the Assembly, for their help and encouragement. My thanks also go to Dr Peter Ingram, Director of SLS, for his extensive and invaluable assistance and to my secretary, Mrs Janice McKee, for her customary cheerful and willing efficiency. For all the flaws and faults in the book, I bear sole responsibility.

The writing of the book was completed in the Spring of 1989, but it has proved possible to include various subsequent developments at the proof--

reading stage. For technical reasons, the chapter notes have had to be included at the end of each chapter rather than at the foot of each page. This is unavoidable, but it is hoped that this may perhaps facilitate both those who wish to read the book on a general level as well as those equally interested in the more detailed information.

Brigid Hadfield
The Queen's University of Belfast
July 1989

# TABLE OF CONTENTS

# INTRODUCTION

Northern Ireland has received of late, for often tragic reasons, a considerable amount of attention. All manner of persons have felt compelled to expound on the Province and its troubles. Historians, seeking to provide long-term explanations, trawl the centuries; political scientists provide their own amalgam of short-term assessments, prognostication and the propounding of political panaceas; and journalists, by very definition, provide that which is ephemeral. By contrast, constitutional lawyers have been hesitant to enter the field. The reasons are various, but revolve around two related explanations, one specific, one general.

First, although the Northern Ireland Parliament and Government were functional for only fifty years, for all but their final years they had an air of durability. Commentary during this time on the Province's constitution,[1] as largely contained in the Government of Ireland Act 1920, therefore, served contemporaneous purposes; the substance of what had been written was not converted into history before the printer's ink had dried. Since 1972, however, this has changed; constitutional lawyers wanting to make their own particular contribution to Northern Ireland have been compelled to become either constitutional historians or mere commentators on the constitutionally transient.

Direct rule (Phase I) began with the dissolution of the Northern Ireland Parliament in March 1972 and lasted until 1st January 1974; a devolved Assembly and Executive operated from January to May 1974 under the Northern Ireland Constitution Act 1973; the subsequent two-month holding operation yielded in July 1974 to direct rule (Phase II). Although the passage of time was to reveal that this system would last longer than its immediate post-1972 predecessors, the Act itself which re-introduced direct rule, the Northern Ireland Act 1974, bore testimony to the intended impermanence of the scheme, that is, to its interim nature. The Act made provision for a Constitutional Convention to be elected to deliberate on the future form of government for Northern Ireland. It duly met and sat for the better part of a year from May 1975 but it failed to achieve an agreed solution, and so direct rule continued. In November 1979 the Conservative Government, which had been returned to power at Westminster earlier that year, produced a "Working Paper for a Conference", which "conference", consisting of the leaders of most of the major political parties in Northern Ireland, met from January to March

1980. Although that conference was somewhat abortive, another White Paper containing "Proposals for further discussion" was published in July 1980, but further discussions led to no change—and so direct rule continued.

These three last-mentioned attempts to find a solution, although in themselves inconclusive, pre-empted any considered assessment of the merits of direct rule and of means of improving it as a system of government *in its own right.* This sequence of failed attempts to find an agreed, and, therefore, workable system of devolution, however, did not deflect the search for this seemingly elusive creature. By 1982 sufficient determination by the Westminster Government finally led to legislation on the matter, the Northern Ireland Act 1982, although it itself did not provide a scheme of devolution but merely provided the means of facilitating discussion geared to finding such a scheme. The 1982 Act provided for an elected local Assembly, possessing at its inception actual powers of scrutiny over both the legislative and executive aspects of direct rule, and bearing the potential, never fulfilled, of developing into a system of devolution as extensive as, although not necessarily identical to, the system which operated in Northern Ireland in the early months of 1974.

Virtually concomitant with the revival of the Assembly had been the formation in November 1981 of an Anglo-Irish Intergovernmental Council and at the third summit meeting of the Council in November 1985 the Anglo-Irish Agreement was signed. It created the Anglo-Irish Intergovernmental Conference into which the Government of the Republic of Ireland was empowered to put its views and proposals on political, security and legal matters as they relate to Northern Ireland and on the promotion of cross-border co-operation.

As a consequence of the signing of the Agreement, the Assembly, which was boycotted from its inception by both the Social Democratic and Labour Party and Sinn Feín, and which had discharged its scrutiny functions from January 1983, effectively ceased to operate other than to produce a report on the Agreement itself. The Assembly was formally dissolved in June 1986.

It is this pattern of constant change, actual or proposed, which has left constitutional lawyers feeling that they are dabbling in the impermanent. That in itself, however, is probably not sufficient to account totally for their current reluctance carefully to consider the Northern Ireland consititution. There is a second, more general but related, explanation and that is this: what, when all is said and done, is the distinctive contribution that a constitutional lawyer can make? This is not a dilemma confined to Northern Ireland. It is best explained in the words of Professor H. W. R. Wade in his 1980 Hamlyn lectures, entitled

*Constitutional Fundamentals*. In the course of these lectures he explained that he would

> wander outside the familiar paths explored by books on constitutional law which are for the most part content to describe in dispassionate detail institutions whose merits may be highly debatable. Perhaps in this respect the attitude of constitutional lawyers is in a transitional phase. The Blackstone-Bagehot-Dicey era was the age of self-satisfaction. Their successors today adopt a stance of fairly strict neutrality. The next era, I hope, will be that of the critics. Their service will be to hammer home the need for constitutional reform. The danger before them is obvious: this path leads straight into politics. But if the price of preserving the purity of constitutional law is that one must ignore the political pros and cons of what are, after all, our essential laws, then I would say that the price is too high and the lack of realism is excessive.[2]

If these comments are of application to the constitution of the United Kingdom as a whole, then *a fortiori* they apply to the constitution of Northern Ireland specifically, except perhaps the first stance: an air of self-satisfaction would scarcely be the most apposite as constitutions rise and fall with frightening rapidity. The choice is not easy. To espouse dispassionate neutrality, as Professor Wade indicates, is to invite the charge of unrealism. This is particularly the case when one is required to consider not only the system of government but also the very constitutional *status* of the country itself—and from status all else flows. To accept or to reject the status quo of Northern Ireland within the United Kingdom must relate to an awareness that goes beyond, or at least precedes, dispassionate neutrality. One also should always remember that the temptation for a constitutional lawyer to wrap up his or her own political preferences in the guise of dispassionate neutrality is great, although it should be resisted.

Yet to enter—overtly at least—the realm of political realism is not without its difficulties either. It becomes only too easy, particularly, again, when the main constitutional consideration is that of national status, to sacrifice law and the rule of law to political expediency.

Yet law still has a part to play. In this book, therefore, the emphasis has been mainly on the law—on how the long series of Acts of Parliament and intergovernmental treaties and agreements have sought to reflect, in one way or another, the various political preferences for Northern Ireland, preferences often passionately held and often fundamentally conflicting, which have also been given expression from a variety of platforms, other than Parliament, and by a variety of means, other than the law. Because much of the ground dealt with in the first three chapters has been comprehensively covered, from one perspective or another elsewhere,[3] the approach in them here has been deliberately selective. The aim has been to concentrate on the factors and on the structures, proposed or operational, which shed light on and assist in an understanding of the institutional developments dealt with in the later chapters. The book as a whole, however, addresses the unanswered question: how does one create an effective, fair and operational constitution for a country of one and a half million people, of whom approximately one million are Protestant and (largely) seek to maintain the Union with Great Britain, and half a million are Roman Catholic and (largely) seek an Ireland united outside and independent of the United Kingdom. The figures are provided with brutal simplicity but the question remains as complex and troubled as ever. Indeed, at the end of the day, the question remains.

## NOTES

1 The word is used here, as elsewhere in the book including its title, to refer to Northern Ireland's system of government. On occasion, the Government of Ireland Act 1920 has been referred to as Northern Ireland's "written constitution" thereby indicating the particular significance of the Act within the Northern Ireland legal system, although that term is not employed in this book. Even if the phrase is of some value, however, with regard to the 1920 Act, it is not appropriate with regard to any of the subsequent Acts of Parliament containing systems of government for Northern Ireland.

2 Pp 1-2.

3 So, for example, the financial relationships between Westminster and London from 1921 to 1972 have been omitted.

# I

# THE HOME RULE DEBATE 1886 TO 1914

## INTRODUCTION

Northern Ireland is part of the United Kingdom. Article 1 of the Union with Ireland Act 1800 enacted that the Kingdoms of Great Britain and Ireland would, from 1st January 1801 and "for ever after, be united into one kingdom, by the name of the United Kingdom of Great Britain and Ireland." Although that Article is now inoperative for the Republic of Ireland, Northern Ireland's status as part of the United Kingdom has continued unaltered to the present day. The most recent statutory reaffirmation of this status is section 1 of the Northern Ireland Constitution Act 1973 which declares that Northern Ireland remains part of Her Majesty's dominions and of the United Kingdom. The legal accuracy of these opening sentences, however, does not guarantee a universal political acceptability. The retention of Northern Ireland within the United Kingdom and its separation from the rest of Ireland in 1920-22 were the results of a compromise, first between the interests of the British Empire and those of Irish Nationalism and later, and more significantly, between Ulster Unionism and an increasingly separatist Irish Nationalism. The tensions inherent in the latter compromise have continued to the present day.

## HOME RULE — 1886

Although a historian may feel constrained to review Northern Ireland's emergence from a longer perspective, the chosen starting-point here is 1886, for that year witnessed the publication by the Liberal Prime Minister, William Gladstone, of the first Irish Home Rule legislative proposals. His opportunity to do this came as a result of the General Election held in November 1885. After it, the Liberals held 335 seats in the House of Commons, the Conservatives 249 and the Irish Nationalists 86. Of these eighty-six seats, one was held by the Member for Liverpool, Scotland Division, the rest being for Irish constituencies. This division of seats amongst the three parties meant that the Nationalists were sufficiently strong numerically so as to be able to keep either of the major parties out of office. In January 1886 they exercised this power and combined with the Liberals to defeat the minority Conservative administration led by Lord Salisbury. He resigned on 26th January and two days later Gladstone was invited to form his third administration.

By now, for whatever reasons, Gladstone was a convert to the cause of Irish Home Rule and on 8th April 1886 he introduced into the House of Commons the Bill designed to provide for internal self-government for the whole of Ireland, as a continuing part of the United Kingdom and subject to the supremacy of the Westminster Parliament.[1] Gladstone stood firm on the latter principle and on the principle of the unity of the Empire, but he believed that a scheme for Irish Home Rule could be accommodated within those two principles. In his preparation of this, the first Home Rule Bill, Gladstone had been greatly influenced by Edmund Burke's hundred-year-old analysis of the functions exercised by Westminster in her relations with the colonies, then most notably America. Burke had argued that Westminster possessed two separate functions, the Imperial and the local. The latter being distinct from the former could, therefore, be devolved to a local legislature without any diminution in the strength of the former.

Gladstone, adopting this division of functions, believed that local autonomy would strengthen not only the Imperial Parliament but also the Imperial ties—"the concession of local self-government is not the way to sap or impair, but the way to strengthen and consolidate unity",[2] he was to announce to the House on introducing his Irish Home Rule proposals. The recent Canadian experience supported him in these views; the British North America Act 1867 which had devolved to home-based institutions legislative and executive powers over matters of Canadian concern was visibly strengthening rather than weakening the Imperial tie.

Gladstone's proposals, therefore, had to combine a delicate and complex intertwining of factors that would both enshrine the amount of autonomy necessary to satisfy those who sought Irish Home Rule and also retain undiminished the supremacy of Westminster and the Imperial connection. Although Gladstone's scheme was unquestionably Imperialist in conception, its political acceptability—certainly outside Ireland—was to depend upon the unequivocal absence of separatist potential.

The leading radical Liberal Joseph Chamberlain, a member of Gladstone's Cabinet from January to March 1886, was deeply suspicious of the Prime Minister's Home Rule scheme, and Chamberlain, with considerable constitutional perspicacity, articulated the four questions which he identified as crucial in terms of their propensity towards separatism. The questions were :

(1) Whether Irish representation at Westminster was to cease;
(2) Whether a power of taxation was to be vested in the Home Rule Cabinet;
(3) Whether the judges were to be appointed by an Irish authority;
(4) Whether the Irish Parliament was to have authority in every matter not specifically excluded from its jurisdiction.[3]

All these questions Gladstone was to answer in the affirmative. The Bill, when published, contained the following scheme. There was to be instituted an Irish "Legislative Body" (note that, significantly, it was not termed a Parliament) with a life of five years and consisting of two Orders. The first Order was to be composed of 103 members, seventy-five elected by registered voters in the constituencies or "electoral districts" as scheduled to the Bill, and twenty-eight peers; the second Order was to be composed of 204 members, two members chosen by each existing Irish constituency, except for the City of Cork which was to return four members. The two Orders were to deliberate and vote together, but with provision made for separate voting if demanded and consequently also for the adjustment of disputes between the two Orders. The Irish Legislative Body was, by clause 2, to be given power "to make laws for the peace, order and good government of Ireland, and by any such law to alter and repeal any law in Ireland". This general grant of power was, however, subject to certain exceptions, listed in clause 3, namely matters of Imperial or national concern or matters on which, for practical reasons, local variation would be undesirable; for example the Crown, peace and war, the armed forces and the defence of the realm, treaties, dignities and titles, treason, trade, postal and telegraph services, beacons, coinage, copyright and patent rights were all to be beyond its competence. The Dublin Metropolitan Police and the Royal Irish Constabulary were to remain subject to the Lord Lieutenant while the forces subsisted, but the Irish legislature was to be empowered to establish and maintain a police force in Ireland under the control of local authorities. Furthermore, any law made in respect of the establishment or endowment of religion or imposing a disability or conferring a privilege in accordance with religious belief was to be void. Clause 37 of the Bill provided that:

[s]ave as herein expressly provided all matters in relation to which it is not competent for the Irish Legislative Body to make or repeal laws shall remain and be within the exclusive authority of the Imperial Parliament, whose power and authority in relation thereto, save as aforesaid, shall in nowise be diminished or restrained by anything herein contained.

Clause 25 conferred on the Judicial Committee of the Privy Council power to resolve any question referred to it by the Lord Lieutenant as to the extent of the powers of the Irish legislature or, on appeal, by any party to an action in which such a question was raised, and when such questions were considered, "there shall be added to the Judicial Committee . . . such members of Her Majesty's Privy Council being or having been Irish judges, as to Her Majesty may seem meet." Clause 36 preserved the appellate jurisdiction of the House of Lords in respect of all other Irish suits and actions.

The Bill provided in clause 24 that, once it came into force, Ireland would cease to return members to the House of Commons or representative peers to the House of Lords; under the fourth Article of the Acts of Union, twenty-eight Lords temporal of Ireland had been entitled to sit and vote in the House of Lords (hence the requirement of twenty-eight peers in the composition of the first Order), and Irish representation in the Commons had been fixed at 100, although that number was later increased. It was further provided by clause 39 of the 1886 Bill, however, that although power to amend the Bill itself remained at Westminster, such amendments had to be made either with the consent of the Irish Legislative Body testified by an address to her Majesty or by an Act for the passing of which there had been summoned to Westminster to vote in their respective Houses the peerage members of the first Order of the Irish legislature and representatives of the Irish "commoners".

Clause 5 provided that the Queen would have the same Prerogatives with respect to the summoning, proroguing and dissolving of the Irish legislature as with regard to the Imperial Parliament. The Executive authority was to remain vested in the Queen to be carried out on her behalf by the Lord Lieutenant, "with the aid of such officers and such council" as the Queen deemed fit. Further the Lord Lieutenant was to be vested not only with these Royal Prerogative powers but also, "subject to any instructions which may from time to time be given" by the Queen, with the power to give or withhold the Royal Assent to Bills passed by the legislature—this is known as the executive veto.

As far as the judiciary was concerned, existing judges at the time of the passing of the Bill, "if they are removable at present on address to Her Majesty of both Houses of Parliament", were to continue to be so removable. A judge appointed after the passing of the Act, however,

> [s]hall not be removed from his office except in pursuance of an address to Her Majesty from both orders of the Legislative Body voting separately, nor shall his salary be diminished or right to pension altered during his continuance in office.

Clause 12 enabled the Irish legislature to impose taxes to be paid into an Irish Consolidated Fund "for the purpose of providing for the public service of Ireland", but excluded from this power were duties of customs and excise, which were reserved to Westminster. Clause 13 provided for the annual contribution by Ireland to the separate Consolidated Fund of the United Kingdom of its share of the Imperial expenditure. This contribution included the yearly sums of nearly £1½ million as Ireland's share of the National Debt (which was reckoned at £48 million); of just over £1½ million on account of the army and navy; of £1 million for the Royal Irish Constabulary and the Dublin Metropolitan Police; and of £110,000 on account of the Imperial Civil expenditure. This arrangement was to continue for thirty years, during which period these annual contributions could be reduced or terminated, but not increased.

Three aspects of the Bill, namely (a) the extent of the legislative powers conferred on the Irish legislature, (b) the virtual termination of representation at Westminster and (c) the taxation of Ireland, caused the greatest difficulty, not only because they might, to the fear of those who supported the Union, have encouraged its dissolution, but also because they were central features in the two constitutional "models" then prevalent, namely, colonialism and federalism. These terms may be briefly defined. The relationship between the United Kingdom and its colonies was to a certain extent, by this time, controlled by the Colonial Laws Validity Act 1865, although the Act was increasingly overlaid by conventional rules and practices enlarging colonial (later dominion) power. The colonies already possessed the extensive power to legislate for the "peace, order and good government" of their territory but what was not clear, prior to 1865, was the extent to which they could legislate contrary to the law of England, both statute and common law, as it applied to the colony. The Act, therefore, in order to clarify the extent of Westminster's powers, provided that any law passed by a colonial legislature, which was repugnant to an Act of the Westminster Parliament expressly or by necessary implication extending to the colony, was to the extent of that repugnancy void and inoperative. This section, section 2, formally preserved Westminster's sovereignty *vis-à-vis* the colony. Otherwise the colonial legislature was free to legislate as it chose (subject to the increasingly obsolescent power of the Governor's veto), although power to deal with defence and external relations remained at Westminster by which, however, the colonies were not taxed and where they were not represented.

Federalism, on the other hand, relates to the internal distribution of legislative powers within a nation. The central legislature is entrusted by the constitution with power to legislate exclusively on matters of national concern; in it the nation as a whole is represented and the matters on which it legislates are financed by the nation as a whole. The "provincial" (for example, Canada) or "state" (for example, Australia) legislatures, which are in a federal system of co-ordinate status with the central legislature, have exclusive power to legislate on matters of regional concern and the relevant region only is represented in that legislature and finances the matters on which it legislates. Any questions arising from the precise distribution of the legislative powers between the federal and provincial parliaments are resolved by the courts.

So, for example and most pertinently here, under sections 91 and 92 of the British North America Act 1867 (now renamed the Constitution Act) the following division of powers was made in Canada. Section 91 gave the Federal Parliament the power to make laws "for the peace, order and good government of Canada" in relation to all matters not coming within the classes of subject assigned by the Act to the provincial legislatures. That is, under the Act the residue was located centrally. There was then enacted as part of this section a list of twenty-nine different classes of subject specified "for greater certainty but not so as to restrict the generality" of the grant of legislative power. The matters there listed included public debt, regulation of trade and commerce, taxation, the postal service, the armed forces, navigation, currency and patents and copyright. Section 92 listed sixteen classes of subject upon which each provincial legislature "may exclusively make laws", including in this enumeration direct taxation within the province in order to raise revenue for provincial purposes, the management and sale of provincial public lands and their resources, provincial prisons, charities and hospitals, and property and civil rights in the province.

In formulating his Home Rule or devolutionary proposals for Ireland, Gladstone was to draw on elements from both the colonial and the federal model. Before considering the difficulties inherent in such a proceeding, however, the three salient features mentioned above require more detailed consideration.

### (a) The extent of the legislative powers conferred on the Irish legislature

The most fundamental constitutional question which Gladstone's proposals raised related to Westminster's sovereign or supreme powers. A detailed constitutional critique of the Bill on this point was given by Sir William Anson.[4] He defined the "two marks or tests of a sovereign legislative assembly" as "first the power to make laws from which there is no appeal; and secondly, the power to alter its own constitution," and then argued that the Bill would "seem to impair the sovereignty of the Imperial Parliament in both these respects". As far as the first aspect of sovereignty is concerned, the 1886 Bill contained no clause similar to that in the Colonial Laws Validity Act 1865 preserving the supremacy of United Kingdom statute law within Ireland. Similarly, the other drafting device which could have been used but which was not was a clause explicitly preserving undiminished Westminster's overall sovereignty. Sovereignty, therefore, could only hang upon an implication, namely that Westminster being sovereign was, by definition, incapable of divesting itself by the Bill of its sovereignty, but even this implication stood uneasily beside the specific wording of clause 37 which seemed to exclude Westminster from those matters to be transferred to the Irish legislature. The crucial words of clause 37 provided that "all matters in which it is not competent for the Irish legislative body to make or repeal laws" shall remain within the exclusive authority of Westminster. From this Anson concluded:

> It seems almost impossible to say that clause 37 does not cast some doubt on the right of the Imperial Parliament to legislate for Ireland in such matters as are not withdrawn from the competence of the Irish Parliament.

It may be, of course, that it was envisaged that Westminster's overall dominance (as contrasted with its sovereignty) over all Irish matters, transferred or not, would have been preserved by, for example, the executive veto over Irish legislation or the power of the Lord Lieutenant under clause 25 to make a reference to the Judicial Committee of the Privy Council on the extent of the powers of the Irish legislature, although clause 25 could have been a double-edged sword, as will be seen below.

On the second aspect of sovereignty—the power of Westminster to amend the Home Rule Bill itself—Anson relied on clause 39 as tending to diminish sovereignty. At the least it imposed a procedural fetter on Westminster, enabling it to amend the Bill by a specific procedure only, that is, after an address from the Irish legislature signifying its consent to the amendment or with the presence at Westminster during the passage of the amending Bill of the representative Irish peers and commoners.

Anson, in order to press home his argument that the 1886 Bill threatened both aspects of Westminster's sovereignty, found a parallel authority not in the colonies (where an extensive grant of power was coupled with a clause expressly retaining Westminster's legislative powers) but in Ireland from 1782 to 1800—although it must be stressed that not all historians would agree with his analysis, not least because Anson seems to ignore the fact that although during this time the Irish had legislative and judicial independence they did not have executive independence, the Irish Parliament having no control over the Irish executive. This, however, is Anson's argument. The Act "6 Geo 1 c5"—better known as the Declaratory Act 1719—had, so that "the dependency of the Kingdom of Ireland on the Imperial Crown of Great Britain, as being inseparably united and annexed thereunto" might be better secured, provided that the Parliament of Great Britain

had, hath and of right ought to have full power and authority to make laws and statutes of sufficient force and validity to bind the Kingdom and people of Ireland.

This Act was repealed by the British Parliament in 1782 by "22 Geo 3 c53" which simply stated that

from and after the passing of this Act, the 1719 Act and the several matters and things therein contained, shall be and is and are hereby repealed.

This 1782 Act, argued Anson, elevated the Irish Parliament—"Grattan's Parliament"—from a subordinate and dependent status to a co-ordinate and independent status, and the fact that Westminster's sovereignty with regard to Ireland had been impaired by the passing of the 1782 Act was amply demonstrated by the bringing about of the Acts of Union of 1800. At all times, Anson pointed out, the British Parliament assumed that it was bound by the provisions of the 1782 Act and that at the time of the Union it was not empowered to legislate for Ireland or unilaterally to reincorporate the British and Irish Parliaments. That being so, Anson continued, the case that the 1886 Bill would also have impaired Westminster's sovereignty was the stronger, given the presence in the Bill of clause 39 particularly, but also clause 37 and clause 25, giving the Judicial Committee power to determine the extent of the Irish legislature's competence. Had the Irish legislature chosen to exercise its legislative powers in a way unacceptable to Westminster, which might then have chosen to counteract such a measure by passing its own legislation extending to Ireland on the same matter, the Judicial Committee could then have been called upon to determine not only the extent of the Irish legislature's powers but also those of Westminster.

For Professor A.V. Dicey also the scheme of the 1886 Bill raised many questions, but the allocation of legislative powers between Westminster and the Irish legislature caused him considerable concern. Not only was the question of sovereignty called in issue but further, he commented,

The powers of the Irish Parliament are, it should be noted, indefinite. The Parliament, that is to say, may pass any law which it is not under the Constitution forbidden to pass... The difference between a legislature of definite and a legislature of indefinite powers is important. In the one case changes of circumstances may diminish but cannot increase the authority of the legislature; in the other case changes of circumstances may increase but cannot diminish that authority. The Irish Parliament is a body whose authority will, from the necessity of things, tend constantly to increase.[5]

It should be noted that Dicey used the word "Parliament" because he believed that the avoidance of that word in the Bill was little other than political cowardice. Given that the Imperial Parliament could have amended the allocation of powers in the Bill only (according to one construction of its terms) with the consent and participation of members of the Irish legislature, Dicey's point becomes of greater significance.

### (b) The termination of representation at Westminster

The arguments of constitutional lawyers, however—even given that Dicey at the least was concerned to espouse no cause that would have encouraged the dissolution of the Union—are rarely decisive of major issues. One slogan of value to both constitutional lawyers and politicians, was, in terms of the 1886 Bill, to prove more immediately decisive and that was the slogan "No taxation without representation" for the Bill through clauses 24, 12 and 13 seemed to achieve just that.

Termination of Irish representation at Westminster undoubtedly carried certain advantages in terms of the proceedings in the House of Commons. The Irish Nationalists, at this time, were conducting an increasingly obstructionist campaign on the floor of the House. How successful these tactics had been in preventing the conduct of Government business can be seen from the procedural changes which were introduced during the 1880s (although the Irish Nationalists' tactics were probably the catalyst rather than the sole cause of the change). 1881 saw the introduction of the closure motion, the device for ensuring that debates could be terminated once a certain period for discussion had elapsed, rather than be allowed to exhaust themselves naturally. In 1882, adjournment motions, previously a much favoured obstructive tactic because they could be used without restriction to set aside regular business, were limited to what, in the opinion of the Speaker, constituted a sudden emergency. In 1886, changes (incorporated in Standing Orders in 1888) were made with regard to Parliamentary questions. Prior to 1886, questions had usually been read in full before the House and no advance written notice of them had been required. Because Parliamentary questions were always set in the timetable to precede public business, any expansion in their number meant an erosion in the amount of time available for Government business. The second half of the nineteenth century had witnessed a massive growth in the number of Parliamentary questions, not least because of the use made of them by the Irish Nationalists. The changes of 1886 terminated the practice of reading questions and required written notice to be given. Their value as an obstructive device was thus weakened.[6] Little wonder it is, therefore, that as Dicey wrote, not a little cynically,

> English statesmen ... first began to think that the demand for Home Rule might have something in it when the refusal to erect a Parliament in Dublin meant the continuance of obstruction in the Parliament at Westminster. The terror of obstruction has, to speak the plain truth, done more to effect the bona fide conversion of English members into advocates of Home Rule than any other single influence.[7]

Procedural difficulties encountered by the House of Commons, however, could—and should—not be the sole determinant of the course of constitutional and political developments, although the converse may often appear to be the case. A more telling argument against the continued representation of the Irish at Westminster after Home Rule was the argument based on the inequity of permitting Irish members to continue to speak and vote on matters of exclusively mainland British concern, whilst equivalent Irish matters were to be decided solely by an Irish legislature. A theoretically possible compromise —Irish representation at Westminster for matters of Imperial concern only, a compromise which would have seemed necessary under the Burkean analysis—was excluded by Gladstone on the ground that it might lead to a House of Commons composed of different political majorities for different purposes. The task of forming and operating a collectively responsible Government in such circumstances would have been both politically undesired and constitutionally undesirable.

An alternative compromise to the "in-and-out" proposal would have been to retain Irish representation for all matters handled at Westminster, but in reduced number, but this compromise likewise had several difficulties. Logically, it did not meet the objection to the influence of Irish members on non-Irish affairs. It was, further, not known what level of representation would be acceptable to both the Irish Nationalists and the British Parliament. More fundamental still was the related objection that the acceptability of this compromise depended upon the numerical balance at Westminster between the two major parties. When the Conservatives and Liberals were finely balanced, even a minimal Irish representation would have been crucial.

### (c) The taxation of Ireland

Both compromises, therefore, contained considerable flaws, but the total exclusion of Irish representation to which Gladstone adhered in 1886 raised the spectre of the constitutional monster of taxation without representation, given the unequivocal meaning and effect of clauses 12 and 13. Politically this combination of clauses was crucial, for it guaranteed the opposition to the Bill of Joseph Chamberlain. Apprised in March 1886 of what the contents of the Home Rule Bill would be, he had already resigned from the Cabinet when the Bill appeared in April. His resignation ensured the split of the Liberal party and the defeat of the Bill in the House of Commons by 343 votes to 313, 93 Liberals voting against the Bill.

Although political opposition to the Bill proved decisive, other interpretations of the Bill should not be ignored and some, at least, were to bear fruit in terms of the details of subsequent Home Rule proposals. Dicey's opposition to the taxation provisions of the Bill was directed to a different consideration from that which persuaded politicians. He argued, using a significantly emotive word:

> If England gives Ireland semi-independence and at the same time makes Ireland pay tribute, all the conciliatory effects of Home Rule will be lost. If Home Rule is to have even a bare chance of producing in Ireland ... contentment... Ireland, the poorest of all civilised countries, must be freed from Imperial taxation, which would not be tolerated by the richest of our colonies.[8]

## Conclusions

A novel constitutional expedient had, thus, been tried and had failed. It had failed inevitably for political reasons, but it is nevertheless worth considering the extent of the novelty of Gladstone's design. The weaknesses of fusing elements from colonialism and elements from federalism were stressed by both Dicey and Anson in virtually identical terms, and to be able to stress constitutional niceties was a luxury which was increasingly to be whittled down by the dominance of political arguments. Dicey explained the constitutional weaknesses of the 1886 Bill as follows:

> From federalism is borrowed the idea of leaving the settlement of constitutional questions to a court. But the conception is spoilt in the borrowing. ... The Privy Council lacks moral authority, for it is an English court sitting in England and representing English opinion. ... From federalism again is borrowed the contribution by Ireland towards meeting the expenses of the Empire. But imposts which under a federal

system are a tax towards the payment of common expenditure are under the Gladstonian Constitution a tribute to a foreign power. From the federal system again is taken that restriction of legislative authority (that is, clause 3) ... which under any circumstances is a source of irritation ... From the Colonial system, on the other hand, is derived the theoretical supremacy of the British Parliament (and) the right of veto (of the Lord Lieutenant) ... From the colonies we therefore bring to Ireland sources of dispute, of friction, and of irritation, which are unknown to a true system of federalism, whilst we do not give to Ireland that practical independence (for example, freedom to make laws affecting trade and freedom to defend the state) and that immunity from taxation, which prevent our ill-arranged connection with the colonies from causing real dissatisfaction.[9]

More concisely and increasingly more prophetically Dicey further warned:

It is not the colonial system, but the conditions which make that system succeed, which ought to engross our attention.[10]

Devolution of power, however, whether it takes a thoroughbred or mongrel form, is only a satisfactory expedient when the value of the Imperial tie or Union is not put in question. It can satisfy only the needs felt for greater autonomy over matters of local concern and that is what has been meant by "Home Rule" so far—the conferment upon Ireland of autonomy over Irish affairs, that autonomy being exercised by local representative institutions and a responsible government. No real opposition, in this first period, certainly amongst parliamentarians, was made manifest against the overall sovereignty of Westminster. Devolution, however, cannot satisfy national that is, separatist, aspirations—nor, for that matter, is total separation a universally satisfactory solution when a significant proportion of people wish to retain the Union. As the Home Rule saga evolved the tensions inherent in attempting to reconcile Irish Nationalism as defined and the sovereignty of Westminster became less important. Irish Nationalism became increasingly separatist and consequently more telling became the tensions between Unionism and that increasingly separatist Nationalism. Indeed, it was on this point that Chamberlain made his most revealing comment. In the second reading debate on the doomed Bill of 1886 he stated:

It is the difficulty, one of the great difficulties of this problem, that Ireland is not a homogeneous community—that it consists of two nations—that it is a nation which comprises two races and two religions.[11]

Meanwhile Anson, well aware that Gladstone, given the opportunity, would attempt again to give Home Rule to Ireland, argued on the need for clarity in constitutional thinking. The constitution proposed for Ireland by the 1886 Bill was, he commented,

> neither a colonial nor a federal constitution, but contained some features of both in a blurred and imperfect form. Mr Bryce (the Under-Secretary of State for Foreign Affairs) treated it as providing for Ireland institutions similar to those of our colonies, but the powers conferred were far narrower than the legislative powers granted to our colonies, while, so far as they went, their subordination to the Imperial Parliament (if it existed) was sedulously veiled. The position assigned to the Judicial Committee of the Privy Council carries with it the suggestion of federation, but there was no provision for the representation of federated Ireland in the Imperial Parliament, nor any machinery for carrying out the judgments of the Court .... It is to be hoped that any future scheme for the better government of Ireland will not halt in this way between irreconcilable forms of constitution.[12]

He argued that a scheme, if it were not to involve separation, should either be strictly colonial, in which case Ireland should be given greater legislative powers but made explicitly subordinate to Westminster, or federal, in which case there would have to be a written constitution carefully delineating legislative powers, to be interpreted by a judiciary and enforced by the Executive, and giving Ireland representation in the Imperial Parliament. A third option would be, he concluded, an extension of local government, but that nobody really wanted.

## HOME RULE—1893

In July 1886, after the defeat of his Bill, Gladstone decided to appeal to the electorate and suffered considerable reverses. 394 seats went to the Conservatives, including 78 dissentient Liberals or Liberal Unionists. Those Parliamentary candidates who supported Home Rule and who were returned numbered 191 Liberals and 85 Nationalists. Lord Salisbury returned to power. In 1892, however, Gladstone embarked upon his fourth term of office as Prime Minister, the election of July 1892 having left the Conservatives with only 268 seats and the Liberal Unionists with 47. In February 1893, Gladstone introduced into the Commons his second "Irish Government" Bill. It differed from the 1886 Bill in certain significant respects. The Preamble to the Bill immediately disposed of any lingering concern regarding the sovereignty of Westminster in connection with Irish Home Rule and proclaimed:

> Whereas it is expedient that without impairing or restricting the supreme authority of Parliament, an Irish Legislature should be created... .

The Irish legislature, with a life of five years, was this time to consist of the Queen, and of two Houses, a Legislative Council, composed of forty-eight directly elected councillors, and a Legislative Assembly, composed of 103 members, returned by the existing Parliamentary constituencies in Ireland. Clause 8 provided for the resolution of disagreement between the two Houses, the powers of which were to be to legislate for "the peace, order and good government of Ireland", subject to certain exceptions relating to matters of Imperial or national concern. Clause 3(7), however, instead of excluding trade *simpliciter* from the Irish legislature's competence, excluded more specifically "trade with any place out of Ireland". Similarly, the powers of the Irish legislature did not extend to the making of laws respecting the endowment or establishment of religion or interfering with the free exercise thereof. That same clause, clause 4, also provided by "subsection" (5) that its powers did not include the making of any law:

> [w]hereby any person may be deprived of life, liberty, or property without due process of law, or may be denied the equal protection of the laws, or whereby private property may be taken without just compensation.

Gladstone, this time, attempted to deal with the question of Irish representation at Westminster by resort to an "in-and-out" clause. The Irish representative peers in the House of Lords were to be retained and there were to be eighty members returned to the Commons to represent Ireland, but clause 9 originally stated that neither an Irish peer nor an Irish member was entitled to "deliberate or vote on" any matter relating exclusively to Great Britain or on any motion or resolution relating solely to some tax not raised or to be raised in Ireland. This restriction was, however, removed from the Bill at its Committee stage.

Clause 10 of the 1893 Bill set up an Irish Exchequer and Consolidated Fund separate from those of the United Kingdom and by "subsection" (2) provided:

> The duties of customs and excise and the duties on postage shall be imposed by Act of Parliament, but subject to the provisions of this Act the Irish Legislature may, in order to provide for the public service of Ireland, impose any other taxes.

All the public revenues raised in Ireland were to be paid into the Irish Exchequer and form an Irish Consolidated Fund, the duties of customs being paid into the Exchequer of the United Kingdom. Clause 12 regulated the financial arrangements between the United Kingdom and Ireland and was less exacting than its 1886 counterpart. It stated:

> The duties of customs contributed by Ireland and ... that portion of any public revenue of the United Kingdom to which Ireland may claim to be entitled ... shall be carried to

the Consolidated Fund of the United Kingdom, as the contribution of Ireland to Imperial liabilities and expenditure as defined in the Third Schedule.

Schedule three defined "Imperial liabilities" as including the National Debt and "expenditure" as including expenditure on Naval and Military expenditure and Civil expenditure, including the Civil List. These arrangements were to be subject to review after fifteen years following an address to the Queen from either the House of Commons or the Irish Legislative Assembly. Although the tenure of the judges was the same as that provided for by the 1886 Bill, the 1893 Bill provided that Irish appeals to the House of Lords would cease, such appeals going instead to the Judicial Committee of the Privy Council, which, when hearing such cases, would be composed of not less than four Lords of Appeal and "at least one member who is or has been a judge of the Supreme Court of Ireland". Clause 23 made special provision for the speedy determination of the question whether any Irish Act or any of its provisions was beyond the powers of the Irish legislature: such questions were to be referred by the Lord Lieutenant or a Secretary of State to the Judicial Committee then constituted as if hearing an appeal from a court in Ireland.

Clause 33 reinforced the declaration of Westminster's sovereignty in the Preamble by incorporating a clause very similar to that operating with regard to colonial legislation, although phrased positively rather than negatively:

The Irish Legislature may repeal or alter any provision of this Act which is by this Act expressly made alterable by that Legislature, and also any enactments in force in Ireland, except such as either relate to matters beyond the powers of the Irish Legislature, or being enacted by Parliament after the passing of this Act may be expressly extended to Ireland. An Irish Act, notwithstanding it is in any respect repugnant to any enactment excepted as aforesaid, shall, though read subject to that enactment, be, except to the extent of that repugnancy, valid.

The provision of the Bill expressly made alterable by the Irish legislature was found in clause 7(3) which enabled it, after six years from the passing of the Bill, to alter, with regard to the Legislative Assembly,

the qualification of the electors, and the constituencies, and the distribution of the members among the constituencies, provided that in such distribution due regard is had to the population of the constituencies.

Clause 9(5), however, expressly withheld from it power to legislate with regard to the election laws and laws relating to the qualification of electors for Westminster elections.

The Executive powers under the Bill were largely the same as under the

1886 Bill. Clause 5(2), however, provided that there "shall be an Executive Commitee of the Privy Council of Ireland to aid and advise in the government of Ireland", appointed as the Queen may think fit "or as may be directed by Irish Act". Clause 5(3) then stated that the Lord Lieutenant shall give or withhold the Royal Assent to Irish Bills on the advice of the Executive Committee "subject nevertheless to any instructions given by Her Majesty in respect of any such Bill." Hence the executive veto over Irish legislation was retained.

The provisions of the 1893 Bill, compared with those of 1886, were clearer, more refined. Their hybrid nature remained, but less markedly, so that one could more easily perceive devolution within a State as a constitutional system in its own right rather than as one simply borrowing mixed aspects of colonialism and federalism. The sovereignty of Westminster was not threatened overtly at least, for devolution must inevitably carry the potential for fostering separatism most particularly where, as here, the devolved legislative power was general, subject to exceptions, rather than consisting of enumerated heads. As Dicey remarked "from the necessity of things" such a distribution of power means that the devolved legislature is endowed with constantly increasing powers. Extensive powers were given to the Irish legislature, which also had greater financial flexibility in order to exercise those powers more effectively and more independently. The Judicial Committee was integrated more fully into the Irish legal system and Ireland itself remained more properly a part of the conduct of affairs at Westminster.

Time, however, was running against both Gladstone and his Irish Home Rule proposals. Although the House of Commons, learning to accommodate party discipline, voted in favour of the Bill, the House of Lords voted against it by 419 votes to 28. In light of the electoral reverses suffered after the July 1886 General Election, the Cabinet advised Gladstone not to seek a further General Election on the issue and the Bill was simply dropped. In March 1894, Gladstone, however, resigned as Prime Minister and in 1898 he died.

## INTERLUDE

Meanwhile it was becoming increasingly clear that to satisfy Home Rule aspirations was not Westminster's sole responsibility. Chamberlain's warning that Ireland was not a homogeneous nation meant that there was good reason to suppose that the whole nation did not support Home Rule, certainly as embodied in one all-Ireland legislature based in Dublin—and it did not. From 1886 Unionist opinion in Ireland began to crystallise as a separate force to be reckoned with in any Home Rule debate. At this stage, it would be premature to talk of the emergence of the Ulster Question, that is, how to accommodate the distinct interests and opinions in the nine counties constituting the northern Province in Ireland (namely Armagh, Antrim, Down, Londonderry, Tyrone, Fermanagh, Donegal, Monaghan and Cavan). For the first fifteen to twenty years after the 1886 Bill, the main Unionist stance throughout Ireland was to identify Unionism with the interests of Ireland as a whole. Increasingly, however, the focus of Unionist thought moved specifically to Ulster, that being where the Unionists were largely concentrated (Unionists in the South being more scattered and less able to "group" and indeed increasingly inclined to define their aspirations differently from those of the Ulster Unionists). The cause of Irish Nationalism seemed to the Ulster Unionists increasingly to militate against their own interests. It would probably not be unfair to state that Irish Nationalists made little effort to define their cause as one embracing *all* Irish people. The main basis of their movement indeed was *territorial* unity or integrity. As a result of the extension of the franchise by the Representation of the People Act 1884 to cover some 60 per cent of the adult male population, the Irish Nationalists were able, as has already been seen, to return some 85 members to Westminster from Ireland. The party, however, already openly supported by the Roman Catholic hierarchy and supporting the principles of Roman Catholicism, seemed to present Home Rule as a Roman Catholic rather than an all-Irish policy. It became increasingly easy for a Protestant to believe that Home Rule meant "Rome Rule". Already the fusion of Nationalist with Roman Catholic and Protestant with Unionist, although not an invariable convergence, was widespread.

Also, the institution both of the Gaelic Athletic Association, formed in 1884 to promote Gaelic sports and to discourage Irish participation in "foreign" sports, including cricket and soccer, and of the Gaelic League in 1893, formed to foster the revival and continuance of the Irish language, served further to alienate the Protestants from the Nationalist movement, although these bodies were not in themselves necessarily sectarian, at least at their inception.

The Unionists themselves, therefore, began to organise in order to resist Home Rule. Already phrases, which were to be of emotive force, if not prophetic value, were to hand. Lord Randolph Churchill had proclaimed in 1886 "Ulster will fight; Ulster will be right" and in 1892, the Duke of Abercorn had declared "We will not have Home Rule". At the national level, the Conservatives, for a multiplicity of reasons, espoused the Unionist cause, and this gave it a national platform from which to be aired. Locally the Orange

Order (formed in 1795 "to maintain the laws and peace of the country and the Protestant constitution")[13] revived from its slumbers of the mid-nineteenth century to give a certain cohesion to Protestant Unionism, which aimed at retention of the status quo. Further in 1905, the Ulster Unionist Council was formed. Although Unionist organisations had developed from 1886, the Council became the focal point of Unionism in Ulster, the central council consisting of two hundred representatives of, for example, local Unionist associations, Orange Lodges, Members of Parliament and Peers. The machinery to resist Home Rule was now ready, if not yet fully operational.

Meanwhile against this background, the quest for Irish Home Rule in Parliament continued at a slower pace although other developments during this time such as land reform and local government reform made Home Rule increasingly inevitable. There was little Government interest in the matter once the Conservatives were returned to power in 1895. During 1903 there was hatched a scheme (by the Irish Reform Association) by which an Irish Assembly might be given power to initiate Public Irish Bills, and by which a "financial council" could control and administer some £6 million per annum for Irish affairs, (subject to the overriding power of the House of Commons). The plans were prematurely leaked, however, and Unionist wrath buried them in their infancy—to mix metaphors. The return of the Liberals to power in December 1905, confirmed by a General Election in January 1906, meant that Parliamentary interest in Home Rule revived, although the formation of the Sinn Féin party in 1905, espousing a more militant, that is separatist, form of Irish Nationalism than that espoused by the Irish (Nationalist) Parliamentary Party, made it increasingly likely that any Home Rule proposals would have to be more rather than less extensive. In 1907, the Irish Chief Secretary, Mr Augustine Birrell, (perhaps best known for his involvement in the legislation which set up the National University of Ireland and the Queen's University of Belfast in 1908) and the Attorney General for Ireland introduced into the House of Commons the Irish Council Bill. It proposed the institution of an Administrative Council in Ireland, consisting of 107 members partly elected, partly nominated. By clause 2, the Irish Council was to be given administrative rather than legislative powers over certain local departments, including the Local Government Board (Ireland), the Department of Agriculture and Technical Instruction for Ireland, the Congested Districts Board for Ireland, the Commissioners of Public Works (Ireland) and the Commissioners of National Education in Ireland. Such bodies were to be required to act in the exercise of their powers in accordance with any resolution of the Irish Council. By clause 3 the Lord Lieutenant had the power to reserve any question concerning the exercise of even these limited powers. The work of the Council was to be financed mainly by an annual grant from the Consolidated Fund of the United Kingdom. This was clearly very far removed in substance from the provisions of the earlier two Home Rule Bills—indeed it cannot with any accuracy be classified as a Home Rule Bill. It incorporated only administrative rather than executive and legislative devolution. It was rejected by the Irish Nationalists and made no further progress.

Subsequent significant developments at Westminster, particularly with regard to the powers of the House of Lords, however, made the enactment of a Home Rule Bill imminent. After the Liberals were returned to power in 1905-6, the House of Commons and the House of Lords, which had a permanent Conservative majority and possessed equal legislative powers to those of the Commons (except, in deference to the Commons' privileges, with regard to the *amendment* of Financial Bills), came increasingly into conflict. In 1909, the House of Lords *rejected* the Finance Bill and after two General Elections were held, virtually solely on the question of the powers of the House of Lords, the Liberal Government once re-elected introduced a Bill to curb the powers of the Upper House. The Liberals, in order to secure a majority in the Commons, generally needed the support of the Irish Nationalists and such was given as a *quid pro quo* for the introduction of a Home Rule Bill. Consequently in 1911, Parliament passed (the House of Lords reluctantly under threat of being flooded with Liberal peers) the Parliament Act which removed from the House of Lords the power of absolute veto over the vast majority of public Bills and substituted the power to delay such Bills for just over two years; that is, the 1911 Act required the House of Commons to approve a Bill in three successive sessions before it could be submitted for the Royal Assent without the Lords' consent. The Act exempts from this provision Bills to prolong the life of Parliament, which Bills must still receive the consent of the House of Lords. Further, the House of Lords from 1911 has possessed with regard to Bills certified by the Speaker of the House of Commons as "money bills" a delaying power of only one month.

## HOME RULE — 1912–14

It was, once this Bill was enacted, quite apparent that the Government could now succeed in translating a Home Rule Bill into law. True to its promise to the Irish Nationalists, the Liberal Government, now led by Herbert Asquith, introduced in 1912 the Government of Ireland Bill. It departed very little from its 1893 predecessor. The legislature to be instituted was, for the first time, termed a Parliament and inserted into the body of the Bill instead of the Preamble—clause 1(2)—was the statement:

Notwithstanding the establishment of the Irish Parliament or anything contained in this Act, the supreme power and authority of the Parliament of the United Kingdom shall remain unaffected and undiminished over all persons, matters, and things in Ireland and every part thereof.

The Parliament was to be bicameral consisting of, first, a forty-member Senate. Under the Bill as finally enacted, the first senators were to be nominated by the Lord Lieutenant, and afterwards were to be elected, according to the principle of proportional representation, by the four Provinces of Ireland (Ulster, Leinster, Munster and Connaught). There was also to be a House of Commons, consisting of 164 members elected on a constituency basis. Irish representation at Westminster was to continue but at a lower level than that proposed by the 1893 Bill—forty-two members rather than eighty. There was, however, no "in-and-out" clause this time; the Irish members were to have powers and functions identical to those who represented British constituencies.

The legislative powers of the Irish Parliament followed in principle the set pattern—the general grant of power to make laws for the "peace, order and good government" of Ireland, subject to specified exceptions, again including defence and trade with any place outside Ireland. Certain other matters were reserved from its powers, including the collection of taxes, the Royal Irish Constabulary and the Post Office, each of which was subject to special regulation—for example, the Royal Irish Constabulary was to be transferred from Westminster to the Irish Parliament after six years had expired from the passing of the Act. The Irish Parliament was also prohibited from enacting any law which interfered with religious equality. Clause 4(5) of the 1893 Bill—the clause reminiscent of the American Bill of Rights—was not repeated. The Executive authority was delineated along the lines of the 1893 Bill albeit in greater detail, and the Executive veto over Irish Bills was again retained. The power of Westminster to legislate for Ireland in respect of all matters, whether within or outside the Irish Parliament's competence, was clearly stated in clause 41:

(1) The Irish Parliament shall not have power to repeal or alter any provision of this Act ...or of any Act passed by the Parliament of the United Kingdom after the passing of this Act and extending to Ireland, although that provision deals with a matter with respect to which the Irish Parliament have powers to make laws.
(2) Where any Act of the Irish Parliament deals with any matter with respect to which the Irish Parliament have power to make laws which is dealt with by any Act of the

Parliament of the United Kingdom passed after the passing of this Act and extending to Ireland, the Act of the Irish Parliament shall be read subject to the Act of the Parliament of the United Kingdom, and so far as it is repugnant to that Act, but no further, shall be void.

The details of the legislation, however, no longer arrest the attention. The intention of the Bill was to devolve power to a home-based Parliament and Government in Ireland, subject to Westminster's sovereignty and with Ireland remaining as an integral part of the United Kingdom. For the Irish Nationalists, particularly that strand of thought represented by Sinn Féin with its aspirations of a sovereign Ireland, it was too little, too late. For the Ulster Unionists, with their distrust of both one all-Ireland Parliament and of the increasingly uncompromising Irish Nationalism, it was, simply, too much. Given the restrictions which the Parliament Act 1911 had imposed upon the House of Lords, the need for those opposed to the Bill to intensify their opposition outside the Parliamentary forum was, therefore, heightened and had to be concentrated into the two years while the House of Lords, as was correctly anticipated, exercised its delaying powers. The extent and the intensity of the, at times unlawful, opposition to the third attempt at Home Rule were dramatically and immediately made manifest in Ulster. A voluntary military force, the "Ulster Volunteers", of some 90,000–100,000 men was raised and later armed, and a Solemn League and Covenant of 1912 declared:

Being convinced in our conscience that Home Rule would be disastrous to the material well-being of Ulster as well as to the whole of Ireland, subversive of our civil and religious freedoms, destructive of our citizenship, and perilous to the unity of the Empire ... we ... pledge ourselves, in Solemn Covenant, throughout this, our time of threatened calamity, to stand by one another in defending ... our cherished position of equal citizenship in the United Kingdom and in using all means which may be found necessary to defeat the present conspiracy to set up a Home Rule Parliament in Ireland.

This (with a parallel declaration for women) was signed by half a million Unionists. In 1913 a "Provisional Government" was formed to take over in Ulster in the event of Home Rule being introduced. These were developments that no Government was likely to ignore, certainly in the climate of the times. The question was, could Ulster be excluded from the provisions of the Bill? Any such move, however, would alienate the Nationalists. The extension of the Bill to the whole of Ireland was the preference of Prime Minister Asquith, although he probably gave greater weight to the difficulties stemming from any exclusion of Ulster to the neglect of those stemming from its inclusion. He did, however, expect that the Bill would be subject to some amendment on this point. The major question in this respect was whether the amendment should be used as a partial concession to Unionist demands—although the substance of the Unionist claims was for Ulster to retain the status quo for itself, there were those in the Unionist camp who also wished to use the Ulster question to thwart Home Rule generally[14]—or as a warning to the Nationalists against over-zealous pursuit of their own demands. Before the Bill was published the Cabinet warned the Nationalists that

> the Government hold themselves free to make changes if it becomes clear that special treatment must be provided for the Ulster counties, and that in this case the Government will be ready to recognise the necessity either by amendment or by not pressing the Bill on under the provision of the Parliament Act.[15]

The problem of exclusion was indeed complex, not only in principle, but also, if introduced, in terms of the precise area to be excluded. The difficulties revolved around majorities and minorities. At least four-fifths of Ireland had voted in favour of Home Rule. Ulster's wishes were minority wishes within Ireland. Nevertheless, within the Province of Ulster itself the majority of the people favoured retention of the status quo, although within that nine-county unit different county groupings could produce smaller or larger majorities—or minorities—on that point. Further, the respect a Government should accord to the wishes of a people for self-determination should, so far as is feasible, accommodate both majority and minority wishes. The virtually unanswerable, unanswered question is, what is feasible? Parliamentary attempts to answer this question were conducted more dispassionately than attempts within Ireland.

The first Parliamentary attempt was made in the House of Commons in 1912 by a Liberal back-bencher, Thomas Agar-Robartes, who, stating that "orange bitters will not mix with Irish whiskey",[16] proposed the exclusion from the Bill of the four counties of Ulster which had Protestant and therefore Unionist majorities—Antrim, Armagh, Down and Londonderry. The amendment was defeated, but the talking had begun.

In June 1914, in accordance with Asquith's opinion that the best time to offer Ulster a compromise was during the final Parliamentary stages of the Bill, the Marquis of Crewe, the Lord Privy Seal, while the Royal Assent was pending introduced into the House of Lords an amending Bill which provided that if a tenth of the electorate of any of the nine counties of Ulster presented a petition requesting it, the Lord Lieutenant should cause a poll to be held amongst the electorate of that county, enabling them to answer this question:

Are you in favour / are you against the exclusion of your county from the operation of the Government of Ireland Act 1914 for a period of six years?

This proposal was very similar to one made by Asquith in the Commons during the third successive second reading of the Bill in March 1914. It had not proved acceptable. Hardly surprisingly and very succinctly it had been rejected by Sir Edward Carson, leader of the Ulster Unionists, with the words, "We do not want a sentence of death with a stay of execution for six years".[17] The same comment applied with equal force to Lord Crewe's amending Bill which was introduced into the House of Lords a month after the House of Commons had passed the Home Rule Bill for the third time. It was a last ditch attempt for the Lords. Time was now short, for even civil war seemed a possibility. The Lords, therefore, did not reject Lord Crewe's Bill but substituted for the temporary county option permanent exclusion for the whole of Ulster. In July 1914 the House of Commons rejected the Lords' amendment.

It was, however, now a possibility that if the Government were to concede to Unionist pressure for permanent exclusion, the Unionists might be prepared to make concessions concerning the area to be excluded. In July 1914, a conference chaired by the Speaker of the House of Commons was convened at Buckingham Palace by King George V. It consisted of representatives of the Government (Asquith and Lloyd George, then Chancellor of the Exchequer), the Opposition (the Marquis of Lansdowne and Bonar Law), the Ulster Unionists (Carson and (Sir) James Craig—later Viscount Craigavon) and the Nationalists (John Redmond and John Dillon). The purpose of the conference was to see if a compromise could be reached on the two issues of the duration of the exclusion and the area to be excluded. No compromise was reached. The question of duration was never discussed and on the question of the area to be excluded, the division between those who sought a county by county option (primarily the Nationalists, in order to ensure that no county with a Nationalist majority was excluded from Home Rule), those who sought the complete exclusion of the whole of Ulster (Sir Edward Carson) and those who sought the exclusion of part of Ulster (for example, Bonar Law) proved too deep. The conference failed. On 18th September 1914 the Bill passed into law as the Government of Ireland Act 1914, without the consent of the House of Lords and without any special provision being made for Ulster, but simultaneously there was passed a Suspensory Act which suspended the operation of the Government of Ireland Act for the duration of the First World War which had begun on 4th August. The War was to give the various parties some five or six years in which to try to reach agreement.

## NOTES

1 See, generally, Bogdanor, *Devolution* (1979), chapter 2.

2 Quoted in Mansergh, *The Irish Question 1840-1921* (3rd ed, 1975), p 137.

3 Mansergh, *op cit*, p 185.

4 "The Government of Ireland Bill and the Sovereignty of Parliament" 1886 *LQR* (vol 2), pp 427-443.

5 Dicey, *England's case against Home Rule 1886* (Introduction by E.J. Feuchtwanger, 1973), p 229.

6 See Walkland (ed), *The House of Commons in the Twentieth Century* (1979), pp 162,170,476-7.

7 Dicey, *op cit*, p 122. It should be noted that the Third Article of the Acts of Union required that "the said United Kingdom be represented in one and the same Parliament, to be styled the Parliament of the United Kingdom of Great Britain and Ireland".

8 *Ibid*, p 253.

9 *Ibid*, pp 271-3.

10 *Ibid*, p 275.

11 Quoted in Mansergh, *op cit*, p 216.

12 See *supra*, *op cit*, at p 442.

13 Quoted in Barritt and Carter, *The Northern Ireland Problem* (1972), p14.

14 See Mansergh, *op cit*, pp 217 *et seq*; Bogdanor, *op cit*, p 43; and specifically Sir Edward Carson: "if Ulster succeeds Home Rule is dead."

15 Quoted in Mansergh, *op cit*, p 219.

16 Quoted in Bogdanor, *op cit*, p 43.

17 Quoted in Buckland, *Irish Unionism: Ulster Unionism* (1973), p 97.

# II

# THE FIXING OF PERIMETERS

In 1916 the Government was given all the impetus it needed to find a solution by the Easter Rising in Dublin, and in May 1916, Lloyd George, then Minister of Munitions, opened negotiations to reach some agreement on the Ulster Question. They were generally unsuccessful, not least because those participating on the Nationalist side were, in many ways, far removed from the increasingly more popular Sinn Féin Nationalism which was essentially both separatist and republican and which would be satisfied by neither Home Rule within the United Kingdom nor by any exclusion of Ulster from an independent Ireland, as involving either the continuation of British rule in a part of Ireland or the denial of the territorial integrity of the Irish nation. At these negotiations, agreement of a sort was, however, reached— or for a while apparently so—on the area of Ireland to be excluded from the Home Rule proposals. The Government's "Headings of a Settlement as to the Government of Ireland" proposed that the 1914 Act should come into force immediately, subject to this modification:

The said Act not to apply to the excluded area which is to consist of the six counties of Antrim, Armagh, Down, Fermanagh, Londonderry and Tyrone, including the Parliamentary boroughs of Belfast (and) Londonderry...[1].

The Unionists accepted with some reluctance the severance of the remaining three Ulster counties which had very clear Nationalist majorities, Cavan, Donegal and Monaghan, but did so on the understanding that the excluded six counties would be permanently excluded from the operation of the Act. Redmond, on behalf of the Nationalists, equally reluctantly accepted the exclusion of those six counties, but did so on the understanding that the exclusion would be temporary. Subject to that exclusion provision, it was hoped that Home Rule could come into operation immediately. The Headings of a Settlement did not, it should be stressed, propose a separate Parliament and Government for these six counties. Paragraphs 3 and 13 read as follows:

As regards the excluded area, the executive power of His Majesty to be administered by a Secretary of State through such officers and departments as may be directed by Order of His Majesty in Council, those officers and departments not to be in any way responsible to the new Irish Government.

A Committee to be appointed in which both of the Irish Parties are to be represented, to assist the Government in preparing the necessary Orders in Council.

All Orders in Council under the new Act to be laid before both Houses of Parliament....

Had the Headings been published sixty years later they would, no doubt, have evoked cries of "Direct Rule", but the full importance of the acceptability of the six-county unit to the Unionists was only to emerge when the post-War Government of Ireland Act proposed to give that unit its own Parliament.

Once the extent of the misunderstanding over the duration of exclusion became apparent the 1916 negotiations broke down. In December 1916, however, Lloyd George himself became Prime Minister, and although sympathetic to the cause of Home Rule, he was also more sympathetic to the Unionist cause than his Liberal predecessors. He had no desire to coerce Ulster into acceptance of the all-Ireland provisions of the 1914 Act:

To place the people of Ulster under national rule against their will would be as glaring an outrage on the principles of liberty and self-government as the denial of self-government would be for the rest of Ireland.[2]

Lloyd George's main concern, therefore, was to consider how he could accommodate the interests of these six Ulster counties within the framework of Irish Home Rule. He first attempted to do this by summoning an Irish Convention, which met in Trinity College, Dublin from July 1917 to March 1918. It consisted of ninety-five members, representing the Irish Parliamentary Party, Southern Irish Unionism (which was generally opposed to the idea of exclusion and was becoming more isolated from Northern Unionism) and Ulster Unionism. The Convention was boycotted by Sinn Féin. The Convention failed to shake the opposition of the Ulster Unionists to the majority Convention support for one all-Ireland Parliament with built-in safeguards for Ulster. Probably by this stage the exclusion of Ulster from Home Rule and hence the partition of Ireland were inevitable but the General Election in December 1918, which saw the formation of a Coalition Government headed by Lloyd George, but with Andrew Bonar Law as leader of the largest party (the Conservatives) in the Coalition, put the ineluctable seal on the events. The 1918 Election also confirmed the extent of the division between the Irish Parliamentary Party (which won only six seats) and Sinn Féin, which won seventy-three; the Sinn Féin members, establishing the Dáil Éireann in Dublin, refused to take their seats at Westminster, and the voice of Irish Nationalism at Westminster was, therefore, effectively muted.

The cessation of hostilities between the United Kingdom and Germany, which had preceded the General Election by a month, meant that the Suspensory Act 1914 could now prevent the coming into operation of the Government of Ireland Act 1914 for an increasingly limited time. By 1919 the position was quite clear—unless an alternative course of action was taken, the 1914 Act would come into operation. A special Cabinet Committee—the Irish Situation Committee—set up on 7th October 1919 considered various alternative courses of action including the possibility of one all-Ireland Parliament with an "Ulster Committee" possessing veto powers over matters of concern peculiar to Ulster. This the Cabinet Committee rejected on the eminently convincing ground that such a device would simply frustrate the interests of an Irish Parliament and Government without providing for the full development of an Ulster interest. It also rejected the "Direct Rule" option, that is, the retention of the Ulster counties—or some of them—under the status quo, on the ground that this would mean the retention of "British rule" in some part of Ireland. The Committee, therefore, having moved inexorably to the conclusion that there should be two Parliaments established within Ireland, next considered the area to be governed by the Northern Parliament—the nine-county unit of Ulster itself or the six counties mentioned in 1916. The decision was not to be an easy one. Of the nine Ulster counties, the four mentioned in the Agar--Robartes unaccepted amendment to the 1914 Act all had solid Unionist majorities. In counties Fermanagh and Tyrone, the Protestant population constituted approximately 45 per cent of the total. In the remaining three Ulster counties, Cavan, Donegal and Monaghan, the proportion of the population which was Protestant ranged from only 18 per cent to 25 per cent. In the nine-county unit, therefore, the Protestants and therefore Unionists would constitute approximately 56 per cent of the population; in the six-county unit, the figure would be closer to 66 per cent. The British Government saw much in favour of the whole province of Ulster being subject to the Northern Parliament, not least because it wanted to do all in its power to ensure the eventual reunification of Ireland. On the other hand, the Ulster Unionists themselves preferred the six-county unit, as being larger than simply the four counties and yet as still containing a clear Unionist majority. As Captain Charles Craig was to explain,

We quite frankly admit that we cannot hold the nine counties. Therefore we have decided that in the interests of the greater part of Ulster, it is better that we should give up those three counties rather than take on a bigger task than we are able to carry out.[3]

In early February 1920 the Government acceded to the pressure of these arguments, and the Bill introduced into the House of Commons on 25th February 1920 sought to achieve a legislative solution that would this time satisfy both Unionist and Nationalist aspirations. Paradoxically, however, the details of the Bill, which was to become the Government of Ireland Act 1920, spelt out a system of government both clearly not acceptable to the dominant and increasingly militant Nationalism of Sinn Féin, and also not generally desired by Ulster Unionists, who sought to retain the Union with Great Britain and the exclusion of Ulster from the jurisdiction of a Dublin Parliament, rather than to obtain their own system of devolved powers.

The Bill proposed a Parliament and Government for the six-county unit, which was given the title Northern Ireland. It also proposed a separate Parliament and Government for the remaining twenty-six counties of Ireland, both Parliaments to possess the power to legislate for the peace, order and good government of the area subject to its jurisdiction. This grant of power was subject to certain exceptions. The Bill thus accepted the principle of Irish autonomy albeit only over the matters transferred to the two Parliaments. Both Parliaments, to sit in Belfast and Dublin respectively, were to be subject to the sovereignty of the Westminster Parliament and the whole of Ireland, both North and South, was to remain within the United Kingdom. In addition there was to be instituted a common High Court of Appeal with final appeal to the House of Lords, and also a Council of Ireland to consist of twenty representatives each from both the Northern and Southern Ireland Parliaments. Provision was made for this Council to be turned into one Parliament for the whole of Ireland. So Ireland was divided. The British Government, compromising between principle and pragmatism, both acknowledged the Unionists' emphasis on the link with Great Britain and their distrust of Dublin-based rule, and also gave some recognition to those whose preferences lay with an Ireland united under a common Irish Parliament and Government.

The long title of the Government of Ireland Act 1920 succinctly stated its purpose to be "an Act to provide for the better government of Ireland" but, as was commonly expected, the provisions relating to both Southern Ireland and to the all-Irish dimension came into only very partial operation for a very limited period. Only with regard to Northern Ireland, where devolution of power had not been sought, did the Act become largely operative. Before turning to the details of what was, therefore, Northern Ireland's constitution for some fifty years, mention must first be made of Southern Ireland's withdrawal from the United Kingdom and the withering away of the all-Ireland dimension.

Although in 1921 amidst much dissension, the Southern Ireland Parliament as constituted under the 1920 Act[4] was elected and summoned, it met only twice. The content and conduct of its two proceedings have been described as follows:

> The Parliament of Southern Ireland was summoned by Royal Proclamation for 28 June 1921, and met on that day in the Council Chamber of the Department of Agriculture and Technical Instruction in Dublin. Fifteen (out of 64) senators and four (out of 128) members of the House of Commons attended. The Parliament was opened by the Lord Chief Justice and the Master of the Rolls, as Lords Justices in the absence of the Lord Lieutenant, and the Lord Chief Justice delivered a short speech on behalf of the Crown, stating that "when a sufficient number of members have taken the oath the causes of His Majesty calling this Parliament will be declared to you" . . . Each House adjourned till the 13 July, the entire proceedings lasting for about fifteen minutes.
>
> Both Houses met again in the same place on the 13 July 1921, when twelve senators and two members of the House of Commons attended. The Lord Chancellor . . . presided in the Senate . . . The House adjourned without day named "until His Majesty shall be pleased to declare his gracious will and pleasure". A similar procedure took place in the House of Commons, which also adjourned for an indefinite period.[5]

This Parliament did not meet again. The attempt to put the Government of Ireland Act into operation in Southern Ireland failed.[6] In July 1921, Lloyd George invited the Sinn Féin leaders to negotiations, which began in October and by the December had reached agreement over the future form of government for Southern Ireland. It was clear, at least at the inception of these bilateral negotiations, that there was agreement that the 1920 Act had settled the status of neither Southern Ireland nor Northern Ireland. This was not, however, a view shared by the Northern Ireland Government, formed after the 1921 elections to the Northern Ireland Parliament had given the Unionists forty seats, the Irish Parliamentary Party six seats and Sinn Féin six. As far as the Northern Ireland Government (Unionist in complexion) was concerned, the aim of the negotiations was for Great Britain and Southern Ireland to reach whatever accommodation of interests with each other was possible, the position of Northern Ireland being in no wise at issue. Sinn Féin, on the other hand, wanted to use the status of Northern Ireland as a bargaining counter—a united Ireland to be the *quid pro quo* for Ireland remaining within the Empire. Their position was a reasonably strong one. First, the close proximity of Southern Ireland to Great Britain meant that from a security or defence point of view

Ireland was something of an advance post, better held by friend than foe. Secondly, Sinn Féin's willingness to accept Dominion status in exchange for a united Ireland was not only likely to meet with international delight but also to mean that lack of co-operation on the part of Ulster[7] could be presented as intransigence against the interests of the Empire.

Ulster, however, was not prepared to move and hence when, in November 1921, the Northern Ireland Government was offered the possibility of becoming subordinate to an all-Ireland Parliament whilst still retaining the powers set out in the 1920 Act, it rejected the offer. Lloyd George had publicly stated that he was not prepared to coerce Ulster and indeed any attempt to do so would have been strongly resisted by many (although not all) Conservatives, such as, for example, Bonar Law. At the same time, Lloyd George also hoped that Ulster would freely make concessions in the Imperial interest. The agreement which he reached, therefore, with Sinn Féin was imbued with a certain amount of ambivalence. This agreement was expressed in the Articles of Agreement for a Treaty (commonly called "the Treaty") and was given the force of law in the United Kingdom by the Irish Free State (Agreement) Act 1922. Article 1 of the Articles of Agreement, which constituted the schedule to the 1922 Act, endowed "Ireland" with

> the same constitutional status in the Community of Nations known as the British Empire as . . . (Canada, Australia, New Zealand and South Africa). . . . with a Parliament having powers to make laws for the peace, order and good government of Ireland and an Executive responsible to that Parliament

and gave "Ireland" the name of the Irish Free State. Article 1's reference to "Ireland" rather than more specifically to Southern Ireland, the term used in the 1920 Act for the twenty-six counties, was part of Lloyd George's compromise, but has been labelled a "legal fiction" for the following reason. The agreement as formulated was designed to cover the whole of Ireland, North and South, but by Article 12 provision was made for an Address to be presented to the King within one month of the passing of the Act—the "Ulster Month"—by both Houses of the Parliament of Northern Ireland, requesting that the powers of the Irish Dominion Parliament and Government be not extended to Northern Ireland. Were such an Address to be presented, the provisions of the Government of Ireland Act 1920 were to continue in full force and effect for Northern Ireland. The Irish Free State Constitution Act 1922 (Session 2) provided that the Ulster Month should run from 5th December 1922. On 7th December 1922, both Houses of the Northern Ireland Parliament unanimously passed the following Address:

We, Your Majesty's most dutiful and loyal subjects . . . do, by this Humble Address, pray Your Majesty that the powers of the Parliament and Government of the Irish Free State shall no longer extend to Northern Ireland.

It was presented to the King, George V, on the following day. The continued operation of the Government of Ireland Act 1920 in Northern Ireland from 31st March 1922, when the Agreement Act 1922 apart from the Ulster Month provisions came into force, until 8th December 1922, when Article 12 and the Humble Address ensured its continuance, was governed by Article 11 of the Articles of Agreement. Article 11 provided that

the powers of the Parliament and the Government of the Irish Free State shall not be exercisable as respects Northern Ireland and the provisions of the Government of Ireland Act 1920, shall, so far as they relate to Northern Ireland, remain of full force and effect

unless the Parliament of Northern Ireland resolved otherwise, which it did not. Hence, the expression "Ireland" in Article 1 is to be construed as excluding Northern Ireland, certainly in terms of United Kingdom law. The Irish Free State (Consequential Provisions) Act 1922, passed on 5th December 1922, made provision for the matters consequential on the ratification of Dominion status for the Irish Free State. The Government of Ireland Act, for example, ceased to apply to any part of Ireland other than Northern Ireland and the Lord Lieutenant for the whole of Ireland, provided for under the 1920 Act, was replaced by a Governor for Northern Ireland.

The actual area to be incorporated within Northern Ireland was one of the last matters to be resolved; it was not finally settled for a further three years. Article 12 of the Articles of Agreement, which had enabled Northern Ireland to opt out of the Irish Free State, also attached the condition, that, in the event (or likelihood) of such choice being exercised, a Boundary Commission was to be set up, consisting of three members appointed respectively by the British (to appoint the chairman), Northern Ireland and Irish Free State Governments, in order to

determine in accordance with the wishes of the inhabitants, so far as may be compatible with the economic and geographic conditions, the boundaries between Northern Ireland and the rest of Ireland.

The Northern Ireland Government refused the British Government's formal request to appoint a representative, partly at least on the ground that it was not bound by the contents of the Articles of Agreement to which it had not been party.[8] This refusal was referred, under the Judicial Committee Act 1833, to the Judicial Committee of the Privy Council, which held, first, that in the absence of a Commissioner appointed by the Northern Ireland Government a proper Commission within the meaning of Article 12 would not be constituted; and secondly, that in the event of such non-appointment neither the British Government nor the Governor of Northern Ireland could appoint the Northern Ireland representative on the Boundary Commission.[9] This opinion was approved by Order in Council of 31st July 1924; a new agreement, therefore, was entered into between the British and Irish Free State Governments and given the force of law by the Irish Free State (Confirmation of Agreement) Act 1924. It provided that in the continued absence of the nomination of a representative by the Northern Ireland Government the power to make such an appointment would pass to the British Government. The latter, therefore, appointed Mr Justice Richard Feetham, a judge of the South African Supreme Court, as chairman of the Commission. He was not the British Government's first choice. Sir Robert Borden, a former Prime Minister of Canada, had earlier refused the appointment, not wanting to proceed with the work of the Boundary Commission without the co-operation of the Northern Ireland Government. The British Government also appointed to the Commission, Mr J.R. Fisher, an Ulster Unionist and editor of the *Northern Whig* newspaper. The Irish Free State Government appointed the Minister for Education in the Dublin Government, Professor Eoin McNeill, who, unlike the other two representatives, served on the Commission in a part-time capacity only.[10]

The most difficult problem confronting the Commission, which met for the first time on 6th December 1924, was the interpretation of Article 12, which laid down the Boundary Commission's terms of reference. The expectations of the Irish Free State Government concerning the functions that the Commission was to serve were explicitly stated by it—it expected that substantial areas of Northern Ireland would be ceded to the Irish Free State. It believed that Article 12 bore a presumption in favour of the inclusion of the whole of Ireland under its own jurisdiction, subject only to the opting out of those areas of Northern Ireland within which the majority of the population favoured such a course. Hence an early submission from the Irish Free State Government read:

> It was not contemplated by the Treaty that any area within "Northern Ireland" should have the right to withdraw permanently from the jurisdiction of the Irish Free State, unless the majority of the inhabitants of such areas were in favour of this course.[11]

It should be noted, first, that this interpretation read into Article 12 the word "areas" of Northern Ireland. The Article itself refers only to the "boundaries".

Secondly, this interpretation assumed that the boundary re-definition would operate to the advantage of the Irish Free State only. Indeed, it carried with it the possibility (for some, the preference) of the total abolition of Northern Ireland. It was not, however, an interpretation that found favour with Mr Justice Feetham. He pointed out that its effect was

> not merely to provide for the determination of the boundaries of Northern Ireland, but to raise, as to every portion of the existing territory of Northern Ireland, the question whether that territory shall be retained within the limits of Northern Ireland, and thus to open up the fundamental question as to whether or not Northern Ireland itself shall continue to exist.[12]

This was so, not because it was envisaged that all areas of Northern Ireland would choose union with the Irish Free State but because Northern Ireland would be so reduced in size as to make its viable operation under the provisions of the Government of Ireland Act 1920 impossible. It is perhaps a matter of no minor importance that while the Boundary Commission was meeting, the Northern Ireland Parliament and Government were already functioning.

Mr Justice Feetham's interpretation of Article 12—unchallenged although not necessarily supported by both other Commissioners—was that it gave the Commission power to shift the boundary line in either direction; that the "wishes of the inhabitants" referred only to the inhabitants of the boundary regions, that is, those people who would be directly affected by boundary revision; and—crucially—that

> Northern Ireland must, when the boundaries have been determined still be recognisable as the same provincial entity; the changes made must not be so drastic as to destroy its identity or make it impossible for it to continue as a separate province of the United Kingdom with its own Parliament and Government for provincial affairs under the Government of Ireland Act.[13]

In accordance with this interpretation, therefore, the three members of the Boundary Commission met, "perambulating the border area",[14] and by October 1925 they were on the verge of producing concrete proposals. On 7th November 1925, however, a British newspaper, the *Morning Post*, prematurely and unauthorised, disclosed the likely details, including a map, of the Commissioners' proposals. These details not only showed comparatively minimal territorial gains for the Irish Free State, but also included some losses of its own territory to Northern Ireland. This disclosure caused a furore in the Irish Free State, probably more because of the likelihood of loss of territory rather than the possibility of only minimal gains. More specifically, the disclosure led the already unhappy Professor McNeill to resign on 20th November and effectively destroyed all the work of the Commission.

When the refusal of the Northern Ireland Government to appoint a representative to the Boundary Commission had been referred to the Judicial Committee of the Privy Council, on Mr Justice Feetham's insistence its opinion had also been sought[15] on a further supplementary question, namely whether

> if a Commission is duly constituted . . . in the event of disagreement (will) the vote of a majority prevail?

The Judicial Committee regarded as conclusive and, therefore, applied the rule laid down by Chief Justice Eyre in *Grindley* v *Barker* in 1798:[16]

> I think it is now pretty well established that where a number of persons are entrusted with powers not of mere private confidence, but in some respects of a general nature, and all of them are already assembled, the majority would conclude the minority and their act will be the act of the whole.

This rule, that in arbitration of matters of public concern the majority will prevails, had already been applied by the Judicial Committee in a Canadian case involving the retirement of an arbitrator from a properly constituted Commission. The rule was, however, phrased sufficiently generally to cover both resignation, as here, and dissent also. The resignation of Professor McNeill from the Boundary Commission, therefore, could not legally invalidate its decision, but politically his resignation rendered the recommendations unenforceable.

In spite, therefore, of the annoyance of Mr Justice Feetham, the British, Northern Ireland and Irish Free State Prime Ministers (Baldwin, Craig and Cosgrave) agreed to withdraw the report and not publish it. Instead the three Governments reached agreement on 3rd December 1925 that the extent of Northern Ireland should be that as laid down in section 1(2) of the 1920 Act, namely the six-county area of Ulster. This agreement was formally enacted in the Ireland (Confirmation of Agreement) Act 1925, which came into operation on 17th December 1925 and amended the Articles of Agreement and the Agreement Act 1922, by revoking the powers conferred by Article 12 on the Boundary Commission.

The reasons for reaching this agreement were recited in the 1925 Agreement itself, which forms the schedule to the 1925 Act:

> Whereas the progress of events and the improved relations now subsisting between the British Government, the Government of the Irish Free State, and the Government of

> Northern Ireland and their respective peoples, make it desirable to amend (Article 12) so as to avoid any causes of friction which might mar or retard the further growth of friendly relations between the said governments and peoples;
> And whereas the British Government and the Government of the Irish Free State being united in amity in this undertaking with the Government of Northern Ireland, and being resolved mutually to aid one another in a spirit of neighbourly comradeship, hereby agree

to confirm the 1920 delimitation of Northern Ireland. As will be seen, however, the question of the ownership of the territorial waters off Northern Ireland was not universally seen as settled until the 1970s.

Subsequent publication in 1968 of the Boundary Commission's Report showed that even if its recommendations had been implemented they would have led to only slight territorial changes, although in light of the incidence of some of Northern Ireland's subsequent troubles, these changes could have had greater significance than simply territorial adjustment. The changes recommended included not only the proposal that parts of South Armagh (around Forkhill and Crossmaglen) and small parts of Fermanagh (around Garrison) and of Tyrone be transferred to the Irish Free State, but also that certain parts of East Donegal be transferred to Northern Ireland.

The 1925 Agreement did not only resolve the question of the border, it also disposed finally of the Council of Ireland, and the rapidly fading all-Irish dimension of the 1920 Act, and of this brief mention must now be made.

Section 2(1) of the Government of Ireland Act 1920 read:

> With a view to the eventual establishment of a Parliament for the whole of Ireland, and to bringing about harmonious action between the Parliaments and Governments of Southern Ireland and Northern Ireland, and to the promotion of mutual intercourse and uniformity in relation to matters affecting the whole of Ireland, and to providing for the administration of services which the two Parliaments mutually agree should be administered uniformly throughout the whole of Ireland ... there shall be constituted ... a Council to be called the Council of Ireland.

The Council was to consist of a President, to be nominated by the Lord Lieutenant—and no such nomination was ever made—and twenty members from both the Northern Ireland and Southern Ireland Parliaments, to be elected by their respective Houses. The representatives from Northern Ireland were elected on 23rd June 1921 by ballot.

Section 3 of the 1920 Act related to the transmutation of the Council into a Parliament for the whole of Ireland, should the Parliaments of both Northern Ireland and Southern Ireland pass identical legislation agreeing thereto.

Certain powers under the Government of Ireland Act 1920, including postal services, savings banks, registration of deeds, land purchase and certain taxes, including customs and excise duties and income tax, were reserved to Westminster, but in anticipation that at least some of them would eventually be transferred to the all-Ireland Parliament, along with some or all of the powers originally devolved under the Act to the two Parliaments, North and South.

The all-Ireland dimension, however, got off to a rather more prosaic start. Section 10(2) of the Act enacted that

> any powers ... exercisable by any department of the Government of the United Kingdom ... with respect to railways and fisheries and the contagious diseases of animals in Ireland, and the power of making laws with respect (thereto) shall ... become powers of the Council of Ireland, and not of the Governments and Parliaments of Southern and Northern Ireland ...[17].

The first steps towards the potentially expanding all-Ireland dimension faltered during the talks between Lloyd George and the Sinn Féin leaders which resulted in the Articles of Agreement of December 1921. They effectively deprived the Council of any powers with respect to the Irish Free State, and by the Consequential Provisions Act 1922, the operation of its functions regarding Northern Ireland were deferred. Paragraph 3(1) of the first schedule to the 1922 Act modified the Government of Ireland Act 1920 by providing that

> [t]he constitution of the Council of Ireland shall, if identical Acts for the purpose are passed by the Parliament of the Irish Free State and the Parliament of Northern Ireland, be altered in accordance with those Acts.

Until such time as a new constitution for the Council could be agreed, however, the powers of the Council under the 1920 Act relating to Northern Ireland continued to be exercised by the Parliament and Government of the United Kingdom. Even this formal preservation of the powers of the Council as regards Northern Ireland did not survive for very long. The agreement reached in December 1925 concerning the border between Northern and Southern Ireland also finally disposed of the Council of Ireland. The Ireland (Confirmation of Agreement) Act 1925, by section l(2) repealed, *inter alia*, paragraph 3 of the first schedule to the 1922 Act and as from lst April 1926 transferred those powers intended for the Council of Ireland to the Parliament and Government of Northern Ireland. As from that date, therefore, the Council of Ireland became a dead letter, for both North and South of the border, although Article 5 of the 1925 Agreement expressed the hope that the Governments of the Irish Free State and of Northern Ireland shall meet together as and when necessary for the purpose of considering matters of common interest arising out of or connected with the exercise and administration of (the powers intended for the Council of Ireland).

The judicial aspect of the all-Ireland dimension, namely the common High Court of Appeal, which was set up by sections 42 and 43 of the Government of Ireland Act 1920, had a briefer although more productive existence. The court consisted of the Lord Chancellor of Ireland and the Lords Chief Justices of both Northern and Southern Ireland (or their nominees) although provision was made for a full court of five judges, were it to be deemed advisable. The function of the Court was to hear appeals from both Courts of Appeal, sitting within Northern Ireland when hearing an appeal from the Northern Ireland Court of Appeal, and similarly for Southern Ireland. A full court was convened in *Leyburn* v *Armagh County Council (No 2)* 1922[18], in which it was held that the new court was not a substitute for the former, that is, the pre-1920 Court of Appeal, but was separate and distinct from all pre-existing courts and indeed had a more extensive jurisdiction than any previous Irish appellate court.

Sections 42 and 43 of the 1920 Act became operative on 1st October 1921[19] and the High Court of Appeal sat for the first time on 15th December 1921. In all it heard nine appeals, sitting for the last time on 5th December 1922, the date from which the Ulster Month started to run. The Consequential Provisions Act 1922 by section 1 and schedule 1, paragraph 6(1) provided that, as from 8th December 1922 (the day of the presentation of the Humble Address from the Northern Ireland Parliament):

the High Court of Appeal for Ireland shall cease to exist, and sections 42 and 43 of the (1920) Act ... shall cease to have effect.

Hence, within five years, the Government of Ireland Act 1920 had ceased to be operative (in so far as it ever became operative) within Southern Ireland and had been shorn of its all-Ireland dimensions.[20] Operating within a very different context from that originally intended, therefore, the Government of Ireland Act 1920 came into effect as the constitution for Northern Ireland only.[21]

## NOTES

1 Cd 8310 (1916), para 2. Para 14 provided for a review of the situation at the conclusion of the War.

2 Quoted in Mansergh, *op cit*, p 228-9.

3 Quoted in Mansergh, *op cit*, p 213; which see also generally for details of the above developments.

4 As stated above, Sinn Féin had already established its Parliament in Dublin in 1918.

5 Quekett, *The Constitution of Northern Ireland* (1928) Vol 1, p 18, footnote 3.

6 *Ibid*, pp 18-19: "The [1920 Act, by section 72] made express provision for the case (which actually arose) in which a majority of the total number of members of the House of Commons should fail to take the Oath of Allegiance. The Parliament was to be dissolved and a form of Crown Colony government set up; the place of Parliament was to be taken by a Legislative Assembly appointed by His Majesty, whilst the Government was to be administered by the Lord Lieutenant with the assistance of a committee of members of the Irish Privy Council, appointed for the purpose by His Majesty. This provision was not put into operation, and the Parliament of Southern Ireland remained in suspended animation until dissolved in ... 1922 ... under the authority of the Irish Free State (Agreement) Act of that year."

7 Although this name historically refers to the nine-county Province, the name is now frequently used to refer to the six counties of Northern Ireland and the terms now will be used interchangeably.

8 See Harkness, *Northern Ireland since 1920* (1983), pp 35-36: "[Article 12] was the article most deeply resented by Unionists and, for all its importance in the signing and ratification of the treaty in Dublin, it had perhaps a more profound impact in Belfast and throughout the North in these years. It was simultaneously a sword of Damocles hanging over the head of unionists and a beam of hope for northern nationalists .... It was at least in part because of the Boundary Commission ... that the first four crucial years of Northern Ireland were so divided, with Protestant determination moulding its every institution, and Catholic aloofness refusing every opportunity to contribute."

9 Cmd 2214, 1924. See Quekett, *op cit*, (1933) Vol 2, pp 170-177.

10 See Report of the Irish Boundary Commission 1925, introduction by Geoffrey Hand (1969) p x.

11 *Ibid*, p 33.

12 *Ibid*, p 34.

13 Draft Conclusions of the Report, *ibid*, paras III, IV and V, pp 65-6.

14 Newark, in Wilson (ed), *Ulster Under Home Rule* (1955), p 25. Newark states that: "Michael Collins's idea of boundary revision was the cession to the Free State of the counties of Fermanagh and Tyrone and parts of the counties of Down, Londonderry and Armagh."

15 See Hand, *op cit*, p xx.

16 1 B & P 229.

17 In the event, some joint bodies were created, for example, Foyle Fisheries and the Great Northern Railway.

18 [1922] 2 IR 15.

19 SR&O 1921/1527 (dated 27th September 1921).

20 The Statute Law Revision Act 1927, section 3 provided that: "Enactments or words in respect of matters exclusively relating to the portion of Ireland within the jurisdiction

of the Irish Free State or to any portion thereof may be omitted from any revised edition of the statutes published by authority."

21 As a final postscript to this chapter on the fixing of perimeters, see Buckland, *A History of Northern Ireland* (1981), at p 46: "the ... violence in Northern Ireland... between 21st June 1920 and 18th June 1922 claimed over 2,000 victims—1,766 wounded and 428 killed. This violence has often been represented as part of a deliberate attempt by Protestant and loyalist forces, official and unofficial, to exterminate Catholics. Certainly, more Catholics were killed than Protestants, but such a simplistic view takes little account of IRA activity in the North and the number of Protestant casualties...; even the most pessimistic statistics covering Belfast in the period 6th December 1921 to 31st May 1922 underlined both the extent and the impossibility of any glib explanation of the violence facing Northern Ireland in its early days. In that period 236 people were killed and 346 injured. Of those killed, 16 were members of the Crown forces, including five Catholics; 73 were Protestants; and 147 were Catholics, many of whom may have been killed by indiscriminate IRA firing in their own areas. Of the wounded, 37 belonged to the Crown forces; 143 were Protestants; and 166 were Catholics." On the 7th April 1922, the Northern Ireland Parliament enacted the Civil Authorities (Special Powers) Act (NI) 1922 to empower "certain authorities of the Government of Northern Ireland to take steps for preserving the peace and maintaining order in Northern Ireland." The Act, originally intended to be in force for one year, was continued in force on an annual basis until in 1933 it was made permanent. The 1922 Act (as amended) was repealed by the Northern Ireland (Emergency Provisions) Act 1973, an Act of the Westminster Parliament. For commentaries on the 1922 Act and its operation, see, *eg*, Calvert, *Constitutional Law in Northern Ireland* (1968), pp 380-386; Edwards, "Special Powers in Northern Ireland" 1956 *Crim LR*, pp 7-18; and Boyle, Hadden and Hillyard, *Law and State: The Case of Northern Ireland* (1975) *passim* and references therein.

# III

# THE GOVERNMENT OF IRELAND ACT 1920[1]

## INTRODUCTION

The withdrawal of Southern Ireland from the United Kingdom and the adoption by it of its own internal constitution led to those amendments to the Government of Ireland Act which were mentioned at the conclusion to chapter II. These amendments did not, however, make any substantial alterations to the system of government which the Act had intended for Northern Ireland. The Act, designed in part to appease Irish Nationalism and Ulster Unionism and to keep Ireland as a whole within the United Kingdom, had failed in two of its objectives. Did it succeed in the third? Although much of the matrix of the system of government intended for Northern Ireland had been destroyed, no attempt was made to adjust the 1920 Act to meet specifically Northern Ireland requirements. This not only left the country with a form of government created for a situation other than that prevailing within its own borders, but also more especially with one not devised to satisfy its own political aspirations. The mood of the Northern majority was not centrifugal—if the "centre" is defined in British not Irish terms. The reverse was the case. The majority had stood in firm defence of the Union and had for long opposed Irish Home Rule on the ground, *inter alia*, that it would tend to the destruction of the Union. Paradoxically, therefore, it was in Northern Ireland where the Act, unsought for and by no means autochthonous, was to make its greatest impact.

With the rejection by Southern Ireland of the system of government contained in the 1920 Act, there were three constitutional options open with regard to Northern Ireland. The first, to unite with Southern Ireland in its new Dominion status, was decisively rejected by the Northern Ireland Parliament in December 1922. It should also be remembered that Lloyd George, during his negotiations with Sinn Féin, had tried to secure the Northern Ireland Parliament's agreement to its own legislative subordination to an all-Ireland Parliament, although still retaining its own 1920 Act powers—and he had failed to secure such agreement.

The second possibility—theoretical rather than realistic—was the total reintegration of Northern Ireland within the United Kingdom. By 1922 it is doubtful whether this was acceptable to anyone. During the long and tortuous debates on the question of the exclusion of Northern Ireland from the Home Rule proposals Lloyd George had commented:

[T]he policy of exclusion is open to one general objection of the most serious kind. It involves the retention of British rule in some part of Ireland . . . If it is retained anywhere in Ireland, the opponents of Great Britain will be able to say either that Great Britain is ruling nationalist majorities against their will or that it is giving active support to Ulster in its refusal to unite with the rest of Ireland.[2]

However convincing this reason, more likely is the argument that total reintegration was completely incompatible with the British Government's desire to extricate itself, as much as was possible, from Irish affairs. Reintegration would have reinvolved the British Government in issues from which it had tried to extricate itself, at a time when already the nascent Northern Ireland "state" was subjected to a considerable amount of politically motivated and sectarian violence. The most telling arguments against reintegration, however, came from the Northern Unionists themselves. Sir James Craig, then Prime Minister of Northern Ireland, in correspondence between himself and the British Government,[3] referred to Unionist acceptance of the 1920 Act as "a final settlement and supreme sacrifice in the interests of peace."[4] Part of the sacrifice made had been the "surrender" of the Protestants in the three Ulster counties severed from the six counties of Northern Ireland and now ruled by a Dublin-based Parliament and Government. This stress on the finality of the 1920 settlement rendered Unionist opposition to the question of reintegration likely, but the likelihood of such opposition was turned into a certainty because of the early appreciation of the Unionists of the purposes which a Northern Ireland Parliament could serve. Representation at Westminster of a reintegrated Northern Ireland would probably have amounted to little more than twenty members,[5] who would not themselves have been able to resist any Labour or Liberal moves made there to coerce Northern Ireland into a united Ireland (although, as in 1912-1914, measures taken outside Westminster may have proved more effective). As against that potentially ineffective representation—ineffective not only on that issue but also equally probably in terms of being able to influence the content of legislation applying to Northern Ireland—the advantages for the Unionists of having a Parliament for Northern Ireland were explained in March 1920 during the Parliamentary debates on the enactment of the 1920 Act. Captain Charles Craig stated:

[W]e feel that an Ulster without a parliament of its own would not be in nearly as strong a position as one in which a parliament had been set up ... We believe that so long as we were without a parliament of our own, constant attacks would be made . . . to draw us into a Dublin parliament ... We believe that if either (the Labour or the Liberal party) or the two in combination were once more in power our chances of remaining a part of the United Kingdom would be very small indeed.

We see our safety, therefore, in having a parliament of our own, for we believe that once a parliament is set up and working well ... we should fear no one, and we feel that we should then be in a position of absolute security ...[6].

That this belief was held strongly and continuously is confirmed by its repetition in 1936 in a report issued by the Standing Committee of Ulster Unionist Councils. It is a quotation often cited and to this day explains the preference of many Unionists for devolution rather than integration:

The cry "Back to Westminster" is a subtle move fraught with great danger. Had we refused to accept a Parliament for Northern Ireland and remained at Westminster, there can be little doubt that now we would be either inside the Free State or fighting desperately against incorporation. Northern Ireland without a Parliament of her own would be a standing temptation to certain British politicians to make another bid for a final settlement with Irish republicans.[7]

This stance was vindicated when in 1949 the Irish Free State, on becoming the Republic of Ireland, left the Commonwealth. The Westminster Parliament consequently enacted the Ireland Act 1949, section 1(2) of which provided that

Northern Ireland remains part of His Majesty's dominions and of the United Kingdom and it is hereby affirmed that in no event will Northern Ireland or any part thereof cease to be part of His Majesty's dominions and of the United Kingdom without the consent of the Parliament of Northern Ireland.

As reintegration was so thoroughly discounted, the third choice available in 1921-22, therefore, was the only feasible option, namely the operation in Northern Ireland of the system of government set forth in the 1920 Act. Even although many of the assumptions on which it had been built had been frustrated, the 1920 Act was to become a reality for Northern Ireland, not only because of Unionist determination to avoid the other possibilities but also because of the British Government's state of enervation with regard to the issue. However inappropriate the 1920 Act was for operation solely within Northern Ireland, therefore, it came into force and lasted for some fifty years, ultimately proving less durable than the forces at work at its inception.

Before dealing in greater detail with some of the salient features of the Government of Ireland Act 1920, as it operated within Northern Ireland from

1921 to 1972, it may be expedient to provide a brief outline of its provisions on legislative and executive devolution.

The 1920 Act established a bicameral Parliament and provided for reduced representation of the Northern Ireland electorate at Westminster. Section 4(1) transferred to the Northern Ireland Parliament the extensive power to make laws for "the peace, order and good government" of the Province. This grant of power was residual in that it was subject to certain limitations. First, excepted matters, which dealt with matters of Imperial or national concern, remained within the exclusive competence of Westminster. Secondly, reserved matters, which included postal services, savings banks, certain major taxes and the Supreme Court, some of which had been intended for transfer to the all-Ireland Parliament had it come into existence, were, for as long as they remained reserved matters, equated with excepted matters and consequently they too stayed within Westminster's exclusive competence. All other matters, other than the excepted and reserved matters, were transferred to the Northern Ireland Parliament. Consequently, the 1920 Act created three categories of legislative power—transferred matters (the responsibility of the Northern Ireland Parliament) and reserved and excepted matters (the responsibility of Westminster). Certain other minor matters were withheld from the Northern Ireland Parliament's competence—for example, sections 64 and 68 made special provision for Queen's University and certain officers of local authorities—and section 5 of the 1920 Act prohibited the making of laws interfering with religious equality and the taking of property without compensation.

As far as the devolution of executive powers was concerned, section 8(1) of the Act provided that the executive power in Northern Ireland would continue to be vested in the King who would discharge with regard to any transferred matter the Prerogative or any other executive powers through a Governor. Section 8(3) of the Act further provided that those powers delegated to the Governor would be exercised through the Northern Ireland departments or ministries (as they were later renamed), which were headed by Northern Ireland Ministers who were drawn from the Northern Ireland Parliament and were also members of the Northern Ireland Privy Council. Indeed the Northern Ireland Cabinet's statutory title was "the executive committee (of the Privy Council) of Northern Ireland."

These general points will now be considered in more detail.

## THE LEGISLATURE

There was established for Northern Ireland a bicameral legislature, which consisted of the Crown, represented by the Governor, a 52-member House of Commons and a 26-member Senate.

### (a) The Governor

The Governor (an office which replaced that of the Lord Lieutenant under the original scheme) was given the functions traditionally associated with the Crown with regard to the legislatures based on the Westminster model. Section 11(2) of the Government of Ireland Act provided that the Governor

> shall, in His Majesty's name, summon, prorogue and dissolve the Parliament of Northern Ireland.

He was given, by section 12, the further power to give or to withhold the Royal Assent to Bills passed by both Houses of Parliament, subject to the requirement of compliance with any instructions given by the Crown in respect of the Bill and subject to the power to reserve any Bill. Reservation served the purpose of suspending the Bill, either until the Royal Assent was given, or for a period of one year on the expiration of which the Bill lapsed. This power to reserve was exercised only once, in 1922,[8] over the Local Government Bill (NI) which provided for the abolition of proportional representation in local government elections. To a certain extent, the requirement of this form of voting in such elections had been by way of a "constitutional guarantee", to protect minority political interests both North and South of the border in the Act as originally conceived. The 1922 Bill completed its parliamentary stages on 5th July 1922 but the Royal Assent was not given until 11th September. This delay was a direct consequence of pressure exerted upon the British Government by the then Provisional Government of the Irish Free State, which argued that the Bill put in jeopardy the Articles of Agreement for a Treaty wrought between the British and Irish in December 1921. More specifically, the Irish Free State argument against the Bill had two planks—first, that it would wreak injustice to the minority in Northern Ireland and secondly, that it was designed to pre-empt the work of the Boundary Commission. Hence in August 1922, Michael Collins, who headed the Irish Free State Provisional Government, informed Winston Churchill, the British Colonial Secretary, of his belief that the Bill not only intended to oust the Catholic and Nationalist people of the six counties from their rightful share in local administration

but, also, was

beyond all question, intended to paint the counties of Tyrone and Fermanagh with a deep Orange tint in anticipation of . . . the Boundary Commission and so try to defraud these people of the benefits of the Treaty.[9]

As against these arguments there should be placed the clear and real difficulties which would have stemmed from the withholding of the Royal Assent from a Bill which fell fair and square within the competence of the Northern Ireland Parliament. There was some merit in the contention that if a power had been transferred by the 1920 Act to the local legislature, then the British Government should not interfere in the exercise of that power. Although Northern Ireland was not a Dominion but, rather, an integral part of the United Kingdom, possessing only a devolved legislature with restricted legislative competence, there were very real fears at Westminster that intervention in the domestic affairs of Northern Ireland would cause unease in the Dominions. So, for example, Winston Churchill warned the Southern Irish Government that to veto the 1922 Bill could create "a precedent limiting for the future the powers of Dominion Parliaments."

How constitutionally correct that argument was will be considered in more general terms below, but it was probably not decisive of the issue anyway. The Northern Ireland Government perceived the threat to withhold the Royal Assent from a Bill which fell within its legislative competence as a fundamental challenge to its own authority. The Prime Minister of Northern Ireland told the Colonial Office:

No government could carry on in Northern Ireland if it knew that the powers of the Parliament ... were to be abrogated.

The British Government was, therefore, informed that if the Bill did not become law, the Northern Ireland Government would have no alternative but to resign. The former, therefore, well aware that, should there be a resignation followed by a local general election, there was no alternative to a Unionist administration, was faced with the choice of either advising the giving of the Royal Assent or of itself taking over the responsibility of governing the Province. The latter course of action was, as has already been seen, effectively closed and, therefore, the British Government exercised the freedom of Hobson's choice and advised that the Royal Assent be given to the Bill. This course of action was, possibly, made easier by the Northern Ireland Government's willingness to defer the holding of local government elections until the Boundary Commission had done its work. Due to the delay in setting up that Commission, however, although the elections were postponed from June 1923 to the summer of 1924, they still preceded the Commission's work. The importance of this episode, therefore, lay with other factors, as Buckland states:

> It starkly revealed the limits of central control, even when the regional administration was a friendly one anxious to maintain the unity of the state. The imperial government could do little to supervise the conduct of government in Northern Ireland. This incapacity was partly self-induced arising from an unwillingness to become once more directly involved in Irish affairs and from a respect for the sovereignty of Parliaments. But it was also, and very largely, based upon an appreciation of political realities. The plain fact was that there was no alternative government to call upon in Northern Ireland should the Unionists resign in protest against the exercise of Westminster's sovereignty.

Certainly, use of the power to reserve was not attempted again, although in 1970 opposition senators and members petitioned the Governor to use section 12 of the 1920 Act against the Public Order (Amendment) Bill (NI) which was debated—heatedly—in the Northern Ireland Parliament for over 100 hours as the opposition fought it clause by clause. The Governor, having consulted with the Home Office, rejected the petition.[10]

The significance of the dispute in 1922 over the exercise of the power to reserve lies in the fact that it unequivocally dictated the course of the relationship that was to develop over the ensuing decades between Westminster and Stormont—the "nickname" of the Northern Ireland Parliament, taken from its location at Stormont, just outside Belfast, from 1932 onwards.[11]

### (b) The House of Commons

The structure of the Parliament of Northern Ireland was based largely, although not totally, upon the Westminster model. The lower House was given a maximum life of five years. As with Westminster, there was no minimum period of duration, section 14(4) of the 1920 Act providing that

> [t]he House of Commons of Northern Ireland when summoned shall, unless sooner dissolved, have continuance for five years from the day on which the summons directs the House to meet and no longer.[12]

The House was composed of fifty-two members, forty-eight of them representing territorial constituencies, the remaining four the Queen's University of Belfast. By section 14 of the Act, Northern Ireland was divided into multi-member constituencies, each constituency returning four to eight members elected through a system of proportional representation.

The 1920 Act became operative on 3rd May 1921 and it was under that electoral system that the first elections were held in Northern Ireland on 24th May 1921. The Unionists won forty seats and the Nationalists and Sinn Féin shared the remaining twelve. The latter two parties, however, boycotted the formal first meeting of the House of Commons, which took place in the City Hall, Belfast on 7th June 1921. At this meeting the Speaker was elected, the members took the oath of allegiance, swearing—

> by Almighty God ... [to be] faithful and bear true allegiance to His Majesty, King George, his heirs and successors according to the law

and the Prime Minister, Sir James Craig, later Viscount Craigavon, and his Cabinet were sworn in. The Senate having then been elected by the House of Commons, Parliament was formally opened by the King on 22nd June 1921.

The electoral system by which the 1921 Parliament had been elected was used again in the election of April 1925. Already by this time, however, the Northern Ireland Government had plans to exercise the power given to the Northern Ireland Parliament by section 14(5) of the 1920 Act. Section 14(5) read:

> After three years from the day of the first meeting of the Parliament of Northern Ireland that Parliament may alter the qualification and registration of the electors, the law relating to elections ... , the constituencies, and the distribution of the members among the constituencies, provided that in any new distribution the number of the members shall not be altered and due regard shall be had to the population of the constituencies other than University constituencies.

It was an important power to be devolved and the exercise of the power proved to be controversial. The Government's plans to abolish proportional representation and to replace it with the method used for Westminster elections—a single-member constituency returning its representative by a simple majority of the votes—were deferred in 1924–25 for fear of prejudicing its case before the Boundary Commission.[13] On 25th February 1929, however, the Northern Ireland Government introduced into the House of Commons the House of Commons (Method of Voting and Redistribution of Seats) Bill (NI), which became law on 16th April 1929, abolishing the system of proportional representation and making consequential revision of constituency boundaries.

The aim of the Government was probably not anti-Nationalist as such, but was directed towards any of the smaller political parties. On an instinctive level, this amendment of the 1920 Act may have reflected a traditional British reaction against proportional representation. Sir James Craig is reported as saying to the Southern Irish:

PR is proving a failure all over the world. Broken down in Australia and New Zealand. You'll probably be driven to abolish it. I can't stand PR. Does not seem to be British. Too continental.[14]

It is, however, worthy of note—albeit parenthetically—that the system of voting used in Westminster elections, the system which the 1929 Act adopted for Stormont elections, was itself at this time subject to intensive review and might well have been replaced by a different electoral system. In 1910 a Royal Commission had rejected proportional representation as a suitable system, but had recommended instead, not the first-past-the-post system, but rather the alternative vote system. In 1917 a Speaker's Conference had recommended the introduction of a mixture of multi-member constituencies, regulated by a form of proportional representation, and single-member constituencies, regulated by the alternative vote system. The House of Commons preferred the latter to be employed throughout the country and the House of Lords the former, and, after some attempt was made to achieve a compromise, a Bill based on the Conference recommendations lapsed. The first-past-the-post system was, therefore, retained for negative as much as positive reasons. In 1931, shortly after the voting system for use with regard to Stormont was altered, the minority Westminster Labour Government attempted to have enacted a Bill that would have introduced the alternative vote system into the United Kingdom. The Bill fell with the Government, having generated hostility amongst both those who favoured the retention of the status quo and those who favoured proportional representation.

We must return now to the 1929 Northern Ireland Act. Although it may have reflected an instinctive dislike of proportional representation as an acceptable voting system, more overtly it served two much more important purposes—stability and clarity:

First of all (Sir James Craig) wanted a strong government, a government with a "strong solid majority" rather than one dependent upon the "whim of two or three independents who do not care which way they give their vote". Secondly, he wanted what he saw as the fundamental issue of Northern Ireland politics—Unionism versus Nationalism—laid clearly before the electors. According to Craig, "the real question at the bottom of the heart of every person in Ulster" was "whether we are going to remain part and parcel of Great Britain and the Empire or whether on the other hand we are going to submerge ourselves in a Dublin Parliament". The only sure way to achieve these two related ends,

Craig believed, was by the encouragement of a stable two-party system in which Unionists and Nationalists, the "two active, alert, vigorous parties in Ulster", opposed each other in a straight fight. General elections would then become what Craig thought they should be: a "referendum on the question which of two Governments shall be returned to power".[15]

Proportional representation can facilitate the proliferation of small parties although not inevitably so and, therefore, whatever the arguments in its favour, it is easily perceived as being conducive to governmental instability. The timing of the abolition of proportional representation and the justification based on forcing the clarity of one issue, however, were—and are—primarily political questions, and hence their advisability depends upon political predilections and, less acceptably, hindsight.

The controversial nature of the 1929 Act was heightened by the redrawing of the electoral boundaries which it entailed, attracting allegations of gerrymandering. As is clear from the parliamentary debates and from the electoral returns, however, the Government was careful to ensure that the balance between Unionists and Nationalists would be virtually the same as under the system of proportional representation. Sir James Craig stated in the House of Commons in March 1929 that the Government hoped to

> secure to this House when it meets again after the next election that it will be composed as nearly as possible of the balance of power which exists today -

and indeed the pattern was preserved.[16] In 1921, 1925, 1929 and 1933, total Unionist representation was 40, 40, 41 and 41 respectively, whilst non-Unionists held 12, 12, 11 and 11 seats respectively.[17]

Possibly much more serious than the changes themselves was the impression which the Government gave the minority community in introducing the changes. The Government failed to enter into any consultations with the opposition over its proposals and this omission led it to believe that the Government was merely "implementing the wishes of its most uncompromising supporters",[18] although had this been the case one suspects that one way or another Nationalist representation would have been reduced rather than maintained. Nevertheless, what matters is the perception rather than the reality, and this impression, when coupled with a consideration of some of the details of the boundary determinations, led to much bitterness amongst the Nationalist population. The Act, however, passed into law in April 1929; Parliament was dissolved in May, and the immediately ensuing general election and all others were conducted under the provisions of the 1929 Act. The Act did not affect the representation in the Northern Ireland Parliament of Queen's University, which continued to return four members, elected by a system of proportional representation until 1968, when the University constituency was abolished and four new single-member constituencies were created.

The other problem caused by the 1929 Act was that it made no provision for a Boundary Commission, so that the constituency boundaries remained unaltered until the Electoral Law Act (NI) 1968, rather late in the day, created one with powers and duties similar to those possessed by the four national Boundary Commissions with responsibility for Westminster constituencies.[19]

### (c) The Senate[20]

Section 13 of the 1920 Act provided that the Senate, the Upper House, should consist of twenty-six members, namely the Lord Mayor of Belfast and the Mayor of Londonderry *ex officio* and twenty-four other senators to be elected by the members of the House of Commons of Northern Ireland according to a system of proportional representation. A senator's term of office, which was not affected by the dissolution of Parliament, was eight years, one half of the senators retiring at the end of every four years.

The first Senate, chosen on 7th June 1921 by the newly assembled House of Commons, was totally Unionist in composition as nominations were made by neither the Irish Nationalists nor Sinn Féin. The Senate met formally for the first time on 20th June, to take the oath and to elect their Speaker and to begin, after the formal opening of Parliament by the King two days later, its limited work in a constitution of which it had not originally been a part. All the Home Rule Bills 1886-1912 had suggested bicameral legislatures of a sort, but they differed with regard to the principle which they incorporated concerning the basis of membership of the Second Chamber. The Irish Legislative Body, proposed by the 1886 Bill, was to have consisted of two Orders, the second Order being directly elected by the Irish people on a constituency basis. The first Order, as has been mentioned, was to have consisted of twenty-eight Irish peers and seventy-five "elective" members. Clause 10(2) provided:

> Each elective member shall at the date of his election and during his period of membership be bona fide possessed of property which—
>
> (a) if realty, or partly realty and partly personalty, yields two hundred pounds a year or upwards, free of all charges; or
>
> (b) if personalty yields the same income, or is of the capital value of four thousand pounds or upwards, free of all charges.

Those entitled to vote for the elective members were, by clause 10(4), to have been required to satisfy certain conditions, one of which was that they be "the owner or occupier of some land or tenement within the district of a net value of twenty-five pounds or upwards". The term of office of elective members was to have been ten years, thirty-seven or thirty-eight of them retiring every five years. Clause 9 provided that the two Orders should deliberate and vote together, although, if requested, the votes could have been taken separately on legislative and procedural matters. Clause 23 provided that where a Bill or a provision of a Bill was lost through disagreement between the two Orders, then after a period ending with the dissolution of the Legislative Body or a period of three years, whichever was the longer, if the resubmitted Bill were to be adopted by the second Order and negatived by the first, it should be submitted to the whole Legislative Body, both Orders voting together, the outcome to be resolved by a simple majority of the members voting together.

These details were changed very little in the 1893 Bill. The proposed Irish legislature was to consist of an Irish Legislative Assembly, directly elected by popular vote on a constituency basis, and an Irish Legislative Council, to be composed of forty-eight councillors, elected for an eight-year term of office (half retiring every four years) on a constituency basis by voters satisfying property qualifications slightly more relaxed than those of the 1886 Bill—to own or occupy any land or tenement in the constituency of a rateable value of more than twenty pounds, rather than the twenty-five required in 1886. Clause 8, providing for the settlement of disagreements between the two Houses, was similar to clause 23 of the 1886 Bill, although the 1893 Bill did not provide for the two Houses normally to deliberate together. Clause 8 reduced the time for starting to settle disagreements from three to two years and made more clear the subordination of the Legislative Council to the first chamber.

The Government of Ireland Bill 1912 produced yet another variation on the same theme. As originally introduced into the House of Commons, it proposed as the second chamber a forty-member Irish Senate, the term of office for each senator to be eight years with ten senators retiring every two years. It was intended that the Lord Lieutenant of Ireland should nominate all the senators. This was a provision deliberately designed to protect minorities, it being the aim of the clause to ensure representation in the Senate of minorities not likely to be represented as a result of popular election. This proposal was, however, amended during the passage of the Bill through the House of Commons to provide for nomination for only the first five-year period of the operation of the Act, to be replaced by a system of popular election on a

Provincial basis, according to a system of proportional representation. The franchise was to be the same as for Westminster elections. The Bill was enacted with this amendment unaltered. Section 11 of the Act provided for the resolution of disagreement between the two Houses. In the event of such disagreement lasting over two parliamentary sessions, the Lord Lieutenant was empowered to convene a joint sitting of the members of the two Houses, matters to be resolved by a simple majority vote at the joint sitting.

By the time of the 1920 Act, therefore, several different bases for the composition of a second Irish chamber had been proposed. The 1886 Bill had combined the heredity principle with popular vote based on property interests; the 1893 Bill had excluded the hereditary element. The 1914 Act had been changed from nomination geared to representation of interests, to popular election geared to Provincial representation. As the sequence of changes might indicate, none of these was generally acceptable. The case for a second chamber when power is being devolved is not easy to make. Indeed, experience seems to have shown that second chambers in a devolved system of government are not necessary or desirable. In a federal system, to put the matter simply, the lower House represents the people directly, the upper House represents them regionally, by granting the States or Provinces a certain number of seats. When devolution is involved, it is not as simple. The nearest approximation to what may be termed the "federal justification" was the second 1914 scheme, that is representation of Irish Provincial interests, but once the principle of regional representation is abandoned, the justification for a second chamber falters. Representation of interests is probably the next most plausible justification. This indeed was not only the system proposed originally in 1912-1914, but was also that preferred by a majority of the Irish Convention in 1917, although not by the Ulster Unionist representatives at that Convention. The majority stated a preference for a 64-member Senate, with some *ex officio* members, some elected with the aim of securing the representation of certain interests and some nominated by the Lord Lieutenant.[21] Such bases of composition are, however, rather contrived, and "nomination" in this context may become associated very quickly with "patronage". When a body composed in such a way is pitted against a democratically elected chamber, it can be endowed with only limited powers.

Although this is the language of the later rather than the earlier part of the twentieth century, it was by 1920 already clear—and the debates concerning the reform of the House of Lords have subsequently strengthened the clarity —that the connection between the powers to be entrusted to a body and the composition of that body is crucial. Similarly, a consideration of the extent of the powers to be given to a second chamber must be placed firmly beside those entrusted to the lower house and the basis of its composition. Unless both are elected on principles equally democratic, the powers of the second chamber have to be so circumscribed as not to be or to become unjustifiably obstructive. Given that this is so, the dividing-line between non-obstructive but useful (rather than superfluous because unnecessary) powers and obstructive powers becomes very hard indeed to draw. If both Houses are elected on principles equally democratic, the search for a formula for resolving conflict between the two Houses is at best fraught with massive difficulties, if it is to be justified as being fair.

The Government in 1920 was already aware of these many difficulties and the Government of Ireland Bill as originally introduced proposed unicameral legislatures for Northern and Southern Ireland. An amendment that there be instituted an all-Ireland Senate serving both Irish legislatures was rejected, but the Government eventually accepted Lords' amendments for separate Senates for both Northern Ireland and Southern Ireland. The Northern Ireland Senate was to be composed as described above; the Southern Ireland Senate was to be composed along the lines recommended by the majority of the 1917 Irish Convention.

The justification for introducing into Northern Ireland a second chamber —received by Sir Edward Carson with the words, "We take no responsibility for it. We did not ask for it and we do not want it"[22]—was the same as that for Southern Ireland, namely, the protection of minority interests. Given that the minority parties made no nominations to the first Senate this was rather ironical and anyway the justification seems rather weak in the first place.

The functions of the Northern Ireland Senate were circumscribed partly by the provisions of the Government of Ireland Act itself, for example section 16, which prevented the Senate from initiating and amending "money" bills. They were also circumscribed by the inevitable difficulties surrounding any second chamber in a non-federal structure and by the fact that the Senate's political complexion remained constantly Unionist—inevitably given the constant Unionist majority in the Commons. This meant that the Senate exercised functions largely similar to those currently exercised by the House of Lords (excluding, of course, the latter's judicial functions), namely, the technical scrutiny of legislation, the initiation of non-controversial legislation and the provision of an extra forum for public debate. The Senate's potentially most important power was not conferred upon it until 1949 when, as has been mentioned, section 1(2) of the Ireland Act of that year declared that Northern Ireland would not cease to be part of the United Kingdom without the consent of the Parliament of Northern Ireland, that is of both Commons and Senate. Given that the election of senators was staggered over four year periods, it would have taken a minimum of four years from the time the Nationalists secured a majority in the Commons before the Senate could also have been composed of a Nationalist majority. Hence the Senate provided a check against the status of Northern Ireland being changed immediately, had there been a Nationalist landslide in a general election.

The 1920 Act borrowed from the Dominions, for example South Africa and Australia, a provision for resolving deadlock between the two Houses should such have arisen. Section 17 gave the Governor the power (which it was never necessary for him to use) to convene a joint sitting of both Houses, and a Bill passed by a majority of the total number of those present was to have been deemed duly passed. Presumably, the section 17 procedure could only have been used, had there been deadlock between the two Houses over the consent of the Northern Ireland Parliament with regard to a change in Northern Ireland's constitutional status, had that consent been sought by way of a Northern Ireland Bill.

### (d) Representation at Westminster

#### *(i) The House of Commons*

The Fourth Article of the Acts of Union 1800 provided that Ireland should be represented at Westminster by 100 seats. Later this had increased to 105. Given that the 1920 Act devolved extensive legislative power, this number was reduced to a total of forty-six for Ireland as a whole. Of these only the thirteen seats allocated to Northern Ireland became a reality, as the thirty-three Southern Irish seats were abolished in 1922. Of these thirteen seats, one seat was that for the Queen's University of Belfast and it, like all United Kingdom university seats, was abolished by the Representation of the People Act 1948, leaving Northern Ireland with twelve members at Westminster. Northern Ireland was thus the only part of the United Kingdom to have a fixed level of representation at Westminster. The House of Commons (Redistribution of Seats) Act 1949 set up for Northern Ireland, as for all regions of the United Kingdom, a Boundary Commission to keep Westminster constituency boundaries under continuous review.

Northern Ireland's level of representation at Westminster was below that to which Northern Ireland was entitled on a *per capita* basis. This, however, was justified by reference to the fact that Northern Ireland possessed a legislature of its own for regional affairs. More problematic, as in 1886 and 1893, was the question of the nature of the participation of the Northern Ireland Members in all matters handled at Westminster. They were, however, granted and they exercised full membership of Westminster. The possible inequities involved in them discussing and voting on, say, English regional affairs when the Northern Ireland equivalent were the concern of Stormont and not Westminster, were reduced by both the limited number of Northern Ireland Members at Westminster and also by their own inclinations largely to pursue only Northern Ireland affairs there. Although in a devolutionary system, any provision for representation, full or partial, at Westminster would both present practical problems and also be logically indefensible, the arguments of 1886 and 1893 had exhausted all avenues and few wanted to tread again well-worn ground. The system introduced by the 1920 Act was probably the fairest and the most generally acceptable.[23]

*(ii) The House of Lords*

The Fourth Article of Union also provided that

> four Lords spiritual of Ireland, by rotation of sessions, and twenty-eight Lords temporal of Ireland elected for life by the peers of Ireland, shall be the number to sit and vote on the part of Ireland in the House of Lords of the Parliament of the United Kingdom.[24]

The disestablishment of the Church of Ireland and its organisational severance from the Church of England by the Irish Church Act 1869[25] terminated the episcopal representation (the four lords spiritual), and the Irish Free State (Consequential Provisions) Act 1922 effectively terminated the representation of the lords temporal. The acquisition by Southern Ireland of Dominion status in 1922 led to the consequential abolition of the post of the Lord Chancellorship of Ireland, the office responsible for administering the election of temporal peers and hence no elections were held after 1922. Those who had been elected to sit prior to 1922 continued to do so, being entitled to sit for life. The last Irish representative peer, the Earl of Kilmorey, died in 1961. In 1966, in response to a petition made the previous year, from twelve Irish peers, the Committee of Privileges of the House of Lords ruled that the provisions of the Acts of Union of 1800

> relating to the election of Irish Representative Peers ceased to be effective on the passing of the Irish Free State Agreement Act 1922; and that the right to elect Irish Representative Peers no longer exists.[26]

Consequently, therefore, from 1921, Northern Ireland was represented at

Westminster by thirteen, later twelve, Members of Parliament and by a dwindling and ultimately non-existent number of peers, some of whom were Southern and not Northern Irish. The Peerage Act 1963 gave Irish peers the privileges of commoners, for example, voting, and removed all their constitutional disabilities. Northern Ireland was during this time also "represented" by any of its peers holding peerages of the United Kingdom, that is those peerages created after January 1801, and—after 1958—life peerages.

## THE EXECUTIVE

The form of the Executive may be dealt with much more briefly. Executive power remained vested in the Crown, but section 8 of the 1920 Act made provision for the exercise of this power with regard to those matters transferred to, that is within the legislative competence of, the Northern Ireland Parliament. The 1920 Act originally envisaged that there would be one representative of the Crown in Ireland, namely the Lord Lieutenant, and that the Governments of both Northern and Southern Ireland would be responsible for his actions to their respective Parliaments. A Lord Lieutenant was appointed in April 1921 and in June 1921 he established for Northern Ireland various departments, namely those of the Prime Minister, Finance, Home Affairs, Labour, Education, Agriculture and Commerce. (In 1944 a Ministry of Health and Local Government was created.) As a result of the Articles of Agreement for a Treaty, the office of Lord Lieutenant was abolished. For that office for the whole of Ireland there was substituted for Northern Ireland the office of Governor and in respect of Northern Ireland he exercised the same functions as had been conferred by the 1920 Act on the Lord Lieutenant.[27] The first Governor was appointed in December 1922.

Section 8 of the Act required that the devolved executive powers should be exercised through the departments, and that the Governor should appoint officers, holding office at his pleasure, to administer those departments. The persons appointed to be heads of the Northern Ireland Government departments, which in 1946 were renamed Ministries, were the Northern Ireland Ministers. Each person appointed Minister was required to be a member of the Privy Council of Northern Ireland (which had replaced the Irish Privy Council) and also to be or within six months to become a member of the Parliament of Northern Ireland. Membership of either the Senate or the House of Commons satisfied this requirement; in practice most Ministers were appointed from the Commons and usually one, *per* Government, from the Senate. Thus, for Northern Ireland, there was a statutory requirement for what is regulated by constitutional convention as far as Westminster is concerned, namely that members of the Government are drawn from the legislature. Section 8(5) of the Act also gave the force of statute to one of the United Kingdom's creatures of convention, namely the Cabinet, by providing that

> [t]he persons who are ministers of Northern Ireland for the time being shall be an executive committee of the Privy Council of Northern Ireland . . . to aid and advise the Governor in the exercise of his executive powers

in relation to Northern Ireland services. This "executive committee" (to use its statutory title) was the Cabinet.

Section 8(6) was by way of a constitutional guarantee:

> In the exercise of power delegated to the Governor in pursuance of this section no preference, privilege or advantage shall be given to, nor shall any disability or disadvantage be imposed on, any person on account of religious belief except where the nature of the case in which the power is exercised itself involves the giving of such preference, privilege or advantage, or the imposing of such a disability or disadvantage.

It should be noted that the 1920 Act was silent on the relationship between the Northern Ireland and the Westminster Governments. In practice the Home Office (eventually) was the Northern Ireland Government's "point of reference" in London and the Home Secretary was the spokesman on Northern Ireland affairs in the Westminster Cabinet. There was also, however, continual contact between the Northern Ireland Ministries and their Westminster counterparts.

This, then, is the skeleton of the form of the Executive that was devised for Northern Ireland under the Government of Ireland Act. In practice it was "fleshed out" by clearly following the Westminster style of responsible Cabinet Government; the Governor became a constitutional figurehead taking the requisite action on the advice of the Prime Minister (about which office the 1920 Act was silent; in practice he was the leader of the majority party at Stormont) or the relevant member of the Cabinet. The members of the Cabinet, in turn, were chosen and dismissed by the Prime Minister and were collectively and individually responsible to the Northern Ireland Parliament.

The doctrine of collective responsibility to the Northern Ireland Parliament clearly had less constitutional bite than its Westminster counterpart. First, the fact that the Unionist party was constantly the majority party in Northern Ireland denied Northern Ireland the type of alternating party government enjoyed, or at least experienced, at Westminster for the United Kingdom as a whole. The significance of this fact was heightened by the way in which the

Northern Ireland Cabinet was formed—the members of it were chosen exclusively from the majority party. It was, thus, a Westminster-style of government—Cabinet Government formed only from the majority party—without the presence of the one factor which made the Westminster system of government so different, namely, the alternation of parties in power. Secondly, the Northern Ireland Parliament was not dominated by "politics" in the British sense of "left versus right wing" politics. Thirdly, the Northern Ireland Government (generally, but by no means invariably) followed the Westminster Government's policies, whether that Government was Labour or Conservative. All this meant not only that scrutiny of the Northern Ireland Government by the Northern Ireland Parliament as a whole lacked vigour; it also entailed the more specific but crucial consequence that the opposition, constantly denied the responsibilities of governing or of partaking in the processes of government, was largely not inclined or encouraged to undertake the role of a responsible opposition. The particular fact that the statutory bones of the 1920 Act were covered with the flesh of Westminster's constitutional practices was to build into the operation of the 1920 Act the seeds of destruction—although, as ever, hindsight endows a picture with greater clarity than contemporaneous vision.

## THE LEGISLATIVE POWERS OF THE NORTHERN IRELAND PARLIAMENT

### (a) "Peace, order and good government"

The legislative competence of the Northern Ireland Parliament was defined in terms identical to those employed by Westminster with relation to its overseas territories. The Act of 1852, which granted a representative constitution to the colony of New Zealand, by its Preamble gave the legislature the power to make laws for the "peace, order and good government" of the colony. This phrase was repeated for the Canadian Federal Parliament in the British North America Act 1867, in the Commonwealth of Australia Constitution Act 1900 and the South Africa Act 1909. In accordance with this colonial tradition, therefore, subsection (l) of section 4 of the Government of Ireland Act 1920 read:

> Subject to the provisions of this Act ... the Parliament of Northern Ireland shall ... have power to make laws for the peace, order and good government ... of Northern Ireland.

The provisions of the Act limiting this grant of power were sections 4(l)(l) to

(14), 5, 6, 9, 21, 22, 47, 64, 65, 68 and 75, which will be considered below. The first question which arises from the wording of section 4(1) is whether, subject to these specific sections, Westminster thereby granted to the Northern Ireland Parliament plenary legislative powers or whether it thereby qualified "the power to legislate by reference to the purpose or at least effect of legislation".[28] That the phrase "peace, order and good government"—sometimes called the "pogg clause"—is capable of bearing a construction limiting legislative competence is clear. If the words are not to be used as a criterion for assessing the *vires* of a statute, they become superfluous, and change the power granted to the power to make laws *simpliciter*.

As against this construction, based on grammatical rules, there must be placed the context of the use of this phrase in statutes prior to 1920, for the construction of the words cannot proceed on grammatical principles only. A more realistic construction must involve a consideration of how much self-government it was intended to devolve to the colony concerned. For New Zealand, Canada, Australia and South Africa, as had become clear by 1920, this grant of power was but one step towards Dominion status. Prior to the Statute of Westminster 1931, these countries were all technically colonies and as such were subject to the Colonial Laws Validity Act 1865 which imposed certain restrictions on their legislative independence. For example, as has been seen, section 2 stated that laws passed by the colonial legislatures were void and inoperative to the extent that they conflicted with a Westminster Act of Parliament expressly or by necessary implication applying to the colony. There was also some uncertainty, as will be seen, as to whether or not colonial legislatures could pass laws having extra-territorial effect. Furthermore, competence to deal with matters of Imperial concern, such as defence and external relations, rested with Westminster. By the early years of the twentieth century, however, the word "Dominion", importing the idea of equality of status with the United Kingdom and hence legislative independence of Westminster, was already being used to refer to these "colonies". By the close of the First World War this colonial status was nothing more than a matter of form, and that this was so was confirmed by the Imperial Conference of 1926. It was then declared that the United Kingdom and the Dominions were

> autonomous communities within the British Empire, equal in status, in no way subordinate one to another in respect of their domestic or external affairs, though united by a common allegiance to the Crown, and freely associated as members of the British Commonwealth of Nations.[29]

By 1926 indeed the Dominions had the right of separate diplomatic representation and the right to make separate treaties with foreign countries in the name of the Crown.

As a result of this Imperial Conference and further ones held at Westminster in 1929 and 1930, the Statute of Westminster was passed in 1931, replacing the conventions, which had adhered to the 1865 Act, with the full force of law. Section 2 of the 1931 Act provided that the Colonial Laws Validity Act 1865 would no longer apply to any laws subsequently passed by a Dominion Parliament, and section 3 declared and enacted that a Dominion Parliament had full power to make laws having extra-territorial operation. The Preamble to the Statute, which applied not only to New Zealand, Canada and Newfoundland, (which did not become a Canadian province until 1949), Australia and South Africa, but also to the Irish Free State, recited that it was in accord

> with the established constitutional position that no law hereafter made by the Parliament of the United Kingdom shall extend to any of the said Dominions as part of the law of that Dominion otherwise than at the request and with the consent of that Dominion.

This matter of the emergent legislative—and national—independence of the original colonies (New Zealand, Canada, Australia and South Africa) was clearly reflected in the opinions of the Judicial Committee of the Privy Council, the Supreme Appeal Court of the Empire[30], when it was called upon to interpret the phrase "peace, order and good government". In 1930 in *Edwards* v *Attorney-General for Canada*, the Lord Chancellor, Lord Sankey, provided this explanation of the general principles upon which the Judicial Committee operated:

> The communities included within the Britannic system embrace countries and peoples in every stage of social, political and economic development and undergoing a continuous process of evolution. His Majesty, the King in Council, is the final Court of Appeal from all these communities, and this board must take great care, therefore, not to interpret legislation meant to apply to one community by rigid adherence to the customs and traditions of another.[31]

Political reality, however, demanded, certainly with regard to those nations which achieved Dominion status, that such meaning should be given to the "pogg clause" as would ensure a considerable amount of internal self-government. This issue was largely determined as early as 1884 by the decision of the Judicial Committee of the Privy Council in *Riel* v *The Queen.*[32] This case came on appeal from the Canadian province of Manitoba and involved the construction of the British North America Act 1871, which had authorised the Canadian Federal Parliament to make provision for the passing of laws for the peace, order and good government of any territory not for the time being included in any Canadian province. Lord Halsbury, the Lord Chancellor, gave the opinion of the Judicial Committee:

It is not denied that the place in question was one in respect of which the Parliament of Canada was authorised to make such provision, but it appears to be suggested that any provision differing from the provisions which in this country have been made for administration, peace, order and good government, cannot as matters of law be provisions for peace, order and good government in the territories to which the statute relates, and further that, if a Court of Law should come to the conclusion that a particular enactment was not calculated as a matter of fact and policy to secure peace, order and good government, that they would be entitled to regard any statute directed to those objects, but which a Court should think likely to fail of that effect, as *ultra vires* and beyond the competency of the Dominion Parliament to enact.

Their Lordships are of opinion that there is not the least colour for such a contention. *The words of the statute are apt to authorise the utmost discretion of enactment for the attainment of the objects pointed to.*[33]

The words of the last sentence extracted require close consideration for they provide part of the background against which the grant of power contained in section 4(l) of the 1920 Act should be viewed. The 1920 Act, however, also contained certain express provisions clearly at variance with the constitutional conventions which in 1920 regulated the relationships between Westminster and the Dominions (conventions which were not given the force of law until 1931).

Section 75 of the 1920 Act guaranteed Westminster's continued supremacy in Northern Ireland as in any part of the United Kingdom:

Notwithstanding the establishment of the Parliament of Northern Ireland . . . or anything contained in this Act, the supreme authority of the Parliament of the United Kingdom shall remain unaffected and undiminished over all persons, matters and things in [Northern] Ireland and every part thereof.

This general assertion of Westminster's sovereignty was reinforced by the more specific content of section 6. It, in effect, introduced into the legislative competence of the Northern Ireland Parliament a qualification similar to that contained in section 2 of the Colonial Laws Validity Act 1865. Section 6(2) of the 1920 Act enacted that

where any Act of ... the Parliament of Northern Ireland deals with any matter with respect to which that Parliament has power to make laws which is dealt with by any Act of the Parliament of the United Kingdom passed after the appointed day (3rd May

1921) and extending to the part of Ireland within its jurisdiction, the Act of ... the Parliament of Northern Ireland shall be read subject to the Act of the Parliament of the United Kingdom, and so far as it is repugnant to that Act, but no further, shall be void.

Section 6(1) reserved to Westminster the power to repeal or alter the 1920 Act, except where the 1920 Act itself permitted the Northern Ireland Parliament to amend certain of its provisions, such as section 14(5), which enabled it to legislate with regard to Stormont elections. It also withheld from the Northern Ireland Parliament the power to repeal or alter any provision of any Act of the Westminster Parliament passed after the appointed day and extending to Northern Ireland, even although that provision dealt with a transferred matter. In practice, however, this section was evaded by a provision in the relevant United Kingdom statute, deeming it to have come into force *before* the appointed day and thus enabling the Northern Ireland Parliament to amend it. This situation arose when for reasons of convenience the Westminster Parliament legislated on a transferred matter having first obtained the agreement of the Northern Ireland Government.

Sections 75 and 6 weaken the presumption that, despite the identical phrasing in the general grant of legislative power, arguments relevant to self-governing Dominions should have been applied to Northern Ireland. The presumption, however, regains its strength not only from the practice of evading the provisions of section 6 but also from the traditional judicial respect for Acts of (any) Parliament and from judicial conservatism—the fact that no Dominion Act had ever been struck down as *ultra vires* for conflict with "peace, order and good government" would have weighed heavily in the judicial mind. Perhaps—as ever—what mattered most is not what Parliament intended by the 1920 Act grant of powers, but what the courts thought it had intended. As it was—and perhaps because all these factors influenced counsel too—the point was never *fully* commented upon in any case concerning the Government of Ireland Act.

The point does seem to have been raised in 1937 in *Gallagher* v *Lynn*[34] in which the validity of the Milk and Milk Products Act (NI) 1934 was challenged. According to the Northern Ireland reports version of the case (but not the Law Reports or All England Reports), one argument presented before the House of Lords was to the effect that

> [i]t has to be shown that this ... Act is for the "peace, order and good government" of Northern Ireland ... The right to legislate for all matters, whether local or general, is still in the sovereign Parliament, the Imperial Parliament.
>
> There is no sovereignty in the Parliament of Northern Ireland, even where local matters

are concerned. The Imperial Parliament still possesses authority to pass legislation even on matters on which the Parliament of Northern Ireland has power to legislate. This distinguishes the present case from the Canadian cases, and the Australian cases, and leaves it open to interpret section 4 of the Government of Ireland Act 1920 much more strictly.

Lord Atkin, delivering the judgment of the House of Lords and resolving the question of the Act's validity on other grounds, merely remarked that the 1934 Act was a law for the peace, order and good government of Northern Ireland in respect of a matter within Stormont's legislative competence.[35] At the strongest this is "hesitantly . . . a tacit assumption of the power to review on this ground".[36] It may indeed be significant that three of the five judges (Lords Thankerton, MacMillan and Wright) involved in *Gallagher* v *Lynn* had been involved in the Judicial Committee's decision in 1933 in *Croft* v *Dunphy*,[37] an appeal from the Supreme Court of Canada. In this case Lord MacMillan said:

Once it is found that a particular topic of legislation is amongst those upon which the Dominion Parliament may competently legislate as being for the peace, order and good government of Canada . . . their lordships see no reason to restrict the permitted scope of such legislation by any other consideration than is applicable to the legislation of a fully Sovereign State.

Traces of this sentiment are to be found in *Gallagher* v *Lynn*. Indeed in *Gallagher* it seemed to be automatically assumed that the type of reasoning employed in *Croft* v *Dunphy* was directly applicable to Northern Ireland. The assumptions inherent in drawing such a parallel were clearly revealed in the later case of *R(Hume)* v *Londonderry Justices*, 1972,[38] which involved a challenge to the validity of a piece of Northern Ireland delegated legislation giving the army power to disperse assemblies of three or more persons if a breach of the peace or public disorder was feared. By the late 1960s and early 1970s arguments drawn from Dominion cases were being rejected as inapplicable to the unique constitutional structure of Northern Ireland—and particularly so as Westminster intervened more and more in the internal affairs of the Province as the Troubles worsened. All this opened up the possibility that the Northern Ireland courts might consider the "peace, order and good government" grant of power as a limited rather than plenary grant. In *Hume*, however, the Northern Ireland Divisional Court did not have to decide whether or not the regulation was compatible with the general grant of power to the Northern Ireland Parliament, as it was held to be *ultra vires* on other grounds. The Lord Chief Justice, therefore, simply commented that the argument that the regulation was not "conducive to peace, order and good government" had been put before the Court, but that it was "unnecessary, having regard to the conclusion I have already expressed to analyse fully the arguments on this point and I will refrain from doing so".[39]

No other attempts were made in the Northern Ireland courts to challenge legislation on the ground that it was not conducive to peace, order and good government. Any conclusions, therefore, concerning the import of the phrase within the context of the Northern Ireland constitution must be tentative. Arguably the phrase was used in the 1920 Act as a borrowing from a known situation to cover new facts, either directly or indirectly because the phrase had been used in the 1886 and 1893 Bills and the 1914 Act and had probably carried over into the 1920 Act without further thought. Arguably, too, the choice of the phrase reflects more consciously the desire on the part of Westminster to extricate itself from the internal government of the whole of Ireland for which the scheme of the 1920 Act was originally intended. It is probable that Westminster deliberately used its relations with New Zealand, Canada, Australia and South Africa, then Dominions in all but legal form, as the basis on which to construct a similar but not identical relationship between Great Britain and Ireland as a whole. The proximity of Ireland to Great Britain and the Unionism of Northern Ireland—a stronger tie than that which bound the Empire—meant that the relationship could not be identical. Had the overall scheme of the 1920 Act not been thwarted at its inception by the withdrawal of Southern Ireland from the United Kingdom and the partition of Ireland, it is probably fair to state that any interpretation of the "pogg clause" should have been in accord with that given it in the context of the Dominions. It is far harder to argue that such an interpretation was correct after 1922 with regard only to the Northern Ireland Parliament. That is to say, as with any such Act of Parliament, the interpretation of a phrase should vary according to the surrounding constitutional and political circumstances. That, however, would have required of the judiciary a role that it is not usually called upon to play within the United Kingdom and, therefore, the Dominion parallel helped the judiciary largely to evade the issue of the extent of the novelty of the Northern Ireland constitution of 1920. The most natural and indeed, arguably, the most constitutionally proper approach of the courts, therefore, to such questions is to be found in *McEldowney* v *Forde* in 1971,[40] in which it was argued that a Northern Ireland regulation was *ultra vires* as being contrary to the 1922 Special Powers Act's requirement of the preservation of peace and maintenance of order. The majority of the House of Lords, by subjecting the regulation to the test recommended by the Privy Council in 1952 in *Attorney-General for Canada* v *Hallet and Carey Limited*,[41] namely, "was it capable of being related to one of (the statute's) prescribed purposes?", held the regulation *intra vires*. The minority test, which looked to the effect of the regulation and not its purpose, was clearly not acceptable to the majority, as requiring them to embark upon a consideration of questions and evidence more appropriately the responsibility of those politically responsible rather than that of the judiciary. Similar reluctance to embark upon such an inquiry probably also explains the dictum of Lord Halsbury, the Lord Chancellor, in *Riel* v *The Queen*, quoted above. The line of reasoning which recommended itself in *Hallet and Carey* would presumably also have been applied, had the occasion arisen, to Acts of the Northern Ireland Parliament. It is not a test which would permit a court easily to replace the assessment of an elected legislature or of a Government Minister as to what worked towards peace, order and good government, with its own judicially-ascertained assessment. As against this, it should be remembered that, as was stated above, political—or at least Parliamentary—control and scrutiny of the Northern Ireland Government's assessments and decisions was not as strong as the systems operating in the Dominions or at Westminster.

It is assumed, therefore, that the Northern Ireland Parliament was granted plenary legislative competence, subject only to the express limitations of the 1920 Act. It was this assumption that prompted Professor Newark to state, in 1953, that

> the Northern Ireland Parliament has a general power to make laws for the good government of Northern Ireland, and it is well to remember that, apart from the excluded and reserved matters, the Northern Ireland Parliament is a Sovereign Parliament. I always tell the students that the proper way to use the Government of Ireland Act 1920, is not to read it to see what the Stormont Parliament can do, but to assume it can do everything and then read the Act to see what it cannot do.[42]

It is interesting, for comparative purposes, to recall here the comment made by the Unionist, Professor A. V. Dicey, concerning the powers to be devolved to the proposed all-Ireland legislature in the 1886 Bill, clause 2 of which gave it the power to make laws for the peace, order and good government of Ireland. Dicey, anxious for the preservation of the Union and concerned about the Bill's separatist potential, commented:

> The powers of the Irish Parliament are, it should be noted, indefinite. The Parliament, that is to say, may pass any law which it is not under the Constitution forbidden to pass ... The Irish Parliament is a body whose authority will, from the necessity of things, tend constantly to increase.[43]

In subsequent devolutionary schemes for Northern Ireland, the Westminster Government and Parliament have been very careful to ensure that comments such as those recorded by Professors Newark and Dicey would be totally inappropriate.

## (b) Express limitations on the legislative competence of the Northern Ireland Parliament[44]

### *(i) No legislation to have extra-territorial effect*

Section 4(1) of the 1920 Act is again the relevant subsection, providing:

> Subject to the provisions of this Act ... the Parliament of Northern Ireland shall ... have power to make laws for the peace, order and good government of ... Northern Ireland with the following limitations, namely, that (it) shall not have power to make laws except in respect of matters exclusively relating to the portion of Ireland within (its) jurisdiction, or some part thereof. ...

This provision was enacted at a time when the law elsewhere was in a state of confusion. Whether or not the colonies possessed the power to make laws having extra-territorial effect was uncertain prior to the enactment of the Statute of Westminster 1931, section 3 of which declared and enacted that the Dominion Parliaments did possess such a power. The main concern of the Colonial Laws Validity Act 1865 had been to clarify what powers, if any, the colonial legislatures had to legislate contrary to English common and statute law. The Act thus provided that such legislatures were subordinate only in respect of United Kingdom Acts of Parliament expressly or by necessary implication applying to the colonies. The 1865 Act, therefore, remained silent on the question of the extra-territorial operation of colonial laws. It was an issue left to the Judicial Committee of the Privy Council to resolve. Two possible alternatives were open to it. The more restrictive alternative was strictly to confine the legislative competence of a colony within its own geographical borders. The second, more expansive, alternative was to accept that, in order for a colonial legislature effectively to administer the colony and provide for its peace, order and good government, its legislative competence should be sufficiently wide as to control persons, matters and things outside the colony but having exclusive relation to it.

In 1891, in *McLeod* v *Attorney-General for New South Wales*,[45] the Judicial Committee opted for the first alternative. The case involved the interpretation of a New South Wales statute enacting that whosoever being married marries another person during the life of the former husband or wife, wheresoever such second marriage takes place . . . shall be liable to penal servitude.

The question before the Judicial Committee involved the ambit to be given to both "whosoever" and "wheresoever" and it was held that these words must be taken to apply only to those actually within the jurisdiction of the legislature and that consequently they did not apply to an offence of bigamy allegedly committed in the United States of America. Lord Halsbury commented that

their Lordships do not desire to attribute to the colonial legislature an effort to enlarge their jurisdiction to such an extent as would be inconsistent with the powers committed to a colony.[46]

This decision was applied in the subsequent New Zealand case, *R* v *Lander*, in 1919[47] by the Court of Appeal of New Zealand. The application of *McLeod* at such a late date is particularly surprising and indeed by this time the Judicial Committee itself would probably have decided differently. The New Zealand decision, however, reflects the general uncertainty concerning the full extent of the extra-territorial restrictions. *McLeod* itself had not been greeted with universal approbation. Sir John Salmond in 1917, two years before *Lander* was decided, stated that *McLeod* was concerned exclusively with a matter of interpretation and that Lord Halsbury's comments on extra-territoriality were *obiter*.[48] That there was some uncertainty arising from the decision in *McLeod* is clear. A Report arising out of the 1926 Imperial Conference mentioned the

difference between the legislative competence of the Parliament of Westminster and of the Dominion Parliaments in that Acts passed by the latter operate, *as a general rule*, only within the territorial area of the Dominion concerned.[49]

At the 1929 Imperial Conference the same doubt was expressed:

It would not seem to be possible in the present state of the authorities to come to definite conclusions regarding the competence of Dominion Parliaments to give their legislation extra-territorial operation.[50]

In *British Coal Corporation* v *The King*[51] in 1935, Lord Sankey called the principle thought to be laid down in *McLeod* a "doctrine of somewhat obscure extent". Whatever the extent of the legal uncertainty of the ruling in *McLeod*, however, there is little doubt that its unacceptability increased co-relatively with the movement of the colonies towards Dominion status. Whether extra-territorial legislative competence was a quality which did or did not inhere in the colonial legislatures was one matter. Whether it was a quality which did or did not inhere in Dominion legislatures was altogether another; and the Statute of Westminster 1931 by section 3 removed all doubts, for the future at least. The impact of this section was tested almost immediately in the Privy Council in *Croft* v *Dunphy*,[52] which involved the interpretation of a Canadian anti-smuggling statute having effect over any vessel hovering within twelve miles of the Canadian coast and having on board dutiable goods. The Judicial Committee refused to consider whether or not section 3 was retrospective, and *per* Lord MacMillan applied the principle quoted earlier, which is worthy of repetition in this context:

> Once it is found that a particular topic of legislation is amongst those upon which the Dominion Parliament may competently legislate as being for the peace, order and good government of Canada . . . their Lordships see no reason to restrict the permitted scope of such legislation by any other consideration than is applicable to the legislation of a fully Sovereign State.[53]

There can be no doubt but that competence to legislate with extra-territorial effect was a quality which was possessed by Dominion legislatures, being a quality which was a necessary component of Dominion status. As is only to be expected, therefore, the stronger the political, conventional or statutory intentions concerning the independence of any legislature from Westminster, the more liberal, the less restrictive, should be the judicial interpretation of its competence to pass laws having extra-territorial effect.

It was in the middle of all the uncertainty concerning the extra-territorial powers of *colonial* legislatures that the Government of Ireland Act was passed. A natural assumption, therefore, is that the explicit wording of section 4(1) was used in order to ensure that the territorial competence of the Northern Ireland Parliament would be strictly confined within its own borders—an assumption reinforced by the fact that there were to be two Parliaments in Ireland, each with its own closely defined area of competence. Also, Westminster had power to amend the 1920 Act, including section 4(1), and when difficulties arose did use the power to amend.[54] To deny the Northern Ireland Parliament the power to make laws having extra-territorial effect, therefore, seemed the preferable interpretation of section 4(1). This was indeed the reaction of the Northern Ireland courts, which resolved the questions which arose with a response redolent of *McLeod*, although the issue arose but infrequently. One illustration will suffice.[55] In the unreported case of *R(Alexander)* v *Ministry of Agriculture*, (discussed in *Gallagher* v *Lynn* in the Northern Ireland Court of Appeal in 1936),[56] Alexander, a producer of milk outside Northern Ireland, sought a milk producer's licence under section 2(2) of the Milk and Milk Products Act (NI) 1934, which provided that

> [t]he Ministry of Agriculture shall, on application being made in the prescribed manner, ... grant to *any person* upon the prescribed conditions a licence under this section.

Having been refused a licence, Alexander applied to the King's Bench Division for mandamus to compel the Ministry of Agriculture to grant him the licence. Mandamus was refused, a decision affirmed by the Court of Appeal on the basis that the powers of the Northern Ireland Parliament were subject to territorial limitations and that the Ministry, therefore, could grant licences only to "any person" who produced his milk on premises within Northern Ireland. In the King's Bench Division, Moore LCJ commented that the Court "had been very much helped" by the decision in *McLeod*. As far as the Northern Ireland courts are concerned, this matter rested there.[57] One question, however, seemingly remained open until the 1970s and that was whether or not the Northern Ireland Parliament had power over the territorial waters surrounding Northern Ireland.

The extent of Northern Ireland, as defined in section 1(2) of the Government of Ireland Act and confirmed by the Agreement in 1925 between Great Britain, Northern Ireland and the then Irish Free State, was the six parliamentary counties and the parliamentary boroughs of Belfast and Londonderry. Section 1(2), before the 1922 amendments, defined Southern Ireland as consisting

> of so much of Ireland as is not comprised within the said parliamentary counties and boroughs.

The Act remained silent on the matter of the territorial waters. According to international law, however, the territory of a State includes the territorial waters. This question was raised in the Westminster House of Commons in November 1922, when the following exchange took place between Captain Charles Craig and the then Attorney General who later became Lord Chancellor as the first Viscount Hailsham:

> *Captain Charles Craig:*
> Am I to understand that the Law Officers have actually considered this question, and that they have given a decision in favour of the theory that the territorial waters go with the counties that were included in the six counties of Northern Ireland?
>
> *Sir Douglas Hogg:*
> If I may be permitted to answer that, I may say that I have considered the question, and I have given an opinion that that is so.[58]

This matter actually came before the courts after the Northern Ireland Parliament had been abolished. The Fishery Limits Act 1964 was one of the Acts passed by Westminster enlarging the powers of the Northern Ireland Parliament under section 4 of the 1920 Act. Section 4(2) of the 1964 Act enacted that

> [r]eferences in the Government of Ireland Act 1920 to the portion of Ireland within the jurisdiction of the Parliament of Northern Ireland shall be construed as including, in relation to any matter concerning or connected with fishing, so much of the fishery limits of the British Islands as is adjacent to Northern Ireland but is not nearer to any point on the coasts of Scotland than to any point on the coasts of Northern Ireland.

As a consequence of this grant of powers, the Northern Ireland Parliament passed the Fisheries Act (NI) 1966 (Reprint to 1969), legislating *inter alia* for sea fisheries. In 1974 the case of *DPP* v *McNeill*[59] (originally *Weaver* v *McNeill*, the case being taken over by the Director of Public Prosecutions in December 1974 on the instructions of the Attorney General in light of the constitutional importance of the Resident Magistrate's decision) arose out of a complaint preferred against the respondents for an alleged breach of a part of the 1966 Act dealing with sea fisheries. The Resident Magistrate queried the jurisdiction of a Northern Ireland court to deal with sea fisheries. He was subsequently asked to state a case for the Court of Appeal. He, therefore, asked the Court whether he had been correct in holding

> (l) that the Parliament of the United Kingdom did not have the power to legislate in respect of the fisheries in the seas around the coasts of Northern Ireland and that, therefore, the Fishery Limits Act 1964 section 4 was *ultra vires* the Parliament of the United Kingdom; and
> (2) that the Fisheries Act (NI) 1966 (Reprint to 1969) was *ultra vires* the Parliament of Northern Ireland in so far as it purported to legislate for sea fisheries.

The basis of the argument of the Resident Magistrate, Mr Patrick Maxwell, was that by the bilateral agreement between Great Britain and the Southern Irish leaders of 6th December 1921 "the fisheries in the seas around the whole coast of Ireland (had been) transferred to the Irish Government" and there they remained. The stages in the reasoning that led to this proposition were (l) the term "Ireland" rather than the more specific terms "Southern Ireland" or "Irish Free State" had been used in the Articles of Agreement for a Treaty and subsequent ratifying legislation; (2) that although the Agreement had given Northern Ireland the right to opt out of the terms of the Agreement, which right Northern Ireland had immediately exercised, the unit opting out was confined exclusively to the landmass of Northern Ireland; and this is (3) confirmed by the tripartite agreement of 1925, which accepted the definition of Northern Ireland contained in section 1(2) of the 1920 Act, which makes no mention of territorial waters. It was, therefore, so this argument ran, outside the competence of Westminster to legislate for the coastal waters off Northern Ireland, and, that being so, it could not devolve the power to the Northern Ireland Parliament as it had attempted to do by the Fishery Limits Act 1964.

*Pace* the European Communities Act 1972, it is still easy for a United Kingdom court to refuse an invitation to question the validity of an Act of the Westminster Parliament. It was, therefore, on the safe constitutional bedrock of the doctrine of Parliamentary Sovereignty that the Northern Ireland Court of Appeal answered negatively both the questions of the Resident Magistrate and upheld the validity of the 1964 Act and hence automatically the 1966 Act. The Court of Appeal, however, was also anxious to meet the substance of the Resident Magistrate's arguments, and did so not only through a detailed construction of the provisions of the Government of Ireland Act 1920 but also by reference to the European Fisheries Convention 1964, implemented in the United Kingdom by the Fishery Limits Act 1964. The Governments of both the United Kingdom and the Republic of Ireland were signatories to the Treaty, which by Article 2 gave each coastal state "the exclusive right to fish and exclusive jurisdiction in matters of fisheries" within the six-mile inner belt of the coastal waters. The Lord Chief Justice remarked:

> In view of the "exclusive right and jurisdiction of the coastal state" in Article 2, there can be no overlapping of states with reference to the waters adjacent to the coasts of Northern Ireland. Since these are part of the coasts of the United Kingdom, they are not part of the coasts of the state described in the (1964) Convention as "Ireland" ... I find it surprising if that state, for no tangible consideration, conceded the exclusive right of fishery in a substantial part of its own territorial waters to the Government of the United Kingdom.[60]

It would, therefore, appear that under the Government of Ireland Act 1920 control over the territorial waters off the Northern Ireland coast either remained with the United Kingdom Parliament (it was not necessary for the Court of Appeal to resolve this question, although both the Lord Chief Justice and Jones LJ assumed that control over the territorial waters had passed to Stormont) or passed to the control of the Northern Ireland Parliament, subject to the explicit limitations contained in the 1920 Act[61] and to the overriding right of Westminster to legislate for Northern Ireland. In support of the latter possibility, Lowry LCJ (as he then was), relying on *Croft* v *Dunphy*, observed that

> the power in section 4 of the 1920 Act to make laws for the peace, order and good government of Northern Ireland ... includes power, provided the subject matter is not reserved or excepted, to make laws for the exercise of jurisdiction over territorial waters.[62]

More categorically, Jones LJ stated that

> were it necessary to do so, I would be prepared ... to express the firm view that the position under the 1920 Act was that the rights over the territorial waters off Northern Ireland passed with the six named counties to Northern Ireland ...[63]

subject to the statutory qualifications and section 75 of the 1920 Act. Jones LJ had earlier commented that

> the powers of a territory over its territorial waters include, at any rate, police powers ... and when a subordinate state is granted powers to provide for peace, order and good government it would be very surprising if such subordinate state had no power beyond its actual land limits.[64]

It is the substantive statutory restrictions on the legislative competence of the Northern Ireland Parliament which now require consideration.

*(ii) Excepted and reserved matters and section 5*

The Government of Ireland Act 1920 created three categories of legislative power—those confined to the exclusive competence of Westminster and known as excepted matters; those originally reserved for the institutions of a united Ireland; and the remaining matters, unlisted and unspecified apart from the grant of power in terms of peace, order and good government, which were transferred to the competence of the Northern Ireland Parliament.

Section 4(l), paragraphs (l) to (14) of the 1920 Act listed the excepted matters, those matters permanently excluded from the legislative competence of Stormont. These—similar to the exceptions of 1886, 1893 and 1914—were the Crown, the making of peace or war, the armed forces, treaties with foreign states, dignities or titles of honour, treason, naturalisation, aliens and domicile, trade with any place outside Northern Ireland, submarine cables and wireless telegraphy, aerial navigation, lighthouses, buoys and beacons, coinage and negotiable instruments, weights and measures, trade marks, copyright and patent rights and any matter declared by the Government of Ireland Act to be a reserved matter. All of these, with the exception of the last-mentioned, were either matters of Imperial concern or the concern of the United Kingdom as a whole, on which regional variations were deemed undesirable.

It was contemplated that most of those powers which were reserved at Westminster and withheld from the legislative competence of Stormont would eventually be transferred to the all-Ireland Parliament. With the removal of all likelihood that such an institution would ever come into existence, the difference between excepted and reserved matters became academic. Under the Government of Ireland Act, the following had been reserved—the postal service, the Post Office Savings Bank and Trustee Savings Banks, designs for stamps whether for postal or revenue purposes, the registration of deeds and the Public Record Office of Ireland, certain aspects of land purchase[65] (section 9), certain major taxes[66] (sections 21 and 22) and the Supreme Court of Northern Ireland (section 47).

Apart from these substantive powers being withheld completely from Stormont's competence, it was further precluded from passing laws having certain *effects*, most especially with regard to religious equality. Section 5, a constitutional guarantee, the legislative counterpart of section 8(6) quoted earlier, provided that

> [i]n the exercise of (its) power to make laws under this Act the Parliament of Northern Ireland shall (not) make a law so as either directly or indirectly to establish or endow any religion, or prohibit or restrict the free exercise thereof, or give a preference, privilege or advantage, or impose any disability or disadvantage, on account of religious belief or religious or ecclesiastical status. ...

Section 5 also protected the property of religious bodies. Any law passed in contravention of section 5 would have been void to the extent of its contravention, but no Act of the Northern Ireland Parliament was ever deemed to be void for contravention of the principle of religious equality. When the then Secretary of State for Northern Ireland was asked in December 1981 by a Northern Ireland Member of the Westminster Parliament to list the provisions enacted by the Parliament of Northern Ireland which discriminated between persons or classes of persons on the ground of religious belief, the answer (given on his behalf) was:

> I am not aware of any such provisions.[67]

The presence of section 5 in the 1920 Act, however, was deemed to be of the utmost importance in 1920 in terms of *assuaging* the fears of religious minorities. Westminster, however, had placed no great reliance on its likely *efficacy.* Austen Chamberlain (then Chancellor of the Exchequer) remarked during the Commons' debates on the 1920 Act:

It is not we who are dividing Ireland. It is not we who made the bitterness of religious strife. It is not we who made party coincide with religious differences. Those are the facts of the situation which have embarrassed every English Statesman who has had to deal with Ireland. Those are the difficulties which no Statesman can remove. The cure lies in the hands of Irishmen themselves. It can only come from them.[68]

The section, which was contained in essence (indeed more widely in 1893) although not always in identical wording in the earlier Government of Ireland Bills, and in the 1914 Act, had its constitutional roots in the first part of the First Amendment to the Constitution of the United States of America, which in full provides that

Congress shall make no law respecting an establishment of religion, or prohibiting the free exercise thereof; or abridging the freedom of speech, or of the press; or the right of the people peaceably to assemble, and to petition the Government for a redress of grievances.

Amendment XIV imposes the same restriction on the State legislatures. The Supreme Court has interpreted the First Amendment in such a way as to ensure that what is outlawed is government support both for particular religions and all religions. At one stage, it had been believed that the Amendment merely precluded support for any particular denomination, still, therefore, permitting support for religion in general.

The Commonwealth of Australia Constitution Act 1900, section 9, article 116 contained a similar, more specific, provision:

The Commonwealth shall not make any law for establishing any religion, or for imposing any religious observance, or for prohibiting the free exercise of any religion, and no religious test shall be required as a qualification for any office or public trust under the Commonwealth.

Section 5 also prohibited Stormont from taking "any property without compensation". The context of this provision raised some doubts as to whether or not it covered all property or only ecclesiastical property.[69] The former interpretation was preferred by the Northern Ireland courts[70] and this part of section 5 was the most fecund part of the 1920 Act, in terms of generating litigation[71] challenging the validity of Stormont Acts. It was eventually repealed prospectively by section 14 of the Northern Ireland Act 1962.

Finally, the 1920 Act imposed three other restrictions, similar in effect but less significant, on Stormont's powers. The Parliament was prohibited from passing laws which would affect certain special provisions relating to the Queen's University of Belfast (section 64), to the Grand Lodge of Ancient Free and Accepted Masons of Ireland (section 65(2)), and to certain pensioned officers of local authorities and of Queen's University (section 68).

Apart from all these matters and Westminster's overriding legislative supremacy and the provision of section 6, which provided that Westminster Acts should prevail over Acts of the Northern Ireland Parliament even when they dealt with a matter within the latter's powers, the 1920 Act transferred to the Northern Ireland Parliament by the phrase "peace, order and good government" the power to legislate on all other matters. Remember, again, Dicey's words concerning an indefinite grant of power. Stormont's legislative powers—the transferred powers—were, therefore, considerable. The Parliament could, for example, legislate on matters

> relating to law and order, to the police, to courts other than the Supreme Court, to civil and criminal law, to local government, to health and social services, to education, to planning and development, to commerce and industrial development and internal trade, to agriculture and to finance.[72]

**(c) Constitutional conventions and judicial reasoning**

Although the limitations on Stormont's powers, if enumerated, may seem substantial, consideration of the expansive legal form of the 1920 Act has also to be supplemented by a consideration both of the conventions which developed from 1921 concerning the relationship between Westminster and Stormont and the principles which the judiciary applied in cases involving challenges to the validity of the Acts of the Northern Ireland Parliament.

Of prime importance for a complete understanding of the extent of the powers of the Northern Ireland Parliament over transferred matters is a consideration of the relevant constitutional conventions. As far as their respective legislative powers were concerned, it was unarguably the position that Westminster not only possessed exclusive competence with relation to excepted and reserved matters, but also, through the doctrine of Parliamentary Sovereignty generally and through sections 6, 12 (the Governor's power to withhold the Royal Assent) and 75 of the 1920 Act specifically, shared with the Northern Ireland Parliament competence over transferred matters. Also unarguably, the Northern Ireland Parliament was precluded from legislating directly or substantially on excepted and reserved matters but, within the confines of the express statutory limitations, had plenary legislative competence over transferred matters. The crucial question, therefore, was under what circumstances or conditions would Westminster exercise its powers over transferred matters? The answer to this question was seemingly the same as that which related to the relationship between Westminster and the Dominions. Section 4 of the Statute of Westminster gave statutory force to a pre-existing and very strong convention (referred to in its Preamble), namely that

[n]o Act of the Parliament of the United Kingdom passed after the commencement of this Act shall extend, or be deemed to extend, to a Dominion as part of the law of that Dominion, unless it is expressly declared in that Act that that Dominion has requested, and consented to, the enactment thereof.

A convention, similar although not identical to this statutory provision, "developed" with regard to the Northern Ireland Parliament—Westminster would legislate over transferred matters only with the consent (either full-blooded or half-hearted) of the Northern Ireland Government. This apparently gave the Northern Ireland Parliament exclusive powers over transferred matters. It was a position reinforced by a ruling of the Speaker of the Westminster House of Commons in 1923, that no questions could be asked at Westminster on matters transferred to the Northern Ireland Parliament on the ground that there was no Minister responsible therefor at Westminster:

With regard to those subjects which have been delegated to the Government of Northern Ireland, questions must be asked of Ministers in Northern Ireland, and not in this House.[73]

A similar ruling was made by the Speaker of the Northern Ireland House of Commons ruling out questions and debate on matters outside its own competence:

Since ... we have no power to make laws on any of these reserved matters, they are not *prima facie* proper subjects for discussion here.[74]

The reasoning that the absence of power to legislate on a matter precluded debate on the matter was not only curious and attracted strong criticism but also heightened the appearance of exclusiveness in the areas of competence of the respective Parliaments. Professor Newark pointed out that the Northern Ireland Speaker's ruling

has rather belied the anticipation, for if you go back to the debate on the Home Rule Bills of the last century you will find that it was generally assumed that though the subordinate Irish would have no powers to legislate on Imperial affairs, there was nothing to prevent them talking: their resolutions would be destitute of legal effect, but of considerable moral significance. ... A Parliament—as the name shows—is a place to talk and, probably, by and large, less harm is done by talk than through legislation. Furthermore, if you give your politician a restricted field he may well lose a sense of proportion. ...[75]

Be that as it may—and the argument has considerable force—the conventions remained, both to bolster the belief that the Northern Ireland Parliament had been given an exclusive competence over matters transferred to it and also to reduce the expression of Northern Ireland opinion on excepted and reserved matters to whatever the then thirteen, later twelve, Northern Ireland Members at Westminster could achieve or felt inclined to try to achieve.

This amalgam of statute and convention which marked the relationship between Westminster and Stormont attracted two inevitable analogies. The first was that based on the conventional relationship which prevailed between Westminster and the Dominions prior to the enactment of the Statute of Westminster. It was an analogy induced by the convention of non-intervention by Westminster without "local" consent. The acceptability of the analogy depends upon the extent to which the convention is deemed to take precedence over the statutory provisions of the 1920 Act, not least section 75, which tended to militate against the Dominion analogy. In turn, of course, the prominence or otherwise of section 75 was largely dependent upon the surrounding political situation. Professor Calvert, writing in 1968, produced five reasons why the Dominion analogy was a fallacious or misleading one:

(l) In all cases to which the convention of non-intervention by Westminster is regarded as applying, the territory in question has been entirely self-governed (which Northern Ireland was not);
(2) In no case has the territory in question been a part of the United Kingdom (as Northern Ireland at all times has been), at the time when the alleged convention developed;
(3) In no case did the territory in question enjoy a say in United Kingdom affairs via the medium of representation at Westminster;
(4) In no case was there financial integration between the territory in question and the United Kingdom;
(5) In the case of none of the Dominions affected by the convention did the constituent Act contain legislation parallel to that of section 75. ...[76]

Unquestionably, however, as far as point (5) is concerned, the convention of intervention only with consent had changed the solemn and potentially real powers of section 75 into a constitutional longstop rather in the way that the saga over the Local Government Act (Northern Ireland) 1922 weakened the force of section l2. The points of distinction, however, which Professor Calvert draws cumulatively show that the Dominion analogy falls through the distortion it induces with regard to Northern Ireland's self-governing powers. The degree of autonomy possessed by the Northern Ireland Parliament could not be equated with that possessed by the Dominions. The movement from colonial to Dominion status reflected a weakening of the ties between Westminster and the Dominions. As it transpired, this was not a movement paralleled—nor generally wanted—in Northern Ireland. The suitability of the Dominion analogy, therefore, depends to a very large extent upon the period which one is considering.[77] In the early years of the life of the Northern Ireland Parliament, it was conceivable, whatever the strict legal provisions of the 1920 Act, such as sections 6, 12 and 75, that the relationship between Northern Ireland and Westminster could ultimately have developed into a Dominion relationship. Certainly as long as the Irish Free State remained in the Empire, which it did until 1949, and as long as the tighter grouping of the Empire existed rather than the British Commonwealth of Nations, the possibility that such a development would take place was greater (without necessarily even being great) rather than smaller. The increasing independence of the Dominions, however, reflected in the emergence of the British Commonwealth, was matched by certain *integrative* tendencies on the part of Northern Ireland, both financial and legal, such as the "step by step" policy pursued by the Northern Ireland Parliament especially in the fields of health and social services. This policy was followed to ensure similarity of treatment for the population of Northern Ireland with that of Great Britain and led to the Northern Ireland Parliament frequently passing Acts virtually identical in substance to those passed by Westminster for Great Britain. The following Acts, for example, were paralleled in Northern Ireland within three years or less of the Westminster original: Legitimacy Act 1926, Adoption of Children Act 1926, Trade Disputes Act 1927, Road Traffic Act 1930, Children and Young Persons Act 1933, Law Reform Act 1934, Road Traffic Act 1934, Hire Purchase Act 1938, Holidays with Pay Act 1938, Evidence Act 1938, Prevention of Frauds (Investment) Act 1939, Truck Act 1940, Family Allowances Act 1945 and the Law Reform (Miscellaneous Provisons) Act 1949.[78] The parity argument should not, however, be overstated. The Kilbrandon Royal Commission on the Constitution in a quantitative, but not qualitative, consideration of the 190 Acts of the Northern Ireland Parliament passed between the beginning of 1965 and February 1970 found that 36 Acts closely followed earlier Westminster statutes, 76 were peculiar to Northern Ireland, 62 fell somewhere in between these two categories and the remaining 16 Acts were technical, such as the Appropriation and Consolidated Fund Acts. Of the 1,602 Statutory Rules and

Orders (delegated legislation) made during the same period, 400 were parity instruments, 613 were peculiar to Northern Ireland, 549 were in the intermediate category and 40 were technical.[79] In broad terms, it was roughly estimated that

> if legislation is divided into two categories only—parity and non-parity matters—about two-thirds of both administrative and legislative time [was] spent on purely Northern Ireland matters.[80]

Parity arguments apart, however, it was increasingly likely that the Dominion analogy would fall as Dominion status itself yielded to the even more inapposite Commonwealth nexus of relationships.

The colonial experience was equally unable to yield a sufficiently accurate analogy. Although it had some relevance, for example, with regard to the extra-territorial operation of Stormont's legislation, the superordinate role of Westminster and sections 6 and 12 of the 1920 Act, it was both politically and generally an undesirable analogy to apply to an integral part of the United Kingdom.

The other analogy that was drawn, in terms of explaining the nature of the relationship between Westminster and the Northern Ireland Parliament, came from federalism, the system of government which allocates exclusive powers as between co-ordinate central and regional or provincial legislatures. In strict legal terms, the relationship was without argument not federal, but the convention of non-intervention by Westminster in transferred matters gave, it was argued, the guise of—or quasi—federalism. This guise of federalism was given an appearance of greater reality, for a while at least, by the attitude of the courts.

In *Gallagher* v *Lynn*,[81] to which brief reference has already been made, the House of Lords was called upon to determine the validity of the Milk and Milk Products Act (NI) 1934. The appellant was a dairy farmer in County Donegal in the Irish Free State and he had, prior to the 1934 Act, been wont to sell his milk in Londonderry in Northern Ireland. The 1934 Act provided that only milk of certain specified grades could be sold for human consumption in Northern Ireland when the Ministry of Agriculture "on application being made in the prescribed manner and on payment of the appropriate fee . . . (granted) to *any person*" a licence to do so. One of the conditions precedent to the granting of a licence was inspection by the Ministry of the dairy premises.

In the unreported case of *R(Alexander)* v *Ministry of Agriculture*, as has been noted, the Northern Ireland Court of Appeal held that mandamus would not issue against the Ministry of Agriculture to compel it to grant licences to persons whose dairies were outside Northern Ireland on the ground that the powers of the Northern Ireland Parliament were subject to the territorial limitation and that the Ministry could only grant licences to "any person" who produced his milk within Northern Ireland. After the passing of the Act and the decision under it in *Alexander*, Gallagher, having applied for and having been refused a producer's licence, continued to sell his milk in Londonderry and was convicted under the 1934 Act. On appeal both to the Northern Ireland Court of Appeal and to the House of Lords, it was argued on his behalf that the 1934 Act was *ultra vires* as being in conflict with section 4(1)(7) of the Government of Ireland Act 1920 which withheld from the Northern Ireland Parliament the power

> to make laws except in respect of matters exclusively relating to (Northern Ireland) or some part thereof and (without prejudice to that general limitation) that (it) shall not have power to make laws in respect of the following matters, in particular, namely ... Trade with any place out of the part of Ireland within [its] jurisdiction ... .

The Court of Appeal held that the primary object of the legislation was not interference with trade and that, therefore, the 1934 Act did not come within the excepted matter of section 4(1)(7). Gallagher, therefore, appealed to the House of Lords. The House, Lord Atkin giving its unanimous decision, dealt first with the point of construction arising from the use of the phrase "any person" and held that the phrase related to any person who chose to sell his milk in Northern Ireland, wherever that milk was produced. This included Gallagher and, therefore, meant that the question of the Act's validity had to be resolved. Lord Atkin stated that

> this Milk Act is not a law "in respect of" trade; but is a law for the peace, order and good government of Northern Ireland "in respect of" precautions taken to secure the health of the inhabitants of Northern Ireland by protecting them from the dangers of an unregulated supply of milk. These questions affecting limitation on the legislative powers of subordinate parliaments or the distribution of powers between parliaments in a federal system are now familiar, and I do not propose to cite the whole range of authority which has largely arisen in discussion of the powers of Canadian Parliaments. It is well established that you are to look at the "true nature and character of the legislation": *Russell* v *The Queen*, "the pith and substance of the legislation". If on the view of the statute as a whole, you find that the substance of the legislation is within the express powers, then it is not invalidated if incidentally it affects matters which are outside the authorised field. The legislation must not under the guise of dealing with one matter in fact encroach upon the forbidden field. Nor are you to look only at the object of the legislator. An Act may have a perfectly lawful object, eg, to promote the health of the inhabitants, but may seek to achieve that object by invalid methods, eg, a

direct prohibition of any trade with a foreign country. In other words, you may certainly consider the clauses of an Act to see whether they are passed "in respect of" the forbidden subject. In the present case any suggestion of an indirect attack upon trade is disclaimed by the appellant. There could be no foundation for it. The true nature and character of the Act, its pith and substance, is that it is an Act to protect the health of the inhabitants of Northern Ireland; and in those circumstances, though it may incidentally affect trade with County Donegal, it is not passed "in respect of trade" and is, therefore, not subject to attack on that ground.[82]

The reliance of the House of Lords on *Russell* v *The Queen*[83] was engendered by a false parallel. Under the British North America Act 1867, the co-ordinate Federal (or Dominion) and provincial legislatures in Canada were given, in order to secure their exclusive areas of competence, separately specified powers; that is, the 1867 Act sections 91 and 92 provided a double enumeration of exclusive powers. In such a case and in the absence of an overall sovereign legislature with plenary powers for the whole nation (as Westminster possessed with regard to the whole of the United Kingdom) the possibility of a legislative gap was real. As Professor Calvert subsequently argued against the application in *Gallagher* v *Lynn* of the *Russell* test:

The pith and substance doctrine in Canada was arguably necessary to avoid a hiatus in legislative power which might otherwise stem from the double enumeration of powers in sections 91 and 92 of the British North America Act 1867 ... It was possible (under this scheme) for a law, in two aspects, to be in relation to matters on each list. Since provincial legislatures cannot legislate in relation to matters on the Dominion Parliament list and vice versa, a strict interpretation might have resulted in there being no body competent to enact many items of legislation. In these circumstances it would be not only reasonable but necessary to resort to some test of characterisation of predominance and this is what was done.[84]

The pith and substance test, inappropriate as it was for Northen Ireland, clearly tended to enlarge the legislative powers of the Northern Ireland Parliament. It ignored the fact that Westminster was empowered to legislate for Northern Ireland should the need arise—for example, to protect the health and well-being of the Northern Ireland population, or to protect its farmers from adverse competition from the Irish Free State, or whatever else might arise and might be outside the general power transferred to the Northern Ireland Parliament. Instead, facilitated by Gallagher's counsel—who chose not to argue that the Act was an indirect attack on cross-border trade—the House of Lords laid down a liberal interpretation of "in respect of" in section 4(1): merely incidentally to affect an excepted matter would not be sufficient to attach invalidity to a Northern Ireland statute. The "pith and substance" test at any rate, given its source and its effects, tended to enhance the impression that the Northern Ireland Parliament was something closely akin to a Canadian provincial legislature. Towards the end of the existence of the Northern Ireland Parliament, the courts would revise their opinions,[85] but by then the political climate had so changed that nothing could gainsay Westminster's supremacy, its power unilaterally to amend the 1920 Act, and the force of section 75, all powers being totally hostile to the federalism analogy.

That is, the acceptability of this analogy of quasi-federalism depended on the extent to which the conventions—and the courts—were allowed to soften the strict legal form. Professor Wheare in his classic, *Federal Government*, strongly denied that the relationship in any way equated to a federal one, but he looked only at the provisions of the 1920 Act:

> ... [T]he relation between the parliament of the United Kingdom and that of Northern Ireland cannot be described as federal. It is true that the people of Northern Ireland are subject to two governments ... just as people in an American state are subject to two governments. But the two governments for Northern Ireland are not co-ordinate.

Professor Wheare then mentioned the grant of power contained in section 4, but placed it in the context of section 75. He then continued:

> There is nothing in law to prevent the parliament of the United Kingdom from passing laws for Northern Ireland not merely on the specified reserved subjects, but on any subject whatever. Moreover, the parliament of Northern Ireland received its powers from the Parliament of the United Kingdom, and the latter can reduce or increase or abolish these powers. Of these two governments in the United Kingdom, one only can be described as independent and that is the government at Westminster. The government at Stormont is a dependent government. There remains the fact that the government of the United Kingdom is also the government of Great Britain, whereas if the federal principle is to be strictly applied, the government of Great Britain should be separate and independent. And thus although great consideration is shown to Northern Ireland and no interference in provincial affairs occurs unless absolutely necessary, there is here no example of federal government.[86]

It almost goes without saying that this is an impeccably correct assessment of the strict legal form; it does, however, seem to pay insufficient attention to the strength of the conventions and the way they operated throughout most of the fifty years of the Northern Ireland Parliament's existence. Those who laid greater emphasis on the conventions found the quasi-federal analogy apposite. Ultimately, however, although political realities can submerge legal form, constitutional conventions must yield to statute and this analogy fell—heavily

—when Westminster used the full force of section 75 and its own inherent sovereignty, dissolved the Northern Ireland Parliament and introduced direct rule in Northern Ireland.

For fifty years Northern Ireland, endowed with all the trappings of a "mini-state"—a Governor, a Parliament passing Acts, a Prime Minister and a Cabinet—had as its constitution one it had never sought, but one to which it had rapidly adapted. In 1972 it all came to an end.

## NOTES

1 Because this Act served as Northern Ireland's constitution for some fifty years, it was felt that it should be considered not only in terms of the light it sheds on subsequent developments but also, in general terms only, in its own right, although in the latter respect emphasis has deliberately been placed upon the less frequently highlighted facets of the Act.

2 Quoted in Bogdanor, *Devolution* (1979), pp 44-5.

3 Cmd 1561 (November, 1921).

4 *Ibid*, p 5.

5 Under the Redistribution of Seats (Ireland) Act 1918 the number of Northern Ireland Westminster constituencies would have been thirty, but this was reduced to thirteen by section 19 and schedule 5 of the 1920 Act. Under the House of Commons Redistribution of Seats Act 1979 (now the Parliamentary Constituencies Act 1986) the number has been increased to seventeen.

6 Quoted in Buckland, *Irish Unionism: Ulster Unionism* (1973), pp 116-7.

7 Quoted in Palley, *The Evolution, Disintegration and Possible Reconstruction of the Northern Ireland Constitution* (1972), p 377, note 37.

8 This power was actually exercised by the Lord Lieutenant, Viscount FitzAlan of Derwent, who had been appointed in April 1921. Consequential upon the establishment of the Irish Free State, the new office of Governor of Northern Ireland replaced that of the Lord Lieutenant and in December 1922 the Duke of Abercorn was appointed as Governor. See further below.

9 This whole account of the 1922 Bill is from Buckland, *The Factory of Grievances* (1979), pp 267-275, from where the quotations are taken. From June 1922 until May 1923, a civil war was waged in the south between the pro-(1921) Treaty and the anti-Treaty forces. Collins himself was killed in August 1922.

10 Wallace, *Northern Ireland: 50 years of Self-Government* (1971), p 28.

11 The Northern Ireland Parliament met first in the City Hall, Belfast and then moved to (as it was then called) Assembly's (Presbyterian) College also in Belfast. Parliament Buildings at Stormont were opened by the Prince of Wales in 1932. The term "Stormont" is usually used, however, with regard to the whole life of the Northern Ireland Parliament and the 1920 Act system of government.

12 Section 11(1) provided that: "There shall be a session ... of the Parliament of Northern Ireland, once at least in every year, so that twelve months shall not intervene

between the last sitting of ... Parliament in one session and their first sitting in the next session."

13 Buckland, *The Factory of Grievances*, p 234, from which the following account is taken.

14 Quoted in Palley, *op cit*, p 394, note 116.

15 Buckland, *op cit*, p 235.

16 *Ibid*, p 240.

17 Bogdanor, *op cit*, p 52.

18 Buckland, *op cit*, p 240.

19 Note that section 14(5) of the 1920 Act required the Northern Ireland Parliament to pay "due regard" to the population of the constituencies.

20 See Donaldson, "The Senate of Northern Ireland" (1958) *Public Law*, p 135, esp pp 135-138.

21 Donaldson, *ibid*, p 136.

22 Quoted in Donaldson, *ibid*, p 137.

23 For another later expedient see the Scotland Act 1978, section 66. Those with short memories called this "the West Lothian question" after the MP for West Lothian, Tam Dalyell, who actively pursued this aspect of representation. It should be noted, however, that it was not intended, had there been devolution to a Scottish Assembly, to reduce Scottish representation at Westminster.

24 The Fourth Article also provided that the method of election would be regulated by Act of Parliament; this Act was passed and incorporated into the Union legislation. See Calvert, *Constitutional Law in Northern Ireland* (1968) pp 80 *et seq*.

25 In *ex parte Canon Selwyn* (1872) 36 JP 54, the applicant sought, unsuccessfully, a means of challenging the validity of the Royal Assent to the 1869 Act on the ground that its terms conflicted with the Queen's Coronation Oath and the Act of Settlement. Cockburn CJ stated: "An act of the legislature is superior in authority to any court of law. We have only to administer the law as we find it, and no court could pronounce a judgment as to the validity of an act of Parliament." The applicant, however, made no reference to Article 5 of the Acts of Union, which united the Churches of England and Ireland established "for ever". The 1869 Act dissolved that union and disestablished the Church of Ireland, contrary to Article 5.

26 The Petition of the Earl of Antrim and eleven other Irish Peers [1967] 1 AC 691. See also Dunboyne, "Irish Representative Peers" (1967) *Public Law* 314 and Lysaght, "Irish Peers and the House of Lords" (1967) 18 *NILQ* 277.

27 Letters Patent constituting the office of Governor conferred the powers of the office: "We do hereby authorise and command the Governor for the time being of Northern Ireland ... to do and execute in due manner as respects Northern Ireland all things which by virtue of the [1920] Act and our Letters Patent of the 27th day of April 1921, or otherwise belonged to the office of Lord Lieutenant at the time of the passing of the Irish Free State Constitution Act 1922 ...". See Quekett, *op cit*, Vol 1, p 35, note 1.

28 Calvert, *op cit*, p 162. On pp 162-72, Calvert thoroughly reviews all the relevant authorities on the question of challenge to the validity of legislation under this head.

29 Cmd 2768 (1926) p 14. See, generally, Wade and Bradley, *Constitutional and Administrative Law* (10th ed, 1985), chapter 24.

30 Section 51 of the 1920 Act made special provision for the decision of "constitutional questions" by the Judicial Committee of the Privy Council. Essentially, the Governor or a Secretary of State, where it was expedient in the public interest to obtain a speedy determination, could refer to the Committee for decision questions on the validity of an Act of the Parliament of Northern Ireland or any provision thereof, questions on the validity of a Bill (or any of its provisions) introduced into that Parliament or a question whether any service was a transferred service within the meaning of the 1920 Act. Technically the reference was made by the Sovereign. Only one such reference was made, the consequence of a petition from Belfast Corporation to the Governor who forwarded it to the Home Secretary: *In re a reference under the 1920 Act: In re section 3 of the Finance Act (NI) 1934* [1936] AC 352. See Quekett, *op cit*, Vol 3 (1946), pp 51-58; Calvert, *op cit*, pp 298-301. Section 51(3) provided that subsection (1) was without prejudice to any other power of the Sovereign in Council to refer any question to the Judicial Committee or the right of any person to petition the Sovereign for such a reference.

31 [1930] AC 124, 135. Quoted in Calvert, *op cit*, pp 166-7.

32 10 App Cas (1884-85) 675.

33 At p 678. Emphasis supplied.

34 [1938] NI 21, 29.

35 At p 39.

36 Calvert, *op cit*, p 170.

37 [1933] AC 156.

38 [1972] NI 91.

39 At p 116. See further below.

40 [1971] AC 632. See MacCormick, (1970) 86 *LQR* 171.

41 [1952] AC 427, 450.

42 "The Constitution of Northern Ireland" in *Devolution of Government* (ed D.G. Neill, 1953), pp 10-11.

43 Quoted in chapter I, above.

44 See Calvert, *op cit*, pp 211-220.

45 [1891] AC 455.

46 At p 457.

47 [1919] NZLR 305.

48 (1917) 33 *LQR* 117. *Cf* O'Connell (1959) 75 *LQR* 318.

49 Cmd 2768.

50 Cmd 3479. Both these quotations are taken from O. Hood Phillips, *Constitutional and Administrative Law* (7th ed, 1987), p 743.

51 [1935] AC 500, 520.

52 [1933] AC 156.

53 At p 163.

54 See, *eg*, the Northern Ireland (Miscellaneous Provisions) Acts 1928 and 1932; the Northern Ireland Act 1947 and the Fishery Limits Act 1964.

55 There are not many other cases cited and analysed by Calvert on pp 213-20; they include *Plumb* v *Fermanagh CC* [1923] 2 IR 54, *Cash* v *Rainey* [1941] NI 52 (where the point was not dealt with directly) and *Duffy* v *Ministry of Labour* [1962] NI 6 (CA).

56 [1936] NI 131, 132-3.

57 Calvert has, however, argued in reliance on the decision of the Privy Council in 1948 in *Wallace Bros* v *Commissioners of Income Tax (Bombay)* AIR (35) 1948 PC 118, that the approach of the NI courts was largely misconceived and unduly restrictive of the powers of the NI Parliament. See pp 213 *et seq.*

58 HC Vol 159, col 451. Referred to in Quekett, *op cit*, Vol II, p 6 and quoted by Jones LJ in *DPP* v *McNeill*—see below.

59 [1975] NI 177. See C.R.Symmons, "Who owns the territorial waters of Northern Ireland" (1976) 27 *NILQ* 48. Symmons points out, on pp 48-49, that one of the arguments put in favour of the territorial waters belonging to the Irish Republic was the presence of the adjective "parliamentary" (counties and boroughs) in section 1(2) of the 1920 Act. Traditionally, the boundaries of parliamentary areas end at the low water mark, and, therefore, the argument ran, the extent of Northern Ireland was confined to the landmass. See further (1983) 32 *ICLQ* 1013 and (1984) 33 *ICLQ* 1064.

60 At pp 182-3.

61 *Eg* section 4 (1)(11).

62 [1975] NI 177, 184. The LCJ immediately prior to this quotation had referred to the NI (Miscellaneous Provisions) Act 1932, section 9(1), which enacted that section 4 of the 1920 Act did not prevent the Parliament of Northern Ireland from legislating with regard to the sea bed.

63 At p 192.

64 At p 190.

65 The "general subject-matter of the Acts relating to land purchase in Ireland" was made a reserved matter pending the completion of land purchase. The NI Land Purchase (Winding Up) Act 1935, by section 1(3), provided that this matter largely "shall cease to be a reserved matter" and transferred power to deal with the matter to the Northern Ireland Parliament and Government. The Royal Irish Constabulary and its management and control were also reserved matters for a period not exceeding three years: see section 9(1). The force was, however, disbanded by the Constabulary (Ireland) Act 1922, an Act of the Westminster Parliament, in August 1922. The Northern Ireland Parliament, by the Constabulary Act (NI) of May 1922, provided for the establishment, management and control of the Royal Ulster Constabulary.

66 The "transferred" taxes were then estate duties, motor licence duties, stamp duties and certain minor excise duties.

67 HC (1981-82) Vol 14, col 376. For a fuller consideration of this area, see Graham "Religion and Education: The Constitutional Problem", 1982 *NILQ* (Vol 33), p 20.

68 Quoted in Calvert, *op cit*, p 254 note 19.

69 This provision was apparently added as a misplaced amendment to the 1920 Act as

it passed through Parliament—see Newark in *Ulster under Home Rule* (ed Wilson, 1955), p 28. It was not in the original Bill; but see clause 4(5) of the 1893 Bill.

70 *O'Neill* v *NIRTB* [1938] NI 104 and *Robb* v *Electricity Board for NI* [1937] NI 103.

71 See the references in Calvert, *op cit*, p 271.

72 Palley, *op cit*, p 389.

73 1923 HC Vol 63, Col 1625. Quoted in Calvert, *op cit*, p 96.

74 HC Debs (NI) Vol 8, Col 490. Quoted in Calvert, *op cit*, p 104.

75 In *Devolution of Government* (ed Neill, 1953), p 12.

76 *Op cit*, p 90.

77 Professor Newark (in Neill ed, 1953) *op cit*, p 16 commented: "Already there are signs of a movement in Northern Ireland in the direction of a dominion status ... It has certain attractions, especially on the financial side, and to some people it may look as if dominion status is the logical goal when any part of Her Majesty's dominions moves away from the complete and absolute control of the Westminster Parliament. Now, though dominion status is a *possibility*, I am convinced myself that it would be a fatal step. Economically, culturally and politically, Northern Ireland is too bound up with England, Scotland and Wales to contemplate an existence as a completely separate constitutional entity. In order to sustain the role of a dominion a country needs not only the desire for independence but the capacity for maintaining that independence, and six counties with one modern city does not, to my eyes, possess the makings of a dominion—at least not a first-class dominion ...".

78 Newark in (Wilson ed), *op cit*, pp 52-3.

79 Cmnd 5460 (1973) Vol 1, para 1261, p 379; see also Maguire, "Parliament and the Direct Rule of Northern Ireland", 1975 *Irish Jurist*, 81,85.

80 Royal Commission on the Constitution, *op cit*, Minutes of Evidence, Vol III, Appendix II, p 176.

81 [1937] AC 863. Quekett, *op cit*, Vol III, p 52, note 1 states that during the course of the various proceedings under the 1934 Act, "applications were made by a milk vendor to have the question of the Act's validity referred to the Privy Council under section 51 of the 1920 Act, but the applications were not acceded to".

82 At pp 869-870. For a fuller consideration of this point, see Calvert, "Gallagher v Lynn re-examined: a legislative fraud?" 1972 *Public Law* 11.

83 (1882) 7 App Cas 829.

84 Calvert, *Constitutional Law in Northern Ireland*, *op cit*, p 194.

85 See *R (Hume)* v *Londonderry Justices* [1972] NI 91. The quotation from Calvert criticising the reliance in *Gallagher* on the *Russell* test was quoted with approval by the LCJ in *Hume*. In *Hume* at issue was a statutory rule made by the Northern Ireland Government in 1970 conferring power on any commissioned officer in HM Forces to require, in certain circumstances, a group of three or more persons to disperse. Section 4(1)(3) of the 1920 Act made the armed forces of the Crown an excepted matter. John Hume and four other persons were convicted at the Magistrates' Court in Londonderry of failure to disperse contrary to the statutory rule. The applicants sought an order of certiorari to quash the conviction on the ground, *inter alia*, that the regulation was *ultra*

*vires* section 4 of the 1920 Act. The NI QBD quashed the conviction. Lowry LCJ (as he then was) observed that he had found "no case where the doctrine of incidental effect has been called in aid of a provision expressly directed to the forbidden topic" (at p 105), considered both the pith and substance test and Professor Calvert's arguments thereon and concluded (at p 111): "Both object and method must be valid, and there is force in the argument that the *method* employed in [the] regulation ... is invalid because, and so far as, it makes use of members of the forces to achieve the lawful *object* of preserving the peace and maintaining order." The decision of the QBD was given on 23rd February 1972. At 10 pm that evening the Northern Ireland Bill had its second reading in the Westminster House of Commons, receiving the Royal Assent at 2.11 am the following day. See Zander, *The Law-Making Process* (3rd ed, 1989), p 55. Section 1 of the Northern Ireland Act 1972 declares that the limitations imposed by section 4(1)(3) of the 1920 Act on the Parliament of Northern Ireland to make laws "shall not have effect, and shall be deemed never to have had effect" to preclude the inclusion in its laws of all provision relating to HM Forces. During the debate on the second reading of the Bill, the Attorney General gave an undertaking that "any prosecution now pending, which would fail if today's judgment stood, will be abandoned or stopped and no new prosecution of that kind will be initiated in relation to the past ... [Further] the Bill will not act retrospectively affecting civil claims based on any matter other than the technical defect in the power of troops, affected by the Bill." Quoted in Bailey, Harris and Jones, *Civil Liberties: Cases and Materials* (2nd ed, 1985), p 204.

86 Wheare, *Federal Government* (4th ed, 1963), pp 31-2.

# IV

# DEVOLUTION REVISITED

## INTRODUCTION

The events from 1968 to 1972[1] may seem to belong more naturally to the previous chapter, affecting, as they did, the demise of the system of government operating under the Government of Ireland Act 1920, but although the 1920 Act has now faded from the constitutional scene, these events and the attitudes they reflect and have engendered have continued to permeate all subsequent constitutional—and other—developments. Until 1968, Northern Ireland and its constitution were, at least relatively speaking, stable. In 1968 the increasingly euphemistically-named "Troubles" began. The first civil rights demonstration on 24th August 1968 from Caledon to Dungannon in County Tyrone passed off relatively peacefully, but the second demonstration in Londonderry on 5th October 1968 did not. The mixture of demonstrators, counter-demonstrators and police proved combustible. The Commission, set up by the Northern Ireland Government in March 1969, under the chairmanship of Lord Cameron, identified the general causes of the October 1968 and subsequent disorders as follows:

(1) A rising sense of continuing injustice and grievance among large sections of the Catholic population in Northern Ireland, in particular in Londonderry and Dungannon, in respect of (i) inadequacy of housing provision by certain local authorities; (ii) unfair methods of allocation of houses built and let by such authorities, in particular refusals and omissions to adopt a "points" system in determining priorities and making allocations; (iii) misuse in certain cases of discretionary powers of allocation of houses in order to perpetuate Unionist control of the local authority.

(2) Complaints, now well documented in fact, of discrimination in the making of local government appointments, at all levels but especially in senior posts, to the prejudice of non-Unionists and especially Catholic members of the community, in some Unionist controlled authorities.

(3) Complaints, again well documented, in some cases of deliberate manipulation of local government electoral boundaries and in others a refusal to apply for their necessary extension in order to achieve and maintain Unionist control of local authorities and so to deny to Catholics influence in local government proportionate to their numbers.

(4) A growing and powerful sense of resentment and frustration among the Catholic population at failure to achieve either acceptance on the part of the Government of any need to investigate these complaints or to provide and enforce a remedy for them.

(5) Resentment, particularly among Catholics, as to the existence of the Ulster Special Constabulary (the "B" specials) as a partisan and para-military force recruited exclusively from Protestants.

(6) Widespread resentment among Catholics in particular at the continuance in force of regulations made under the Special Powers Act, and of the continued presence in the statute book of the Act itself.

(7) Fears and apprehensions among Protestants of a threat to Unionist domination and control of Government by increase of Catholic population and powers.[2]

This catalogue must also be placed against the broader findings of the Cameron Commission:

It is plain from what we have heard, read and observed that the train of events and incidents which began in Londonderry on October 5th 1968 has had as its background, on the one hand a widespread sense of political and social grievance for long unadmitted and therefore unredressed by successive Governments of Northern Ireland and, on the other, sentiments of fear and apprehension sincerely and tenaciously felt and believed of risks to the integrity and indeed continued existence of the state. These opposing sentiments had by that time built up tensions and pressures within the community of such a kind that incidents comparatively small in themselves could readily lead to explosions of violence of a dangerous and serious character. We have also no doubt whatever that the sentiments of grievance expressed in the representations and evidence placed before us were dispassionately and sincerely held, and supported by a formidable catalogue of supporting facts... At the same time ... it very soon became plain to us that in such a situation as we have described, politically subversive and mischievous elements could and in the event did, for their own purposes deliberately inflame passions on all sides and either irresponsibly or deliberately invoke violent incidents to their own assumed advantage. And we were not without ample evidence and information which have led us to conclude that such elements were and are present and were ready to foment and exploit and did foment and exploit for their own ends genuine grievances or complaints.[3]

There were two direct and related consequences of this outbreak and then upsurge in violence. First a series of legislative and other measures were provided by the Northern Ireland Government and Parliament on its own initiative or as a result of active prompting by the Westminster Government.[4] These included electoral reform in 1968-69 (the provision of adult universal suffrage for local council elections to replace the franchise previously restricted to ratepayers, the abolition of the "Business Vote" in Stormont elections, and the establishment of a Boundary Commission to scrutinise the Northern Ireland House of Commons constituencies); the establishment in 1969 of the offices of Parliamentary Commissioner for Administration (to investigate complaints of injustice suffered as a result of maladministration by the Northern Ireland Departments)[5] and the Commissioner for Complaints (with a similar remit for local councils and other public bodies); the transfer in 1969 of the powers of the County Borough Council of Londonderry and Londonderry Rural District Council to the Londonderry Development Commission; the creation in 1969 of a Ministry of Community Relations and an independent Community Relations Commission; the disbandment in 1969 of the "B" Specials and their replacement with the RUC Reserve;[6] the enactment in 1970 of the Prevention of Incitement to Hatred Act (NI); the creation in 1970 of an independent Police Authority, (representative of the whole community and with a remit which included scrutiny of the handling by the "Inspector-General"[7] of complaints made by members of the public against members of the RUC); and the institution, as from 1971, of the Northern Ireland Housing Executive, a central housing body responsible for all public authority house building and allocations. Furthermore, the whole system of local government was reorganised by the Local Government Act (NI) 1972.

The second consequence of the onset of the "Troubles" was the greater involvement of the Westminster Government in Northern Ireland affairs. This manifested itself most clearly on 14th August 1969 with the deployment in the Province, and specifically in Londonderry and Belfast, of large contingents of the Army at the request of the Northern Ireland Government to assist a police force exhausted by both nationalist and loyalist violence. The convention of the non-intervention of Westminster in Northern Ireland affairs already weakened now inevitably disappeared. From August 1969 the General Officer Commanding the Armed Forces in Northern Ireland had been given overall responsibility for security operations in Northern Ireland, including control of the deployment of the RUC when they were used in a security role, and this effectively meant that the Westminster Government (specifically the Prime Minister, the Home Secretary and the Secretary of State for Defence) assumed full responsibility for security within Northern Ireland. Virtually simultaneously on 19th August 1969 there was issued what is commonly called the Downing Street Declaration,[8] a communiqué issued after a meeting between the United Kingdom Prime Minister, Harold Wilson, and other members of the Cabinet, and James Chichester-Clark, the Northern Ireland Prime Minister[9] and his senior colleagues. Part of the Declaration reads as follows:

4. ... In the context of the commitment of these troops, the Northern Ireland Government have reaffirmed their intention to take into the fullest account at all times the views of Her Majesty's Government in the United Kingdom, especially in relation to matters affecting the status of citizens of that part of the United Kingdom, and their equal rights and protection under the law.
5. The United Kingdom Government have welcomed the decisions of the Northern Ireland Government relating to local government franchise, a revision of local government areas, the allocation of houses, the creation of a Parliamentary Commissioner for Administration in Northern Ireland and machinery to consider citizens' grievances against other public authorities ... as demonstrating the determination of the Northern Ireland Government that there shall be full equality of treatment for all citizens. Both governments have agreed that it is vital that the momentum of internal reform should be maintained.

Internal reform along the lines indicated could assuage those grievances of the civil rights movement as were identified in the Cameron Report, quoted above. What they could not do was satisfy the claims of those Irish Nationalists who sought—by whatever means—a united Ireland. That is, changes in the law could not meet the demands of those who sought far-reaching structural and/or constitutional change—and the latter and not the former increasingly dominated *all* aspects of the Northern Ireland situation. In the summer of 1970, the Social Democratic and Labour Party was formed as a means of organising opposition to the Northern Ireland Government and of giving voice to aspirations for Irish unity by constitutional methods. The previous December-January, however, the IRA had split into its Official and Provisional wings and later in 1970 the Provisional IRA bombing campaign began in Belfast. Meanwhile in September 1971, Ian Paisley (a member from 1970 of both the Northern Ireland and Westminster Parliaments) announced the formation of the Democratic Unionist Party[10] and the same month the Ulster Defence Association emerged as the co-ordinating body for various loyalist (para-military) organisations. These developments were taking place against a severely deteriorating security background which placed great strain upon the relationship between the Northern Ireland and Westminster Governments. Any provision of facts and figures has necessarily to be selective but the following should indicate the magnitude of the problem. In the years 1969 to 1972 inclusive there were respectively:

| | | | | |
|---|---|---|---|---|
| *Deaths* | 13 | 25 | 174 | 468 |
| *Injuries* | 711 | 1056 | 2507 | 4857 |
| *Bomb attacks* | n.a. | 173 | 1515 | 1851[11] |

In a situation already very fraught, the introduction of internment without trial on 9th August 1971 and the shooting dead by soldiers of the First Parachute Regiment of thirteen people in Londonderry on January 30th 1972 ("Bloody Sunday") led not only to considerable escalation in the violence but also to a widespread feeling of disaffection and a more limited campaign of civil disobedience on the part of the Province's half a million "minority community".[12]

The hostility, both national and international, engendered particularly by the introduction of internment, and concern at the generally increasing levels of violence led the United Kingdom Prime Minister (then Edward Heath) in February 1972 to embark upon talks with the Irish Prime Minister (then Jack Lynch of Fianna Fáil). The Republic's official position at this stage towards Northern Ireland was essentially one of both insisting upon an Irish dimension in some unspecified form in any proposed solution to the "Troubles" and also of seeking to "protect" the half a million Roman Catholics from both the policies of the Northern Ireland Government and the effects of the violence. The Irish dimension would become increasingly more prominent. Of more immediate concern, however, were the negotiations which took place between the United Kingdom and Northern Ireland Prime Ministers in February and March 1972. The deployment of British troops in Belfast and Londonderry and their (actual and supposed) *modus operandi* had inflamed feelings in Republican and Nationalist quarters; ironically, the greater involvement of Westminster in security matters within Northern Ireland was also to alienate the Unionists. The consultations between the two Prime Ministers as to the future form of government of Northern Ireland foundered on the United Kingdom Government's insistence on removing all law and order matters from Stormont. The proposals were, said the Northern Ireland Prime Minister,

> to appoint a Secretary of State and to transfer to Westminster vital and fundamental powers which we have exercised for over half a century. The proposition put to us was that all statutory and executive responsibility for law and order should be vested in the United Kingdom Parliament and Government. These included criminal law and procedure (including the organisation of and appointments to the courts); public order; prisons and penal establishments; the creation of new penal offences; special powers; the public prosecuting power, and the police. Even these radical changes were simply to pave the way for further, entirely open-ended discussions with continuing speculation and uncertainty as we have seen it in recent weeks.[13]

On 22nd March 1972, the Northern Ireland Government warned the United Kingdom Prime Minister that, if such a transfer were to take place, it would resign. On 24th March, Edward Heath announced that resignation; a Bill to suspend the Parliament and Government of Northern Ireland was introduced at Westminster (its second reading taking place on 28th March) and the Northern Ireland Parliament sat for the last time, amidst huge loyalist demonstrations protesting against the introduction of what is usually called direct rule. The problem of finding a new constitution for Northern Ireland had begun.

## DIRECT RULE — PHASE I

The Act which provided for the suspension of the system of devolved government established by the Government of Ireland Act 1920 was the Northern Ireland (Temporary Provisions) Act 1972 which received the Royal Assent on 30th March 1972. This Act by section 1 suspended the Northern Ireland Government and vested all powers of the Governor of Northern Ireland, of the Government of Northern Ireland and of any member of that Government in the Secretary of State for Northern Ireland (a newly created office), and all departmental functions were to be discharged by him or by the department on his behalf and subject to his direction and control. In order to assist the Secretary of State, the schedule to the Act established a Northern Ireland Commission, composed of persons, ordinarily resident in Northern Ireland, appointed to it by the Secretary of State and entrusted with the task of giving "advice to [him] on such matters connected with the discharge of his functions relating to Northern Ireland as he may refer to them". The schedule also provided that any requirement stipulating that the Governor should act on the advice of any Minister or of the Privy Council of Northern Ireland should cease to have effect with regard to the discharge of those functions by the Secretary of State.[14]

Section 1 of the Act also provided that the Parliament of Northern Ireland was to stand prorogued and that the Queen in Council should have the power to legislate "for any purpose for which the Parliament of Northern Ireland has power to make laws." This included the power to confer, by such Orders in Council, powers or duties on the Secretary of State for Northern Ireland or any other Minister or department of the Government of the United Kingdom. The schedule imposed the duty on the Secretary of State to refer to the Commission for their advice, "unless in any case it appears to him impracticable by reason of urgency or otherwise so to do", any proposed Order in Council to be made under the 1972 Act.[15] These Orders in Council were given, by the 1972 Act, "the same validity and effect" as an Act of the Northern Ireland Parliament enacted under the Government of Ireland Act 1920. Orders in Council were to be made according to Westminster's affirmative procedures; that is, before the Order could become law a draft had first to be approved (being a form of delegated legislation, it could not be amended) by both Houses of the Westminster Parliament. Provision was also made for an emergency procedure under which an Order in Council could become law immediately but was required to be approved subsequently by both Houses of Parliament within forty sitting days. If it was not subsequently approved, it would then cease to have effect, but without prejudice to anything previously done under the Order or to the making of a new Order.[16] Special mention was made in the 1972 Act of the status of Northern Ireland as part of the United Kingdom. As mentioned in chapter III, the Ireland Act 1949 (passed by the Westminster Parliament to deal with the consequences of the Republic of Ireland's departure from the Commonwealth)[17] by section 1(2) declared

> that Northern Ireland remains part of His Majesty's dominions and of the United Kingdom and it is hereby affirmed that in no event will Northern Ireland or any part thereof cease to be part of His Majesty's dominions and of the United Kingdom without the consent of the Parliament of Northern Ireland.

Given that the 1972 Act prorogued that Parliament section 2 provided that "nothing in this Act shall derogate or authorise anything to be done in derogation from the status of Northern Ireland as part of the United Kingdom". Specifically, the schedule by paragraph 4(5) provided that the general dispensing with those statutory provisions which required a resolution of the Northern Ireland Parliament would have no application to the consent required by section 1(2) of the Ireland Act 1949.

The system of legislating for Northern Ireland under the 1972 Act was inadequate in that minimal Parliamentary time was given to the scrutiny of laws intended for Northern Ireland,[18] and input into the formulation of policy was vested in the non-elected Commission.[19] As the short title of the 1972 Act indicated, however, this was intended only as a temporary expedient.[20] During the course of the remainder of 1972 and 1973 the United Kingdom Government embarked upon a series of negotiations and discussions, designed to lead to the return of (a new system of) devolved government to Northern Ireland. Meanwhile the Troubles continued unabated.[21]

## THE SEARCH FOR A NEW FORMULA

In September 1972, the Secretary of State convened an inconclusive three-day conference at Darlington, at which representatives of the Official Unionist, Alliance[22] and Northern Ireland Labour Parties were present, other political parties (including the DUP and the SDLP) having declined the invitation to attend; and in October 1972 the Government published a document setting out its own thinking on the future form of government for Northern Ireland.[23] It is worth dwelling on this document because it—and a subsequent White Paper[24]—articulates most clearly the thinking of the Government with regard to Northern Ireland, from which thinking there has in fact been but little deviation by successive British Governments.

First, the Government stressed that both under statute law (section 1(2) of the Ireland Act 1949) and under clear, repeated and solemn declarations of the United Kingdom Government, Northern Ireland was and would remain (as long at least as there was majority consent) a part of the United Kingdom and of Her Majesty's Dominions. A partial transfer of sovereignty, either geographical (a re-definition of the border) or jurisdictional (for example, joint sovereignty or a condominium), was excluded as incompatible with the wording of section 1(2) of the 1949 Act. The Government also further repeated the undertaking which it had given on the introduction of direct rule that there would be a plebiscite on the border issue. Within those perimeters, however, the Government called for an examination of both the nature of any future affirmation of Northern Ireland's constitutional status and also of the possibilities of cross-border co-operation, at executive or consultative levels, that is, of the need for an "Irish dimension".

Secondly, the Government proceeded to consider the various possibilities for a future form of government for Northern Ireland against the background of the reminder that "insistence upon Northern Ireland as a part of the United Kingdom involves accepting unequivocally the ultimate sovereign authority, in all circumstances, of the United Kingdom Parliament over Northern Ireland as over all other parts of the country".[25] The various possibilities canvassed included "total integration", that is that Northern Ireland would effectively be treated at Westminster on a par with the other regions of the United Kingdom, particularly Scotland. The Government's own attitude to this option, although technically neutral, was clearly luke-warm:

In considering the possibility of 'total integration' account must ... be taken of the fact that the majority of parties in Northern Ireland are opposed to it, that it would represent a complete reversal of the traditions of half a century, that it would impose a substantial new legislative burden on the Westminster Parliament, and that it would be unacceptable to the Republic of Ireland and would make co-operation with the Republic more difficult.[26]

Whatever may be said of the other reasons, the third reason, that it would impose a heavy burden on Westminster, seems patently unacceptable—there is no inherent reason why Northern Ireland affairs should not occupy proportionately the same amount of Westminster time as those of England, Wales or Scotland.

The other possibilities all related to the creation of a local body of varying powers, either a Council (a purely executive authority), a Convention (a limited law-making authority), or a powerful legislature ("Parliament" or "Assembly") *and* Executive. Each of these involved a differing allocation of powers between Westminster and Northern Ireland; consequently, the discussion document next considered the allocation of functions between Westminster and the Province and the degree of autonomy which the latter might possess. Again, although the Government remained technically open-minded on these matters, it gave a clear indication that those powers which had previously been within the competence of the Northern Ireland Parliament and the exercise of which had proved divisive should be withheld in future from any locally-elected body. The matters specified included "electoral law and boundaries, the courts and the general administration of justice, security and public order, emergency powers and the police".[27] The Government further made it clear that, with regard to the exercise of powers which might be devolved, there would be supervision at Westminster tighter than that which had actually operated under the Government of Ireland Act 1920, whatever the precise requirements of the legislation on, for example, the Governor's veto, section 75 (the supremacy clause) and judicial review. The discussion document mentioned the possibility of providing for the approval of both the United Kingdom Government and Parliament to proposed laws of the local Assembly.

On the precise form, structure and composition of any future locally-elected body, the Government in the discussion document mainly rehearsed the various options although it did put down a few markers (some of which had emerged out of their discussions with the Northern Ireland political parties): that the new body should (probably) be unicameral rather than bicameral; that attention should be paid to the support, expressed by some of the political parties, for the use of a system of proportional representation in the elections to the body; and that the working of the body should include a counterpoise to the undiluted exercise of majority power (for example, through a powerful committee system, with the chairmanships of some of the committees allocated to the minority parties, or through a "proportional representation" government).

The first matter to be clarified—if clarification were necessary—was the border issue. On 8th March 1973 under the terms of the Northern Ireland (Border Poll) Act 1972, the Northern Ireland electorate was given the opportunity to answer this question: "Do you want Northern Ireland to remain part of the United Kingdom?" To this 591,820 people voted "yes"; while 6,463 voted "yes" to the question "Do you want NI to be joined with the Republic of Ireland outside the UK?" Some 425,800 people (including the SDLP) abstained—approximately 41.3 per cent of the electorate.

## THE CONSTITUTION ACT 1973

The Northern Ireland Assembly Act 1973 provided for the holding of elections to a unicameral Northern Ireland "Assembly", it being the preferred word over "Parliament".[28] Section 1(1) of the Act simply stated that "there shall be a Northern Ireland Assembly which shall consist of 78 members" and section 2(3) provided that the electoral system to be used would be "the single transferable vote"[29] form of proportional representation. Consequently, the then twelve Westminster constituencies were, by section 1(2) and the schedule to the Act, converted into multi-member constituencies, returning between five and eight members depending upon their size. The elections to the Assembly were held in June 1973, with this result: Official Unionists led by Brian Faulkner, 22; SDLP 19; Alliance Party 8; Northern Ireland Labour Party 1; DUP 8; Vanguard 7; Official Unionists opposed to power-sharing 12;[30] other loyalists, 1. These figures are listed in terms of those who were prepared to countenance power-sharing in government (the first four parties) and those who were not.

The 1973 Assembly Act made no provision at all for the powers of the Assembly and for the nature and powers of the Executive to be drawn from it. This was done by the Northern Ireland Constitution Act 1973, which drew on the contents of a White Paper[31] which the Government had published in March 1973 and which reflected the extensive consultations surrounding the discussion document of October 1972 as well as the document itself. The salient features of the Act, as explained in the White Paper, are these: first what is often called the "constitutional guarantee". Given that the 1973 Act, by section 31, abolished the Northern Ireland Parliament, which had been standing prorogued since March 1972, a new form of wording to replace section 1(2) of the Ireland Act 1949 had to be found. Consequently, section 1 of the Constitution Act 1973 states:

It is hereby declared that Northern Ireland remains part of Her Majesty's dominions and of the United Kingdom, and it is hereby affirmed that in no event will Northern Ireland or any part of it cease to be part of Her Majesty's dominions and of the United Kingdom without the consent of the majority of the people of Northern Ireland voting in a poll held for the purposes of this section in accordance with Schedule 1 to this Act.[32]

The 1973 Act repealed the Northern Ireland (Border Poll) Act 1972 and by its first schedule, paragraph 1 enabled the Secretary of State for Northern Ireland to direct the holding of border polls at minimal intervals of ten years running from 9th March 1983 (ten years after the first border poll). There is no requirement to hold a poll at those ten-yearly intervals and indeed no poll has been held since the original poll in 1973.

It is often overlooked that section 1 is *not* itself the constitutional guarantee; the guarantee is rather Article 1 of the Anglo-Irish Acts of Union, which provides

that ... the kingdoms of Great Britain and Ireland ... shall upon [1st January 1801] and for ever after, be united in one kingdom, by the name of the United Kingdom of Great Britain and Ireland... .

Section 1 of the 1973 Act (which contains no attempt at an entrenching formula,[33] even if such, under the doctrine of Parliamentary sovereignty, were possible) actually envisages the possibility of an alteration in the status of Northern Ireland as contained in Article 1 of the Acts of Union 1800, albeit that the possibility of change is expressed in terms of a negative proposition: section 1 does not actually state what should or will happen if there were to be consent for change expressed in a border poll.[34]

The 1973 Constitution Act should be read in terms of its balancing of both majority and minority interests within Northern Ireland: section 1 was designed to placate the Unionists; provisions on the form of the devolved government and the allocation of legislative powers between Westminster and the new Assembly were designed to placate those who had opposed many elements in the previous form of devolution operative within the Province. Section 2 of the 1973 Act made the formation of a broadly-based Executive the prerequisite for the devolution of legislative power to the Assembly. Under the 1920 Act, there had been a Prime Minister and a single-party Cabinet in control of the Northern Ireland Ministries. The 1973 Act re-named the existing Ministries departments and established a Northern Ireland Executive, consisting (mainly) of the political heads of the departments, and presided over by a "chief executive member", who was also to act as leader of the Assembly. The members of the Executive were to be appointed by the Secretary of State for Northern Ireland largely from amongst the existing members of the Assembly. In making his appointments the Secretary of State was required to comply with section 2(1)(*b*) of the 1973 Act. It provided that an Executive was to be formed which, "having regard to the support it commands in the Assembly and to the electorate on which that support is based, is likely to be widely accepted throughout the community." Further, in order to ensure a "strong link between the Assembly and the Executive, to involve majority and minority interests alike in constructive work and to provide for the active participation of all its members",[35] the Assembly was, by section 25, required to establish, by its standing orders, consultative committees to advise and assist the head of each of the Northern Ireland departments in the formulation of the policy of each department.[36] The head of each department was also to be the chairman of the relevant consultative committee which, in its membership, was, so far as was practicable, to reflect the balance of the parties in the Assembly. The office of Secretary of State for Northern Ireland (Her Majesty's principal officer in Northern Ireland and a member of the Westminster Cabinet) was to continue; and once he had determined that a power-sharing Executive could be formed and to it had transferred the responsibility for "Northern Ireland" matters, to him was entrusted the main responsibility for those matters not devolved but reserved at Westminster.[37] Section 32 of the 1973 Act provided that the office of Governor of Northern Ireland should cease to exist and that no further appointments were to be made to the Privy Council of Northern Ireland.[38]

Certainly as regards the terms employed, even without consideration of the substantive changes, read chief executive for Prime Minister, Executive for Cabinet, Assembly for Parliament and so forth, the "psychology" of the 1973 Act is clear in that it imports no suggestion at all that Northern Ireland is the (effective) equivalent of a province within a federation of (virtually) co-ordinate status with the central authorities. The status of the devolved institutions as subordinate to those of Westminster and subject to their control may be equally clearly seen in the proposed devolution of legislative power, although here, somewhat strangely, the 1973 Act retained much of the terminology of the Government of Ireland Act 1920. The 1973 Act, like the 1920 Act, created three categories of legislative power, identically-named but different in some respects in both substance and rationale: these are the excepted, reserved and transferred matters. Schedule 2 to the 1973 Act lists the excepted matters which were to be the matters outside the competence of the Northern Ireland Assembly[39] and which included "matters of national importance inappropriate for consideration other than by Parliament, e.g. the Crown, foreign affairs, the Armed Forces and honours and titles".[40] This is the same as under the 1920 Act. The 1973 Act, however, also added to the list of excepted matters those matters which when exercised by the Northern Ireland Parliament had caused division or controversy, for example, the appointment of magistrates and non-Supreme Court judges,[41] elections including the franchise in respect of both local elections and elections to the devolved legislature, prosecutions[42] and "special powers and other provisions dealing with terrorism or subversion".[43] These matters too were permanently excluded from the Assembly's legislative competence.

Under the 1920 Act the second category of legislative powers, a relatively small category of reserved matters, were those which were largely intended for transfer to an all-Ireland Parliament had one come into existence. In the absence of such a Parliament, responsibility for the reserved matters remained at Westminster. Although the 1973 Act also created a category of reserved matters, its content and its rationale[44] were different from the 1920 scheme. Under the 1973 Act reserved matters were those "excluded for the present from the normal legislative competence of the Assembly but in respect of which the Assembly may exceptionally legislate with the agreement of the United Kingdom Government".[45] Schedule 3 to the 1973 Act listed what are termed "minimum reserved matters" and included what are broadly "law and order" powers, for example, the maintenance of public order, the criminal law, the establishment, organisation and control of the RUC, and firearms and explosives. The adjective "minimum" relates to the fact that in the *original* order devolving power to the Assembly no matter listed in schedule 3 could be included, although the Government had a discretion as to whether or not to transfer any other non-excepted matter. Section 3 of the 1973 Act, however, provided that in any *future* devolution order (other than the original order) a minimum reserved matter could be transferred to the legislative competence of the Assembly. It was envisaged that such a transfer would only come about once the Assembly had enjoyed a settled and productive existence. As long as any matter was reserved, however, the Assembly could legislate on it only exceptionally and even then only with the consent of the Secretary of State (section 5) and Westminster (section 6).

All matters other than those listed in schedules 2 and 3 were capable of being transferred to the Assembly and indeed all were transferred to it in the first devolution order. The transferred matters included health and social services, employment and training, education, the environment and agriculture. With regard to these matters, the Assembly was, subject to one important provision on anti-discrimination, given an unrestricted legislative competence. Assembly laws were to be known as "Measures" and were enacted by being passed by the Assembly and approved by the Queen in Council (section 4). The channel to the Queen in Council was through the Secretary of State; there was no direct access from the Assembly to the Crown. Measures were, subject again to the anti-discrimination provision, given "the same force and effect as an Act of the Parliament of the United Kingdom".[46]

The equivalent of sections 75 and 6 of the Government of Ireland Act 1920[47] is section 4(4) which reads:

This section does not affect the power of the Parliament of the United Kingdom to make laws for Northern Ireland but, (subject to the anti-discrimination section), a Measure may amend or repeal any provision made by or under any Act of Parliament in so far as it is part of the law of Northern Ireland.

The inclusion of the first part of this subsection is not legally necessary—Westminster would anyway have retained its inherent sovereignty over an integral part of the United Kingdom—but its exclusion may have been regarded as significant, especially in light of the debates over the Home Rule Bill in 1886 and the specific inclusion of such a clause in the 1920 Act. The second part of the subsection is not, unlike section 6 of the 1920 Act, limited by any time reference, and, therefore, it avoided any resort to the device of deeming the Westminster legislation to have preceded the Northern Ireland law.

The anti-discrimination provision is to be found in section 17(1) and it provides that:

[a]ny Measure, any Act of the Parliament of Northern Ireland[48] and any relevant subordinate instrument shall, to the extent that it discriminates against any person or class of persons on the ground of religious belief or political opinion, be void.

Discrimination is, by section 23, defined as "less favourable treatment", but the terms "religious belief" and "political opinion" are not defined.[49] Section 18 of the Act provides for questions on the validity of any provision in legislation of the nature specified in section 17 to be resolved by the Judicial Committee of the Privy Council (in those cases where it appears to the Secretary of State expedient in the public interest that such a step should be taken for the speedy resolution of the issue). That section further enabled the Judicial Committee to rule on the validity of *proposed* Measures. By section 18(4) any decision of the Judicial Committee under section 18 is binding in all subsequent legal proceedings.[50]

The 1973 Act contains three other major provisions designed to curb discrimination. Section 19 of the Act makes unlawful discrimination by "public authorities". Included under the banner of "public authorities" are United Kingdom Government Ministers in relation to their functions exercised in Northern Ireland, members of the Northern Ireland Executive, the Post Office, the Northern Ireland departments and district councils and such other public bodies as are subject to the jurisdiction of the Parliamentary Commissioners for Administration or the Commissioner for Complaints. Section 19(1) makes it unlawful for such public authorities:

> to discriminate, aid, induce or incite another to discriminate in the discharge of functions relating to Northern Ireland against any person or class of persons on the ground of religious belief or political opinion.

The remedies available to a person discriminated against include an injunction (particularly to prevent continuous discriminatory conduct as opposed to a single unlawful act) and damages.[51]

The Act also established the Standing Advisory Commission on Human Rights, its membership appointed by the Secretary of State (the Northern Ireland "Ombudsman" and since 1976 the Chairman of the Fair Employment Agency are *ex officio* members), and with the remit under section 20(1)(*a*) of the 1973 Act of

> advising the Secretary of State on the adequacy and effectiveness of the law for the time being in force in preventing discrimination on the ground of religious belief or political opinion and in providing redress for persons aggrieved by discrimination on either ground....

The Advisory Commission makes annual reports (it also issues other reports) which are laid by the Secretary of State before each House of Parliament.[52] According to the White Paper of March 1973 which preceded the 1973 Act, the main contribution of the Advisory Commission would be the "effective co-ordination of the activities of all the agencies working in this field" and to ensure that the Westminster Parliament and Government "should have a continuous flow of information enabling them to discharge their responsibilities for human rights in Northern Ireland." These agencies include the Northern Ireland Parliamentary Commissioner for Administration and the

Commissioner for Complaints, (the two offices being held by the same person), the Community Relations Commission (abolished in 1975, never really having played a central role) and from 1976, as created under the Fair Employment (NI) Act, the Fair Employment Agency.

The 1973 Act, as well as rendering discriminatory laws void and discriminatory executive action unlawful and as well as establishing the Advisory Commission, by section 21[53] makes it unlawful for a public body to require any person to make an oath or equivalent affirmation "as a condition of his being appointed to or acting as a member of that authority or body, or of serving with or being employed under that authority or body". Effectively this section applies to the Assembly[54] and to any body subject to the jurisdiction of the Northern Ireland Parliamentary Commissioner for Administration or the Commissioner for Complaints. This provision was designed to bring the law in Northern Ireland into line with that in Great Britain,[55] particularly with regard to local government.

Members appointed to the Northern Ireland Executive under section 8 were themselves required to make an oath or affirmation which by schedule 4 to the Act ran as follows:

> I swear by Almighty God, [or affirm] that I will uphold the laws of Northern Ireland and conscientiously fulfil [as a member of the Northern Ireland Executive] my duties under the Northern Ireland Constitution Act 1973 in the interests of Northern Ireland and its people.[56]

This contrasts with the position under the Government of Ireland Act 1920, as amended by the Irish Free State (Consequential Provisions) Act 1922 under which Northern Ireland Ministers were members of the Privy Council of Northern Ireland.[57] As such, on taking office, they were sworn in and consequently took the oath of allegiance to the Sovereign and the Privy Councillor's (or Counsellor's) oath.

## THE SUNNINGDALE AGREEMENT

The 1973 Act thus laid down the structures and requirements governing the Northern Ireland Assembly and Executive. Little of it, however, would have become operative[58] had a power-sharing Executive not been formed. After the elections to the Assembly had been held in June 1973, therefore, the Secretary of State invited all parties represented in the Assembly to take part in negotiations as to how an Executive complying with the requirements of section 2 on power-sharing could be formed. The Alliance, SDLP and the

Official Unionists led by Brian Faulkner participated in these discussions, which were boycotted by the other parties represented in the Assembly, and eventually on 22nd November 1973, William Whitelaw, the Secretary of State, was able to announce the formation of an Executive-designate, composed of six Official Unionists (Brian Faulkner being Chief Executive), four from the SDLP (Gerry Fitt being deputy Chief Executive), and one from the Alliance Party.[59] As the prerequisite for the introduction of devolution had now been satisfied, the whole machinery was ready to be brought into operation. One further crucial matter had still to be confronted, however, particularly on the insistence of the SDLP, namely the Irish dimension. The discussion document, the White Paper and the 1973 Act all had something to say on this matter. First, the discussion document clearly articulated the Government's commitment to ensuring an Irish dimension to the new system of devolution:

> whatever arrangements are made for the future administration of Northern Ireland must take account of the Province's relationship with the Republic of Ireland: and to the extent that this is done, there is an obligation upon the Republic to reciprocate. Both the economy and the security of the two areas are to some considerable extent inter-dependent, and the same is true of their relationship with Great Britain. It is therefore clearly desirable that any new arrangements for Northern Ireland should, whilst meeting the wishes of Northern Ireland and Great Britain, be so far as possible acceptable to and accepted by the Republic of Ireland which, from 1 January 1973, will share the rights and obligations of membership of the European Communities. It remains the view of the United Kingdom Government that it is for the people of Northern Ireland to decide what should be their relationship to the United Kingdom (sic) and to the Republic of Ireland: and that it should not be impossible to devise measures which will meet the best interests of all three. Such measures would seek to secure the acceptance, in both Northern Ireland and in the Republic, of the present status of Northern Ireland, and of the possibility—which would have to be compatible with the principle of consent—of subsequent change in that status; to make possible effective consultation and co-operation in Ireland for the benefit of North and South alike; and to provide a firm basis for concerted governmental and community action against those terrorist organisations which represent a threat to free democratic institutions in Ireland as a whole.[60]

The White Paper provided a little more detail.[61] Referring to the general welcome with which the above principles had been received in the Republic and to the fact that virtually all the Northern Ireland political parties had envisaged some form of institutional arrangements between Northern Ireland and the Republic, it then referred to such a scheme by the name "Council of Ireland" and added:

As far as the United Kingdom is concerned, it favours and is prepared to facilitate the formation of such a body. The constitutional proposals would permit the new Northern Ireland institutions to consult and co-ordinate action through a Council of Ireland. There are undoubtedly many matters of substantial mutual interest such as tourism, regional development, electricity and transport.[62]

The Government decided against writing the full scheme into the Constitution Act 1973 in order to involve the political representatives of both communities within Northern Ireland in the process of determining the Council of Ireland's "form, functions and procedures". It was, however, already envisaged that such a body might operate at both intergovernmental and interparliamentary levels. Consequently, the 1973 Act itself contains only one—albeit an exceedingly broad—provision on North-South relations, namely section 12 which by subsection (1) provides:

A Northern Ireland executive authority may—

(*a*)consult on any matter with any authority of the Republic of Ireland;

(*b*)enter into agreements or arrangements with any authority of the Republic of Ireland in respect of any transferred matter.

Section 12 further gave the Northern Ireland Assembly the power (subject to sections 5 and 6 of the Act relating to the consent of the Secretary of State and of the Westminster Parliament) to make provision by Measure to give effect to any such agreement or arrangement "including provision for transferring to any authority designated by or constituted under the agreement or arrangement any function which would otherwise be exercisable by any authority in Northern Ireland or for transferring to an authority in Northern Ireland any functions which would otherwise be exercisable by any authority elsewhere." Under schedule 3, paragraph 8 the exercise of such legislative powers was made a minimum reserved matter.

Against the background of that facilitative provision and the Government's broad commitment to an Irish dimension, talks took place at Sunningdale in Berkshire from 6th to 9th December 1973 between representatives of the Westminster Government, of the Northern Ireland Executive-designate and of the Government of the Republic of Ireland. At the conclusion of this Conference agreement in principle on the establishment of a Council of Ireland was reached, subsequent study being required on the functions and finance of the Council.[63] The communiqué issued from the Conference on 9th December 1973—the Sunningdale Agreement—contained the following provisions.

First on the status of Northern Ireland, Article 5 of the Agreement contained a parallel declaration:

The Irish Government fully accepted and solemnly declared that there could be no change in the status of Northern Ireland until a majority of the people of Northern Ireland desired a change in that status.

The British Government solemnly declared that it was, and would remain, their policy to support the wishes of the majority of the people of Northern Ireland. The present status of Northern Ireland is that it is part of the United Kingdom. If in the future the majority of the people of Northern Ireland should indicate a wish to become part of a united Ireland, the British Government would support that wish.

Secondly, Article 7 recorded the agreement that a Council of Ireland should be established, confined to representatives of the Northern and Southern Ireland Governments, but with appropriate safeguards for the British Government's financial and other interests. The Council of Ireland was to comprise a

Council of Ministers with executive and harmonising functions and a consultative role, and a Consultative Assembly with advisory and review functions.

The Council of Ministers, which would act by unanimity, was to be composed of seven members each from the Northern Ireland Executive and the Irish Government, with a rotating chairmanship. The Consultative Assembly would consist of sixty members, thirty chosen by the Northern Ireland Assembly on the basis of the single transferable vote system of proportional representation and thirty chosen by the Irish Parliament on the same basis.

The Conference further resolved that studies should immediately be set in hand "to identify and, prior to the formal stage of the Conference, report on areas of common interest in relation to which a Council of Ireland would take executive decisions", and, in particular, on the following matters: exploitation, conservation and development of natural resources and the environment; agricultural matters, forestry and fisheries; co-operative ventures in the fields of trade and industry; electricity generation; tourism; roads and transport; advisory services in the field of public health; and sport, culture and the arts.[64]

These provisions deal with the first two objectives formulated in the discussion document, namely to secure agreement on the status of Northern Ireland[65] and on cross-border co-operation on social and economic matters. The third, the need for co-operation on security measures, was provided for largely in Articles 10 and 15. Article 10 promised further discussion between the British and Irish Governments, via a special commission, on the amendment of the laws on extradition, the possibility of creating a common law enforcement area in which an all-Ireland court would have jurisdiction, and the extension of the jurisdiction of domestic courts in order to enable them to try extra-territorial offences. Article 15 provided that the Republic of Ireland would set up a Police Authority to which appointments would be made after consultation with the Council of Ministers[66] and that the Northern Ireland Executive would make appointments to the Northern Ireland Police Authority after like consultation. The two Police Authorities would then seek to improve "policing throughout the island and [to develop] community identification with and support for the police services".

It was the Sunningdale Agreement which effectively caused the collapse of the Northern Ireland Assembly. On 1st January 1974 the Government devolved to the Assembly legislative responsibility for all transferred matters, that is, all those matters other than excepted and minimum reserved matters, and the Northern Ireland Executive began to operate under the legislation. Already in the Republic of Ireland, however, Article 5 of the Sunningdale Agreement was being challenged before the courts on the ground that it was unconstitutional as conflicting with the Irish Constitution's provisions on the national territory of Ireland.[67] More immediately, within Northern Ireland, the Agreement was totally repudiated by the DUP, the Vanguard Unionist Party and by large numbers of the Official Unionists, leaving Brian Faulkner increasingly isolated on the Unionist side.

In terms of the Unionist reaction against the Agreement, it is probably futile to speculate on the influence which the choice of the title "Council of Ireland" may have had on the course of subsequent events. The answer is probably "very little", but it should at this stage be recalled that under the Government of Ireland Act 1920 an identically-named body, consisting of representatives of both Parliaments, had been created with at first limited powers, but with the potential for developing into an all-Ireland Parliament. Indeed the discussion document 1972, in a paragraph immediately preceding paragraph 78 on the Irish dimension quoted at length above, stated:

> No United Kingdom Government for many years has had any wish to impede the realisation of Irish unity, if it were to come about by genuine and freely given mutual agreement and on conditions acceptable to the distinctive communities. Indeed the Act of 1920 itself ... explicitly provided means to move towards ultimate unity on just such a basis; but the will to work this was never present... .[68]

The discussion document also quoted extensively from the Explanatory

Memorandum to the Government of Ireland Bill 1920, which explained the purpose behind the then Council of Ireland in these terms:

> Although at the beginning there are to be two Parliaments and two Governments in Ireland, the Act contemplates and affords every facility for union between North and South, and empowers the two Parliaments by mutual agreement and joint action to terminate partition and to set up one Parliament and one Government for the whole of Ireland. With a view to the eventual establishment of a single Parliament, and to bringing about harmonious action between the two Parliaments and Governments there is created a bond of union in the meantime by means of a Council of Ireland... .[69]

Although the Sunningdale scheme was in certain respects different,[70] focusing specifically on an Executive (the Council of Ministers), with an accompanying Consultative Assembly, and although there had during the life of the Northern Ireland Parliament been some cross-border co-operation[71] although not under or through one formal structure, the choice of title was bound to alienate Unionist opinion. That stated, however, it cannot be claimed that the reaction would have been very different had the body been labelled, for example, the "North-South Committee" or "the Executive Council" or any other title (and "neutral" but accurate terms are not easy to find). It may also be, of course, that from the point of view of the SDLP and the Republic's Government the choice of that title was of considered significance. Indeed Bew and Patterson provide the following account of the developments:

> The focus of disagreement [between the SDLP and the Coalition Irish Government of Fine Gael and the Irish Labour Party] became the very different interpretations which the party and the Coalition wished to put on the [British White Paper's section on the] "Irish Dimension". This section had been implicitly minimalist ... The British government and the Coalition government in Ireland were initially agreed that the SDLP should participate in a reconstructed northern regime, with a weak Council of Ireland serving to express the "Irish Dimension". By the end of the summer [of 1973], however, the SDLP had forced the Coalition into a complete *volte-face* ... The Coalition government [now] supported the SDLP's notion of a Council of Ireland with substantial powers; it would also make it clear that the whole complex of new institutions was intended to be a transitional stage on the way to unity.[72]

While the further talks on the fleshing out of the details of the Sunningdale Agreement were being held, however, a General Election was called by Edward Heath for 28th February 1974. Whilst the miners, the economy and the three-day working week absorbed the electorate in Great Britain, in Northern Ireland the issues were both the Sunningdale Agreement and specifically the Council of Ireland, and the power-sharing Executive in so far as the two strands can be regarded separately. Of the then twelve Northern Ireland Westminster constituencies, eleven returned the UUUC Coalition candidate.[73] Gerry Fitt of the SDLP retained his West Belfast seat. The full figures are as follows:

| *Party* | *Votes cast* | *% of total poll* |
|---|---|---|
| UUUC | 366,703 | 50.8 |
| Pro-Assembly Unionists | 94,301 | 13.1 |
| SDLP | 160,437 | 22.2 |
| Alliance | 22,660 | 3.1 |
| NILP | 15,483 | 2.1 |
| Republican Clubs | 12,106 | 1.7 |
| Others | 45,936 | 6.4 |
| *Total valid votes* | 717,626 | 99.4 |
| (*Spoiled votes* | 4,656 | 0.6)[74] |

The newly returned Westminster Labour Government, with Merlyn Rees now as the Secretary of State for Northern Ireland,[75] was prepared to continue with power-sharing,[76] but events in Northern Ireland dictated a different course of events.[77] Those Assembly members who supported the UUUC's opposition to Sunningdale were still in a minority within the Assembly—on 14th May the Assembly voted by 44 votes to 28 to support the Sunningdale Agreement; but on the same day the loyalist Ulster Workers' Council[78] threatened and then the following day carried out power cuts in protest at the Agreement. The UWC strike had begun. It was to last until the end of the month, in those fourteen days halting much of industry, largely through the power cuts and also, for example, through a strike of the Belfast shipyard workers, and eventually through limiting the supplies of oil and petrol.[79] On 22nd May, Brian Faulkner announced to the Assembly that the Northern Ireland Executive now intended to implement the Sunningdale Agreement in two stages: the Council of Ireland would be established immediately with consultative and co-operative powers over various social and economic matters; but the other aspects of the Council of Ireland, namely the Consultative Assembly, the transfer of executive functions to the Council and the appointment of a Secretariat, would only be introduced after the opinions of the Northern Ireland electorate had been tested at a further Assembly Election. On 28th May, however, Brian Faulkner and the other Unionist members of the Executive resigned and the following day the UWC called off the strike.[80] The Sunningdale Agreement never reached the formal final stage it had envisaged, and Westminster again became responsible for all Northern Ireland affairs. The resignation of the Unionists from the power-sharing Executive meant that the statutory precondition for the exercise of devolved power could no longer be met and on 29th May 1974 the Government by Order in Council made under the then section 27(6) of the Constitution Act 1973 prorogued the Assembly for a period of four months. During its short life it had passed four Measures, none of them particularly vital in its import—the Consolidated Fund Measure, the Electricity and Gas Undertakings (Financial Provisions) Measure, the Financial Provisions Measure and the National Insurance Measure. The responsibility for all laws for Northern Ireland now lay at Westminster. The transfer of executive power from the Northern Ireland Executive to Westminster took place under section 8(6) of the 1973 Act:

> If at any time after [1st January 1974] it appears to the Secretary of State that it is not possible to make an appointment which complies with the requirements [of section 8(4)][81] he may make an appointment which does not comply with those requirements but any person so appointed shall not hold office for more than six months.

Using this power the Secretary of State appointed four junior Ministers at the Northern Ireland Office to be the political heads of the Northern Ireland departments.

This was clearly only an emergency holding operation: these Ministers were "responsible for [their] duties not to Parliament but to an Assembly which [was] prorogued and of which they [were] not themselves members",[82] the Assembly stood prorogued for only four months and Westminster did not then have available to it the simplified way of legislating for Northern Ireland which had existed under the Northern Ireland (Temporary Provisions) Act 1972. Direct Rule, Phase I, had come to an end on 31st December 1973. Direct Rule, Phase II, however, was about to begin and to last for a considerably longer period of time.

## NOTES

1 See Palley, 1972, *op cit*, pp 406-444.

2 Cmd 532, (1969), para 229(a).

3 *Ibid*, para 6.

4 See *eg* chapter 2 of the Standing Advisory Commission on Human Rights Report of November 1977 Cmnd 7009; and Annex 3 of The Future of Northern Ireland. A Paper for Discussion. HMSO. 1972.

5 An office closely modelled on the UK Ombudsman set up under the Parliamentary

Commissioner Act 1967. The two offices of NI PCA and Commissioner for Complaints tend to be held by the same person.

6 The Ulster Defence Regiment, an Army regiment recruited within Northern Ireland, was created by Westminster Act of Parliament in 1969.

7 Now Chief Constable.

8 Cmnd 4154, 1969.

9 He had become Northern Ireland Prime Minister in May 1969, replacing Terence O'Neill. He was succeeded in March 1971 by Brian Faulkner.

10 The fragmentation of Unionism was further illustrated by the creation of the Vanguard (Unionist Progressive) Party in March 1973. Throughout the text, the Ulster Unionist Party is referred to by its popular name of "Official Unionist Party". This is effectively the party which constituted the Northern Ireland Government from 1921 to 1972.

11 Source: SACHR Report. Cmnd 7009, November 1977. Table A, p 6.

12 The SDLP had begun a boycott of the Northern Ireland Parliament in July 1971 over the refusal of the Westminster Government to hold a judicial inquiry into two shootings by the army in Londonderry earlier that month. The introduction of internment undoubtedly reinforced their decision.

13 Quoted in Palley, *op cit*, pp 442-3.

14 The Act also provided that the Attorney General for England and Wales should be the Attorney General for Northern Ireland.

15 Birrell and Murie, *Policy and Government in Northern Ireland: Lessons of Devolution* (1980), at p 71 state that the Commission met on 36 occasions between June 1972 and March 1973, but add that it "seems generally to have been a low-key" body. It was largely boycotted by the Unionists who believed that the introduction of direct rule was to treat the Province, in the words of Brian Faulkner, like a "coconut colony". Quoted in Buckland, *A History of Northern Ireland* (1981), p 159.

16 Delegated legislation which had previously required approval by the Northern Ireland Parliament was "taken down" a step so that under the 1972 Act it was laid before Westminster subject to its negative procedures, that is, it would come into effect unless voted against within forty days.

17 For example, it provided that that part of Ireland previously known as Eire would be known as the Republic of Ireland. The Republic is not, under section 2 of the 1949 Act, regarded as a foreign country, nor are its citizens aliens: see the British Nationality Act 1981, section 50(1). For a further consideration of section 2 of the 1949 Act, see *ex parte Molyneaux* [1986] 1 WLR 331, discussed in chapter VII.

18 Birrell and Murie, *op cit*, pp 71-72 state that: "Some of the Northern Ireland Orders in Council received only a few minutes debate, for example, a superannuation order in July 1972. A complex planning order with one hundred clauses and seven schedules was debated for only one and a half hours. A number of orders did receive more favourable treatment ... The order establishing area boards to deal with education and libraries received more than three and a half hours of debate, and the order introducing proportional representation for local government elections received seven hours ...".

19 A much fuller consideration of direct rule will be given in chapter V.

20 By section 1(5) of the Act, section 1 was to expire after one year, subject to a power for its further extension.

21 In 1973 there were 250 deaths, 2651 injuries and 1520 bomb attacks.

22 Formed in April 1970, the Alliance Party aimed to be a party of the middle ground, appealing to both sides of the sectarian divide.

23 The future of Northern Ireland. A paper for discussion. HMSO. 1972.

24 Northern Ireland Constitutional Proposals. Cmnd 5259. March 1973. See further below.

25 *Op cit*, p 20, para 44.

26 *Ibid*, p 21, para 44(a).

27 *Ibid*, p 23, para 48.

28 See the discussion document, considered above, p 25, para 52: "... there is a view that any new legislature should not be called a Parliament. It is argued that the title and the adoption of elaborate Westminster procedures have not only been out of proportion to the real functions independently performed and to the size of the population covered by them, so that these arrangements have led to what may be described as 'over-government', but also have promoted a false view of 'Stormont sovereignty' which has been positively harmful. Amongst those who hold this view there is strong support for the title of 'Assembly'."

29 This is defined by section 2(3) as being a vote "*(a)* capable of being given so as to indicate the voter's order of preference for the candidates for election as members for the constituency and (*b*) capable of being transferred to the next choice (i) when the vote is not required to give a prior choice the necessary quota of votes, or (ii) when, owing to a deficiency in the number of votes given for a prior choice, that choice is eliminated from the list of candidates."

30 Some sources allocate 23 seats to the pro-Faulkner Official Unionists and 11 to the Official Unionists opposed to power-sharing.

31 Northern Ireland Constitutional Proposals. March 1973. Cmnd 5259. Published before the Assembly elections were held, its contents had had a considerable bearing on the various manifestos.

32 Section 43(2) of the Act provides that "Northern Ireland" has the same meaning as for the purposes of the 1920 Act.

33 For example, there is no provision that section 1 itself could not be repealed until after a similar procedure had been followed.

34 These arguments are expressed more fully in Hadfield, "Learning from the Indians? The Constitutional Guarantee revisited," 1983 *Public Law*, pp 351-365.

35 Cmnd 5259, para 44.

36 Section 7(4) of the 1973 Act also provided that: "A member of the Northern Ireland Executive who is head of a Northern Ireland department shall, in formulating policy with respect to matters within the responsibility of that department, consult so far as practicable with the consultative committee ... and where such policy is to be implemented by a proposed measure, [an Assembly law], he shall consult as aforesaid before the proposed measure is introduced."

37 The terms "transferred" and "reserved" are explained more fully below.

38 The 1973 Act repealed extensive parts of the 1920 Act, including (of the provisions mentioned in chapter III) sections 4-6, 8, 9, 11-19, 22-24, 47, 64(1) and 65(2). It also repealed the Irish Free State (Consequential Provisons) Act 1922, schedule 1, para 1(1) (so far as it established the office of Governor), section 1(2) of the Ireland Act 1949 and the Northern Ireland Act 1972 (the Act passed after the decision in *Hume*). Section 42(1) of the 1973 Act enacted that except as otherwise provided by or under the 1973 Act, "nothing in this Act shall affect the continued operation in or in relation to Northern Ireland of any law in force at the passing of this Act or on [1st January 1974]." Section 42(2) preserved the 1920 Act's criteria for testing the validity of Stormont Acts: "Without prejudice to [section 42(1)], neither the abolition of the Parliament of Northern Ireland nor the repeal by this Act of any provision relating to that Parliament shall affect the validity or otherwise of any Act of that Parliament."

39 The Assembly could only legislate on an excepted matter in an ancillary way—see section 5(7) of the 1973 Act.

40 Cmnd 5259, para 56(*a*).

41 The Supreme Court had, under the 1920 Act, always been a reserved matter.

42 Under the Prosecution of Offences (NI) Order 1972 the office of an independent Director of Public Prosecutions was introduced. The appointment and the office of the DPP and deputy DPP for NI are excepted matters under para 10 of schedule 2. See also section 34 of the 1973 Act, and schedule 3, para 4(*c*) which makes prosecutions a reserved matter.

43 Para 14 of schedule 2. Para 4 of the same schedule makes an excepted matter "the armed forces of the Crown but not any matter within paragraph 3 of Schedule 3 to this Act." Schedule 3 deals with reserved matters and para 3 provides that subject to schedule 2, para 14, "the maintenance of public order, including the conferring of powers, authorities, privileges or immunities for that purpose on constables, members of the armed forces of the Crown and other persons" is a reserved matter. This is a further postscript to the decision in *Hume,* discussed in chapter III, note 85.

44 The Irish dimension in this new scheme of things was largely not in the 1973 Act itself—section 12 being the only provision on North-South relations—but in the Sunningdale Agreement. See below.

45 Cmnd 5259, para 56(*b*).

46 Section 4(3). The first Devolution Order was SI 1973/2162.

47 On the supremacy of Westminster and the clash between Westminster and Northern Ireland Acts, see chapter III. Para 15 of schedule 2 to the 1973 Act made amendment of the 1973 Act itself an excepted matter.

48 That is, the section has retrospective effect to 1921.

49 Section 23 makes it clear that these provisions do not render unlawful anything authorised or required to be done by any Act of the Westminster Parliament. Section 23 also provides for certain exceptions to section 17 in the fields of national security, and public order and public safety.

50 The general tenor of the 1973 Act was to avoid judicial review other than with regard to the anti-discrimination provisions. Consequently, section 4(5), reinforcing section

4(3), declares "for the avoidance of doubt that a measure is not invalid by reason of any failure to comply with the provisions of sections 5, 6, 14 or 18(2), (5) or (6) ... and no act or omission under any of those provisions shall be called in question in any legal proceedings." The 1973 Act repealed section 51 of the 1920 Act. The equivalent of section 18(4) of the 1973 Act was section 53 of the 1920 Act, also repealed by the 1973 Act.

51 An injunction for a single act of discrimination would also be available: section 19(3). For a case dealing with section 19, see *Purvis* v *Magherafelt DC* [1978] NI 26.

52 The 1973 Act also required its reports to be laid before the Assembly. For a consideration of the first six annual reports of SACHR, see Maguire, "The Standing Advisory Commission on Human Rights 1973-1980" (1981) 32 *NILQ* pp 31-61.

53 Part III of the 1973 Act, that is, sections 17 to 23, deal with "The Prevention of Religious and Political Discrimination." Section 21 is, then, the fourth and last specific anti-discrimination provision.

54 Assembly members were, for example, simply required to sign the Assembly's Roll of Members: NI Assembly Standing Orders 1973, SO 6.

55 Where any oath was required "in comparable circumstances in the rest of the United Kingdom", such oaths would continue to be lawful in Northern Ireland: see Cmnd 5259, para 64.

56 Brian Faulkner, in *Memoirs of a Statesman* (1978) chapter 18 on the power-sharing Executive, linked the swearing-in of the Executive with the Secretary of State's powers under section 2 of the 1973 Act: "[On 31st December 1973 there was] a slightly absurd little ceremony at Stormont Castle when we all received our "Warrants of Appointment" from the Secretary of State, Francis Pym, on behalf of HM The Queen, after being sworn in by the Lord Chief Justice, Sir Robert Lowry ... The school prize-giving atmosphere at this ceremony, mildly embarrassing though it proved, was less important than the damaging impression given to the public that the Executive was the child of the Secretary of State. It was an important part of the loyalist argument that the new Constitution and the power-sharing Executive had been forced on Northern Ireland against the wishes of its population by British politicians and that the Executive therefore lacked any democratic status. We knew that the Executive was a freely agreed coalition of elected politicians, supported by a strong majority in the Assembly, but this appointment ceremony can in retrospect be seen as making the loyalist misrepresentation that little bit easier."

57 Section 3 of the Union with Ireland Act 1800 relates to the Privy Council of *Ireland*: "And be it enacted, that the great seal of Ireland may, if his Majesty shall so think fit, after the union be used in like manner as before the union, except where it is otherwise provided (in the Acts of Union) within that part of the United Kingdom called Ireland; and that his Majesty may, so long as he shall think fit, continue the Privy Council of Ireland to be his Privy Council for that part of the United Kingdom called Ireland." No appointments were made to it after 1922. The NI Privy Council was established by the 1922 Consequential Provisions Act, schedule 1, para 2(1).

58 Section 1 on the constitutional guarantee and Part III on the anti-discrimination provisions became and remain law, irrespective of the existence of the Assembly and the Executive themselves.

59 "The Executive was supported by some twenty Official Unionists, nineteen members of the SDLP and eight members of the Alliance Party, [and so] the coalition had a clear majority in the Assembly even though the loyalty of some of Faulkner's nominal followers was doubtful:" see Buckland, *History of Northern Ireland* (1981), p 168. There were, in addition, four members of the Administration outside the Executive. See the NI Constitution (Amendment) Act 1973, section 1. Barry White in his book on *John Hume* (1984) at p 156 writes: "Even the signing on ceremony on 1 January, in the shadow of Craigavon's statue in the Stormont Great Hall, was not uneventful. There were two swearing-in formulae [see the second set of square brackets in schedule 4, above], one for the eleven full members of the Executive and one for the four members of the administration, but the Lord Chief Justice used only the first. After lunch apologetic civil servants asked the four administration members to go through the signing ceremony a second time."

60 Para 78, p 34. This paragraph has been quoted in full not only because of its significance then but also in light of subsequent developments: see chapter VII on the Anglo- Irish Agreement.

61 Cmnd 5259, chapter 5: Relations with the Republic of Ireland.

62 *Ibid*, para 110. The White Paper also implicated in this process the three objectives mentioned in the discussion document, namely those on the status of Northern Ireland, cross-border co-operation and security measures.

63 These meetings were all regarded as preliminary rather than formal. Article 6 of the Agreement records that: "The Conference agreed that a formal agreement incorporating the declarations of the British and Irish Governments would be signed *at the formal stage of the Conference* and registered at the United Nations." This formal stage did not take place.

64 Article 8. Section 12 of the Constitution Act 1973 is particularly relevant here.

65 See further below.

66 The Council was also, by Article 11, given a recommendatory role with regard to the implementation of the principles of the European Convention on Human Rights in the domestic law of both Northern Ireland and the Republic.

67 *Boland* v *An Taoiseach* 1974 IR 338. The proceedings, initiated in December 1973, were heard in the Irish High Court in January 1974 and in the Irish Supreme Court on February 20th-22nd 1974. Judgment was given by the Supreme Court on March 1st, holding that the Sunningdale Agreement owed its existence to an exercise of executive (rather than legislative) power and so was not subject to judicial review for unconstitutionality. In the course of their judgments, however, both Fitzgerald CJ and O'Keefe P stressed that the phrase "the status of Northern Ireland" in Article 5 referred only to the *de facto* status of Northern Ireland; that it did not, and could not lawfully, derogate from the Irish Constitution's claim to jurisdiction over Northern Ireland. See Articles 2 and 3 of the Irish Constitution.

68 It was in the White Paper, Cmnd 5259, para 109 that the phrase "Council of Ireland" specifically emerged. Given that the United Kingdom Government assiduously changed other terms under the Government of Ireland Act scheme—"Parliament" to "Assembly" etc—the inference that the phrase "Council of Ireland" was retained for a

purpose becomes stronger although not irrefutable. It is also pertinent to consider here why the three categories of legislative power retained the 1920 "labels".

69 Quoted in Annex 1, para 2, p 40.

70 The provisions of section 12 of the Constitution Act should again be borne in mind here.

71 For example, with regard to the Lough Foyle Fisheries Commission, the Great Northern Railway, Lough Erne, and on tourism.

72 Bew and Patterson, *The British State and the Ulster Crisis*, (1985), p 57-58.

73 The United Ulster Unionist Council was set up to fight the Sunningdale Agreement ("Dublin is just a Sunningdale away"). It comprised those Official Unionists led now by Harry West (in January 1974, the UUUC voted by 427 votes to 374 to reject Sunningdale, Faulkner resigned and West was elected to succeed Faulkner as leader of the OUP), the DUP and the Vanguard Unionist Party: see Flackes, *Northern Ireland: A Political Directory* (1980, 1983).

74 *Ibid*, p 271.

75 He replaced Francis Pym who had been the Secretary of State from early December 1973.

76 The Sunningdale talks also continued.

77 The fact that the judgment of the Irish Supreme Court in *Boland* above was given on 1st March, immediately after the UK election results became clear, is also relevant here.

78 The UWC consisted of both politicians (including Harry West and Ian Paisley, as well as William Craig of Vanguard) and members of the paramilitary Ulster Defence Association and other loyalist organisations.

79 It should be recalled that all law and order powers at this time were vested in Westminster. On 19th May, the Prime Minister, Harold Wilson, declared a state of emergency but crucially the Westminster Government was either not willing or able (in terms of expertise) to deploy the army to maintain power supplies. The extent to which the army could or should have been used (to try) to defeat the strike remains a debated issue.

80 On 17th May 1974, twenty-two people were killed in Dublin and five in Monaghan by car bombs. Although the explosions are generally believed to have been the work of loyalists, no organisation claimed responsibility for them.

81 They were that members of the Executive shall be members of the Assembly and that the composition of the Executive shall meet the statutory requirements on power-sharing.

82 Cmnd 5675, Government White Paper of July 1974 on the Northern Ireland Constitution, para 29.

# V

# DIRECT RULE

On the collapse of the Northern Ireland Assembly, there was no immediate new thinking or reassessment of the situation on the part of the United Kingdom Government. The White Paper[1] which preceded the Northern Ireland Act 1974—the Act which reintroduced direct rule—rehearsed past events, particularly from March 1972, and then stated:

> There is therefore a need to make better *temporary* arrangements for the orderly government of Northern Ireland.
>
> In the short term, the most pressing problem is that of legislation. The Northern Ireland Executive had prepared an extensive programme of future legislation over a wide range of matters devolved to them. To proceed with a programme of this kind entirely by way of Bills in the United Kingdom Parliament is out of the question. Inevitably, any less pressing legislative proposals for Northern Ireland, however desirable in themselves, will now have to be deferred, to the disadvantage of various groups in the Northern Ireland community. There are, however, measures which cannot be put off if orderly government is to be carried on, for example to appropriate money for the public services. The Government will therefore be bringing forward legislation which would reintroduce *temporarily* procedures for making laws for Northern Ireland by Order in Council on matters within the legislative competence of the Assembly.
>
> The *temporary* legislation will also make the Secretary of State responsible to Parliament for the devolved services. These *temporary* arrangements will supersede, for the time being, various provisions of the Constitution Act concerned with the legislative functions of the Assembly and the executive functions of the Heads of Departments and others.[2]

The Government, stressing that these temporary arrangements did not offer a permanent solution to the problém of finding a constitution for Northern Ireland, announced that the next attempt at finding a solution should rest with the representatives of the Northern Ireland electorate themselves. Consequently, the Government in its White Paper announced that legislation would also be introduced to provide for elections within Northern Ireland to a "Constitutional Convention", with the task of considering "what provisions for the government of Northern Ireland would be likely to command the most widespread acceptance throughout the community there".[3] Although the Government stated that it would play no part in the proceedings of the Convention, the White Paper (although not the subsequent implementing Act) gave a clear indication of the policy perimeters within which the Convention would be free to formulate its own proposals:

There must be some form of power-sharing and partnership because no political system will survive, or be supported, unless there is widespread acceptance of it within the community. There must be participation by the whole community ... any pattern of government must be acceptable to the people of the United Kingdom as a whole and to Parliament at Westminster ...

Northern Ireland ... shares a common land frontier and a special relationship with ... the Republic of Ireland. Any political arrangements must recognise and provide for this special relationship. There is an Irish dimension.

It would be premature at this stage to say that the approach embodied in the Constitution Act 1973 is untenable ... No possible solution need be excluded from [the Convention's] discussions but any proposed solution must recognise [these] realities... The Government continues to believe that the best and most desirable basis for political progress in Northern Ireland would be the establishment of local institutions enjoying broad-based support throughout the community. ...[4]

## THE CONSTITUTIONAL CONVENTION

The Northern Ireland Act 1974, which received the Royal Assent on 17th July, had two main sections, section 1 and schedule 1 providing for the dissolution of the Assembly (which at that time was still standing prorogued) and for the introduction of direct rule, and section 2 and schedule 2 providing for the Constitutional Convention. Although the two provisions were effectively related—temporary direct rule would, it was hoped, yield to the system of government to be recommended by the Convention—the latter was of far shorter duration than the former. The elections to the Convention were held on 1st May 1975, on the lines of an election to the Assembly itself: Northern Ireland's then twelve Westminster constituencies returned a total of 78 members, elected by the single transferable vote system of proportional representation. The result was as follows:

| *Party* | *Seats* | *Votes* | *% of total poll* | |
|---|---|---|---|---|
| UUUC | | | | |
| Official Unionists | 19 | 169,797 | 25.8) | |
| DUP | 12 | 97,073 | 14.8) | |
| Vanguard | 14 | 83,507 | 12.7) | |
| Others | 2 | 10,140 | 1.5) | 54.8 |
| SDLP | 17 | 156,049 | 23.7 | |
| Alliance | 8 | 64,657 | 9.8 | |
| UPNI[5] | 5 | 50,891 | 7.7 | |
| Republican Clubs | 0 | 14,515 | 2.2 | |
| NILP | 1 | 9,102 | 1.4 | |
| Independents | 0 | 2,052 | 0.3 | |
| Communist | 0 | 378 | 0.1 | |
| | 78 | 658,161 | 100.00[6] | |

The Convention, which was presided over by the Lord Chief Justice (then Sir Robert Lowry) as non-voting "chairman appointed by Her Majesty",[7] began its deliberations on 8th May 1975[8] at Stormont. By this time the Government had published three discussion papers, one of which, entitled "Government of Northern Ireland: A Society Divided",[9] had set forth for the consideration of the Convention various possible constitutional safeguards in any new devolved system. These safeguards included weighted (rather than simple) majority voting on certain key issues; blocking mechanisms to delay or prevent legislation on certain vital matters; special representation of minority groups in the legislature; an increased use of referenda; power-sharing within the Executive; and government by *executive* committees, that is committees with greater powers than the advisory or consultative committees provided for under section 25 of the Constitution Act 1973.[10]

The chances of a successful outcome to the Convention's deliberations were probably not high even from its inception. The parties united under the United Ulster Unionist Council or Coalition (UUUC) were, as their manifesto and subsequent policy documents made clear,[11] opposed to both power-sharing and to any "imposed institutionalised association with the Irish Republic". Their Convention members supported the return of a Northern Ireland Parliament, with responsibility for policing and internal security, and from which a single-party Government should be formed. It supported watchdog committees (on the lines of Westminster's current Select Committees but with a legislative role too) as a means of enhancing the influence and effectiveness of the opposition parties in the Parliament. Those parties which had formed the Northern Ireland Executive, however, namely those Official Unionists who had supported Brian Faulkner (and now called the Unionist Party of Northern Ireland), the Alliance Party and the SDLP all also advocated devolution but with power-sharing in any devolved government that would be formed. The UPNI had by now rejected the idea of a Council of Ireland and the Alliance Party accepted the need simply for "practical co-operation" between North and South on matters of common concern. The SDLP, however, remained firmly committed to an Irish dimension.

The Convention, by a Resolution of 24th June 1975, committed itself

> to devising a system of government for Northern Ireland which will have the most widespread acceptance throughout the community … .

That is, it undertook to discharge its statutory function as provided in section 2(1) of the Northern Ireland Act 1974. The non-statutory criteria, contained in the Government's White Papers of 1973 and 1974, could not, however, ultimately be ignored with impunity.[12] Although before the Convention began its summer recess, informal talks started between the UUUC and the SDLP and continued throughout July and August, they ended without agreement. In September, William Craig, leader of the Vanguard Unionist Party, suggested that the emergency facing Northern Ireland was such as to warrant a voluntary coalition with the SDLP. This was rejected by the UUUC and the following month split the Vanguard Party itself.[13]

In the event, the Convention, which had effectively been given six months in which to complete its deliberations,[14] produced a majority report in November 1975, the conclusions of which reflected the political preferences of the UUUC. Section 2(2) of the 1974 Act required the Secretary of State, Merlyn Rees, to whom the report was transmitted, to lay that report before Parliament. This he did on 20th November 1975 and in an adjournment debate in the Commons on 12th January 1976, the Secretary of State told the House that the Report was unacceptable to the Government on the grounds that it did not "command sufficiently widespread acceptance throughout the community to provide stable and effective government".[15] He added, however, that the Government believed that the Convention could yet make further progress and so should be reconvened for a month in order to reconsider its recommendations in the light of the Government's response. The Secretary of State stressed that all parties participating in the Convention wanted to see a devolved unicameral Assembly and a devolved Executive and that the Government welcomed this and was prepared, he said, to devolve all matters transferred to the previous Assembly. He added, however, that the devolution of law and order powers could only be done on a very gradual basis (related largely to the withdrawal of the army from Northern Ireland). Furthermore, the Government was not, he stated, prepared to devolve responsibility for judicial appointments and the administration of justice. On the question of the form of the Executive, the Secretary of State saw value in the proposed committees but only "*as part of* a wider and acceptable constitutional framework which provides adequately for partnership and participation on a basis which commands the most widespread acceptance."[16] Finally, the Secretary of State, on the Irish dimension, made some concessions to the UUUC:

> The Government do not consider it necessary or appropriate to create an institutional framework such as a Council of Ireland for relations with the Republic. Arrangements for co-operation should evolve positively and naturally as and when the need for them arises and is generally recognised and accepted.[17]

Consequently, the Convention reconvened on 3rd February 1976 but the talks between the UUUC and the SDLP broke down almost immediately, and on 5th March 1976 Merlyn Rees announced to the Commons[18] that he had advised that the Convention should be immediately dissolved by Order in Council made under the 1974 Act.[19] This left section 1—the section reintroducing direct rule—as the sole operative provision of the Northern Ireland Act 1974. In many ways, therefore, the constitutional principles and framework for the next ten to twelve years were, as it transpires, now settled. The Government's position on some form of power-sharing was absolute; less so (at that stage, at any rate) was its insistence on the need for an institutionalised Irish dimension. Under the 1973 Act and the Sunningdale Agreement the Government had tried out its own constitutional formulae; under the 1974 Act it had transferred the responsibility for finding a new formula to the representatives of the Northern Ireland electorate, but the exercise of that responsibility was confined within quite clearly-drawn perimeters. There was comparatively little room for movement away from the principles contained in the 1972 discussion document and the 1973 White Paper. The Westminster Government was and is legitimately concerned with not only the Provincial but also the wider national and international aspects of the Northern Ireland constitution. The main difficulty it has in terms of finding a widely acceptable constitutional formula lies in attempting to harmonise its own perspective with those of the Northern Ireland political parties. To put the matter starkly, the Unionists largely dislike power-sharing and are opposed to an institutionalised

Irish dimension; the SDLP rejects majority rule and is (increasingly) insistent upon a formal Irish dimension in any constitutional settlement. It is hard to see how there can be any compromise between these views without massive concession on, or indeed surrender of, a fundamental aspect of party policy, and further this scenario takes no account of the rise of political support for Provisional Sinn Féin (the political wing of the Provisional IRA),[20] which advocates a total and immediate withdrawal of the British presence in Ireland, which, it believes, should be undivided.

## DIRECT RULE — PHASE II

With the chances of devolution slim, therefore, the scene was set for a prolonged continuation of direct rule,[21] the "temporary" expedient which has outlasted all other constitutions for Northern Ireland, other than the Government of Ireland Act 1920. What section 1 and schedule 1 of the 1974 Act do, as far as laws for Northern Ireland are concerned, is as follows. They provide that in what is known as the "interim period", which however long it lasts[22] is the period between the introduction of direct rule and the commencement of the next devolutionary scheme of government, legislation for Northern Ireland within the areas devolved by and under the Constitution Act 1973 may be made by Order in Council. This requires some elaboration based upon a reading of the 1973 and 1974 Acts together. Under the 1973 Act there were three categories of legislative power: excepted, reserved and transferred matters. Excepted matters were substantially outside the powers of the Assembly. Section 5(1) of the 1973 Act provided that

> the Secretary of State shall not give his consent in relation to a proposed Measure which contains any provision dealing with an excepted matter unless he considers that the provision is ancillary to other provisions (whether in that Measure or previously enacted) dealing with reserved matters or transferred matters.[23]

Consequently, such matters under the 1973 Act remained at Westminster and were legislated on there by way of Act of Parliament. This is retained under direct rule. Matters listed under schedule 2 of the 1973 Act, the excepted matters, must be legislated on by full Act, for schedule 1, paragraph 1(2) of the 1974 Act requires that

> [n]o recommendation shall be made to Her Majesty to make any Order in Council [during direct rule] containing a provision in relation to which the Secretary of State would be precluded by section 5(1) of the Constitution Act from giving his consent if it were contained in a proposed Measure.

This requirement explains why many of the emergency laws applying within Northern Ireland are to be found in Acts of the Westminster Parliament—the Northern Ireland (Emergency Provisions) Acts 1978 and 1987. Schedule 2 of the 1973 Act makes an excepted matter "special powers and other provisions for dealing with terrorism or subversion." Consequently, such matters cannot be dealt with by Order in Council under the 1974 Act. By contrast, transferred matters under the 1973 Act were capable of being devolved and were in fact devolved to the Assembly. Reserved matters were outside the Assembly's *normal* legislative competence, but nevertheless the 1973 Act did provide a procedure by which the Assembly could have legislated on them provided that the Westminster Government and Parliament agreed. Consequently, schedule 1, paragraph 1(1) of the 1974 Act provides that during the interim period

> (*b*) Her Majesty may by Order in Council make laws for Northern Ireland and, in particular, provision for any matter for which the Constitution Act authorises or requires provision to be made by Measure.[24]

Under direct rule, therefore, laws *may* be made for Northern Ireland on any matter falling within the transferred and reserved areas by Order in Council. This is a facilitative not a mandatory provision, but the Order in Council procedure has been almost invariably used, with the notable exception of the fair employment legislation.[25] Northern Ireland is, therefore, the only part of the United Kingdom where the vast majority of its laws are enacted in the form of delegated legislation, for that is what these Orders in Council are, being a sub-species of the more general category of "statutory instrument".

When Westminster legislates by way of an Act of Parliament—as it does for laws for the whole of the United Kingdom, for Northern Ireland excepted matters, and for Great Britain (or specifically England or Scotland) on those matters which in Northern Ireland would be labelled "transferred" or "reserved"—it uses a procedure which is designed to ensure that both Houses of Parliament are given the opportunity of considering both the principle(s) enshrined in the Bill and its details. Provision is made for, if necessary, lengthy debate particularly at the second reading and for amendments to be proposed and debated particularly at the Committee stage.[26] Delegated legislation, that is legislation made usually by Government Ministers under the authority of a "parent" or "enabling" Act, is accorded a much more perfunctory procedure, for often perfectly sensible reasons. Use of delegated legislation relieves Parliament of the minor details of law-making. Time is a precious commodity at Westminster; it is better spent by concentrating on the *principles* involved, leaving the relevant Government department(s) to provide for the consequential detail by delegated legislation. Parliament approves the outline; delegated legislation fills in the interstices. There are other, subsidiary or specific, justifications: delegated legislation enables speed of action, where this is thought to be necessary, particularly in time of war, when wide powers of delegated legislation are conferred, or other emergency; it enables a Government department to deal with unforeseen circumstances which are particularly likely to occur after the introduction of extensive law reform measures; and it has particular advantages in dealing with the details of exceptionally technical subjects, where the Government needs to consult with outside experts before regulating all the "fine points" of the legislation.[27]

None of these reasons justifies the use of the Order in Council procedure for Northern Ireland. Although there may be a tendency to assume that the "need for flexibility and speed in time of emergency" covers Northern Ireland, most Orders in Council for Northern Ireland deal with "ordinary" or non-emergency situations such as sex discrimination, roads, animals, rent, property and family law matters.[28] The main justification for the use of this procedure for Northern Ireland is that it was designed only as a temporary expedient pending the reintroduction of a new devolutionary scheme of government for the Province. More specific reasons are also given although in many ways they all stem from this first justification. It is probably true to state that the continued existence of direct rule reflects the Government's refusal or at best a reluctance, articulated as early as October 1972 in the discussion document considered in chapter IV, to accept a "substantial new legislative burden".[29] A further minor justification occasionally articulated is that use of delegated legislation preserves what is sometimes rather quaintly called "the integrity of the Northern Ireland statute book". This is the idea that all Northern Ireland laws should be gathered together in one series and all subject to, for example, the Interpretation Act (NI) 1954 rather than the United Kingdom Interpretation Act 1978. In this way the Northern Ireland "statute book" is kept discrete from the United Kingdom "statute book" to the advantage of the consumers of the law—or so the argument goes.

What, then, is the Parliamentary procedure to which these Orders in Council made under the Northern Ireland Act 1974 are subject? The first point to note is that delegated legislation cannot be amended by Parliament; it must be accepted or rejected in its entirety, although if Parliamentary criticism is levelled at only part of a draft Order, then the Government may, if it is so inclined, withdraw it and lay a newly drafted instrument before the House. Secondly, the Northern Ireland Act 1974, schedule 1, paragraph 1(4) lays down that Orders in Council are made once "a draft of the Order has been approved by Resolution of each House of Parliament". This procedure is known as the "affirmative" procedure and it requires the Government to ensure that time is made available to each House for it to consider the draft Order and then to approve (or reject) it. Paragraph 1(4)(*b*) also provides for an emergency procedure, which enables an Order to be made immediately; such an Order, however, lapses, but without prejudice to anything done under it or to the making of a new Order, unless subsequently approved by each House within forty sitting days of its being made. The time which is made available to each House under the affirmative procedure is a matter of at most a few hours and the debate usually takes place at the end of the Parliamentary day, that is after 10 o'clock in the evening. The consideration given to Northern Ireland Orders in Council is thus slight but even this has been reduced, in certain circumstances, by a development subsequent to the Northern Ireland Act 1974. When the Government now introduces a Bill for Great Britain with the intention of introducing virtually identical changes, in whole or in part, to Northern Ireland law, it is increasingly commonplace for that Bill to include a clause stating that an Order in Council will be made on that matter for Northern Ireland subject to Westminster's negative procedures for delegated legislation. That is, the 1974 Act's affirmative procedure applies generally unless overridden in this specific respect by a subsequent Act. The negative procedure allows for even less Parliamentary scrutiny than does the affirmative procedure. Under the negative procedure a draft Order will come into force unless within forty sitting days of its being laid before each House, one or both Houses votes against it, and the onus to stimulate a debate on such an Order is on the backbenchers not the Government, which can otherwise simply wait for the forty sitting days to run. One illustration of the use made of this procedure may be given. The Education (No 2) Act 1986, an Act applying to Great Britain, provided by section 47 for the abolition of corporal punishment in state schools. Section 47(11) of this Act reads:

> An Order in Council [under the 1974 Act] ... which states that it is made only for the purposes corresponding to those of this section—
>
> (*a*) shall not be subject to ... [the affirmative procedure of both Houses of Parliament], but
>
> (*b*) shall be subject to annulment in pursuance of a resolution of either House.

Consequently, the Education (Corporal Punishment) (NI) Order 1987 recited that it was "made only for purposes corresponding to those of section 47" of the 1986 Act and was, therefore, made subject to the negative procedure.

The effect of all this is that laws, which when made for the rest of the United Kingdom are amendable and subject to lengthy and detailed scrutiny by Parliament, are made for Northern Ireland under a procedure which allows for no amendments at all and which provides but little time for debate. This is a most unsatisfactory state of affairs, although it has been ameliorated by an informal procedure often resorted to by the Government. This informal procedure, which cannot apply to Orders made under the urgency procedure, involves the publication and wide circulation of what is known as "a proposal for a draft Order in Council." This proposal has to be distinguished from (although in lay-out it is identical to) the draft Order itself which is the formal document actually laid before each House of Parliament. The proposal instead relates to the *pre*-parliamentary stages of legislating for Northern Ireland and so predates the draft Order. The Government circulates to all interested parties, including the Province's political parties, the proposal for a draft Order accompanied by an explanatory memorandum and invites the submission of comments within a specified period, usually six weeks. In this way, suggestions for amendments may be made and, if they are acceptable to the Government, may be incorporated in the draft when finally made. The proposal, not being a formal draft, but only an "informal" pre-parliamentary document, is amendable. There has, therefore, been built into the procedure of legislating for Northern Ireland by Order in Council a pre-parliamentary "amendment" stage, to replace (in effect) the Parliamentary amendment stage given to Bills. It should be noted, however, that there is no statutory requirement that there should be a "proposal" stage and that this procedure is not always used. Most notably—or infamously—the Criminal Evidence (NI) Order 1988 dealing with the "right to silence"/"wall of silence" issue was *not* preceded by a proposal for a draft Order. The Standing Advisory Commission on Human Rights in a paper published on 19th January 1989, after this Order had been brought into operation, had this to say about the way in which the Government chose to proceed:

> The denial to ... interested parties of any opportunity to make effective comments on such an important piece of legislation is ... of concern to the Commission. It is generally accepted that human rights are often most at risk when legislation or other governmental measures are introduced by abnormal or "emergency" procedures. The Commission accepts that there may be occasions when the exigencies of the situation require immediate action to be taken. The measures included in the Criminal Evidence (NI) Order 1988 cannot by any stretch of the imagination be regarded as of that kind. The legislation was apparently considered a means of dealing with the "wall of silence" encountered by the RUC in questioning members of terrorist organisations. It is also

directly related to the working party established by the Home Secretary in May 1988 on which an official of the Northern Ireland Office participated, and which issued a consultation document in September 1988 calling for comments by November 1988. The Commission is not convinced that there was any need for a more compressed time schedule in respect of legislation in Northern Ireland, especially since the essentials of the legislation had apparently already been prepared... The Commission is concerned about reports that the mode of legislation adopted was deliberately chosen to avoid the need for detailed discussion and possible amendment in Parliament. In so far as there was any need for expedited procedures in Northern Ireland it was in respect of the "wall of silence" experienced in the questioning of terrorist suspects. The natural mode of enactment for such legislation would have been in the current Prevention of Terrorism (Temporary Provisions) Bill [now 1989 Act] which could readily have incorporated an appropriate amendment of the NI (Emergency Provisions) Acts. General legislation applying to all crimes and offenders could then have been adopted at a more leisurely pace. Instead the Government chose to apply the new legislation to all crime in Northern Ireland with the result that the legislation could be enacted by the Order in Council procedure without the need for detailed debate and possible amendment in Parliament.

The other way in which the Government has sought to improve the consideration given to laws for Northern Ireland is to provide more time in the Commons itself, although through use of committees,[30] not on the floor of the House. In 1975 there was instituted a Northern Ireland Committee, a standing committee of the House of Commons, consisting of the Members representing the (now) seventeen[31] Northern Ireland constituencies and up to (now) twenty-five others to ensure representation of other parties in the Commons and a Government majority. This Committee being a standing committee lacks the select committee powers to appoint specialist advisers, send for persons, papers and records and to adjourn from place to place, that is, meet outside Westminster. It is a deliberative committee with the sole powers of considering a matter or matters relating exclusively to Northern Ireland referred to it by the Government and of reporting back to the House that it has done so. Since 1976, this deliberative function has included the consideration of *proposals* for draft Orders in Council (not the draft itself). Hence the Committee has been able to discuss the proposed law before it is finalised and formally laid before Parliament. The Committee not only has very limited powers but also very limited use has been made of it in this respect although not solely because of its limited powers.[32] The members of the Committee representing Great Britain constituencies do not regard it as their number one priority; many Northern Ireland members of differing political hues have at one time or another been involved in a boycott of Westminster; the Committee's sole power to "consider" the proposal is weakened by a lack of powers (such as the power to question civil servants or appoint specialist advisers) which would enhance the deliberative or recommendatory role;[33] and given the involvement of the wider public in the consideration of proposals for draft Orders it is not always easy to appreciate or assess the nature of the contribution which the Northern Ireland Committee[34] is expected to make.

The other Parliamentary means by which the Government has sought to provide for fuller consideration of laws for Northern Ireland at Westminster is by resort to the Standing Committees on Statutory Instruments, usually nick-named "Merits" Committees. These Committees have been in existence since 1973, in composition they reflect the party political complexion of the House, and their work is not confined to Northern Ireland Orders. They are called "Merits" Committees (there is usually more than one), because they were introduced to facilitate fuller debate on the merits of delegated legislation, laid subject to either the affirmative procedure, or to the negative procedure and there is a desire in the House to debate the instrument. The Committees are empowered to debate Northern Ireland draft Orders (that is, the formal draft and not the proposal), for a maximum of two-and-a-half hours (other statutory instruments only receive one-and-a-half hours, so some sort of special provision is made here for Northern Ireland).[35] In order to ensure that important or contentious instruments are not removed from the floor of the House, provision is made in the House of Commons' Standing Orders that if more than twenty members object to the instrument being referred to the Committee the "Noes have it" and the debate is taken on the floor of the House. Only a Government Minister may propose that an instrument be referred to the Committee. The Committee's powers are strictly limited, the debate on the instrument being taken on the Motion: "That the Committee has considered the instrument." Thus the debate takes place in the Committee, which has no effective way of indicating any disapproval it may have of the instrument short of (somewhat inconsistently) disagreeing to the Motion, but the vote, if any, takes place on the floor of the House, which does not debate an instrument considered in Committee. This is not the most sensible of procedures.

It should be noted that the Joint Select Committee on Statutory Instruments, the "Scrutiny Committee", does not consider Northern Ireland draft Orders in Council.[36] This Committee, consisting of members from both the Lords and the Commons, was established with select committee powers in 1973 for the purpose of scrutinising the technical quality, not the merits, of delegated legislation, for example, to ascertain whether or not its drafting is defective, its form or purport calls for elucidation, it purports to have (apparently unauthorised) retrospective effect, it may be *ultra vires* or it excludes judicial review. To this Committee (draft) Orders in Council made during the early stages of direct rule were referred, but, at its own request, the Scrutiny Committee's orders of reference were amended in June 1977 to exclude Northern Ireland Orders in Council. The Committee made the crucial point that since these Orders "are 'disguised' as delegated legislation but are really primary legislation ... [t]he normal questions about *vires*, purport and drafting are, therefore, inapplicable."[37]

The deficiencies in the legislative aspects of direct rule are clear to see: there is only limited debate on the principle enshrined in the Northern Ireland draft Orders, there is no provision for amendment during the *Parliamentary* stages, although this may be compensated for to a certain extent by the circulation of a proposal for a draft Order,[38] and there is inadequate technical scrutiny.

In this context, attention should be drawn to the legal status which Northern Ireland Orders in Council enjoy. Under schedule 1, paragraph 1(7) of the 1974 Act,

> [r]eferences to Measures in any enactment or instrument (whether passed or made before or after the passing of this Act) shall, so far as the context permits, be deemed to include references to Orders in Council under this paragraph.

It will be recalled that, under section 4(3) of the Constitution Act 1973, Measures had (subject to the anti-discrimination provisions of section 17) "the same force and effect as an Act of the Parliament of the United Kingdom." Consequently, (where the context permits) Orders in Council have the same force and effect as a Westminster Act, other than with regard to discrimination on the grounds of religious belief or political opinion. This is clearly designed to make Orders in Council "judge-proof". Delegated legislation may usually be challenged in the courts on the ground that it is *ultra vires*, that is that the person on whom the power has been conferred has gone beyond or exceeded the grant of powers in the parent Act. Such a challenge cannot be made to an *Act* of the Westminster Parliament and clearly the intention of the 1974 Act is to confer a similar status on Northern Ireland Orders in Council.[39] Although there is considerable judicial aversion to these ouster clauses,[40] it is not easy to see how a challenge to the validity of such Orders could be successfully mounted.

Direct rule has its executive as well as its legislative aspects. Schedule 1, paragraph 2 provides:

(1) During the interim period —

(*a*) no person shall be appointed or hold office under section 8 of the Constitution Act; and

(*b*) any functions of the head of a Northern Ireland department may be discharged by that department and any functions of any other person appointed under that section may be discharged by the Secretary of State.

(2) During the interim period any functions of a Northern Ireland department, including functions discharged by virtue of sub-paragraph 1(*b*) above, shall be discharged by the department subject to the direction and control of the Secretary of State.

The "Northern Ireland departments" are those which deal with matters falling under the transferred list, that is, those matters which were devolved on 1st January 1974 and which, in all probability, would be devolved again in any future scheme of devolution. There are currently six Northern Ireland departments: Agriculture, Economic Development, Education, Environment, Health and Social Services and Finance and Personnel. Under direct rule, the administrative edifice of devolution is retained, with a separate Northern Ireland civil service, but the political direction and control rest with the Secretary of State, a member of the Westminster Cabinet, and with the Northern Ireland Office, which itself deals largely with reserved and some excepted matters. The remaining excepted matters rest with the relevant Westminster department, for example, Defence or the Treasury. In order to assist the Secretary of State, there are five (previously four) junior Ministers, at Westminster but not of Cabinet rank, to whom is allocated responsibility for the various transferred matters.

Before turning to consider scrutiny of the executive functions, it should be noted that within Northern Ireland there is a not inconsiderable gap between the powers of the Government and those of the district councils (local authorities) which gap is filled by nominated (non-elected) public bodies discharging functions which in Great Britain would be discharged by local government. Education and Library Boards, the Northern Ireland Housing Executive, the area Health and Social Services Boards, the Northern Ireland Police Authority exercise very considerable public functions, but are largely beyond public influence in terms of its expression in the ballot box. Northern Ireland's twenty-six district councils, elected every four years by the single transferable vote system of proportional representation, have very limited powers indeed. When consideration is given, therefore, to scrutiny of the Government during direct rule, it has to be borne in mind that the political sub-structure with its various forms of accountability, which exists elsewhere in the United Kingdom, is very largely absent in Northern Ireland.

Given that the political direction and control of Northern Ireland affairs are vested in the Secretary of State and the five junior Ministers, scrutiny of the exercise of their powers takes place at Westminster, according to Westminster's usual procedures. Only limited special provision is made for Northern Ireland. Northern Ireland takes its place in the rota for Oral Question-Time in the House of Commons, approximately once every three weeks. This is supplemented by whatever number of Written Questions happen to be submitted on Northern Ireland affairs. There are occasional debates on Northern Ireland—on the annual renewal of direct rule or of the Emergency Provisions legislation, or as and when the latest atrocity or emergency demands. The Northern Ireland (Standing) Committee may, if it so chooses, deliberate, its sole power being deliberative, on any Northern Ireland matter which, with its agreement, is referred to it. There the list ends. There is *no* Select Committee on Northern Ireland affairs. A select committee shadows all the other major departments of state, including the Welsh and Scottish Offices, but for a variety of reasons the Northern Ireland Office and the six Northern Ireland departments are exempt. The other departmental select committees may, where relevant, investigate a matter of general United Kingdom concern and into that investigation there may be a specific Northern Ireland input. They may indeed investigate an exclusively Northern Ireland matter, and sporadically they have done so, for example, the investigations into the Gas Industry (the Select Commitee on Energy) or Further and Higher Education (the Select Committee on Education). There are two main reasons why a Select Committee on Northern Ireland affairs has not been established. First, all select committees are required to have government party majorities. The two regional committees have (at least until the 1987 General Election)[41] been able to ensure this whilst still retaining a membership derived exclusively from their respective region. This would not be possible with regard to Northern Ireland. Secondly, as long as direct rule continues to be perceived as a "temporary" expedient pending the (re-)introduction of devolution, successive Governments have seemed reluctant to introduce changes at Westminster to improve the scrutiny of Northern Ireland affairs. This was the reason advanced in 1979 when the current departmental select committee structure was instituted, and indeed the Select Committees on Scottish and on Welsh Affairs were only established because of the lack of the statutorily requisite popular support, as expressed in the referenda in March 1979, for the systems of devolution contained in the Scotland Act 1978 and the Wales Act 1978. The existence of the Northern

Ireland Assembly, elected in 1982, whose work will be considered in chapter VI, further precluded the creation of a Select Committee for Northern Ireland, whatever practical difficulties there may be in terms of an acceptable and feasible composition and remit.

Whatever the reasons for the non-existence of such a Select Committee —and it has to be accepted that the practical difficulties are formidable although not necessarily compelling—the unfortunate consequence is that there is a marked imbalance at Westminster in the scrutiny of Northern Ireland affairs, on the one hand, and those of the rest of the United Kingdom, on the other.

Consideration will be given in chapter VIII to the question of the reform of direct rule. In the meantime this assessment suffices. It has been stated that

> Direct Rule has advantages. It is the least unacceptable mode of government for both communities, which acquiesce in it as neither frustrating their aspirations nor causing them to feel threatened. Thus a concurring majority exists about the acceptability of direct rule, not as the form of government most preferred, but as tolerable in default of agreement on new institutions. From a United Kingdom standpoint, direct rule neutralises much inter-community competition for power, ensures little opportunity for public sector discrimination and leaves policy options open.[42]

## POLICY OPTIONS

From the inception of direct rule in 1974, successive United Kingdom Governments have made various attempts to explore "policy options". The first was the Constitutional Convention of 1975-1976. During 1977, Roy Mason, having succeeded Merlyn Rees as Secretary of State, began a new series of separate talks with the Northern Ireland political parties, but the talks came to nothing. Roy Mason explained to the House of Commons in February 1977 that he had begun these talks in the hope ultimately of seeing the establishment within Northern Ireland of a system of devolved government which would command widespread acceptance throughout the community. He foreshadowed the later rolling devolution proposals by stating that he was prepared to countenance, as an interim possibility, some form of administrative non-legislative devolution or even partial devolution.[43] In November 1977, the Secretary of State, in order to inject some life into the failing or flailing talks, sent a letter to the leaders of the four main parties, the OUP, SDLP, Alliance and DUP, setting out the Government's preferred framework, but it was essentially unchanged from the 1973 position, except that the Government had by this time dropped the term "power-sharing" as too emotive, preferring to speak instead in terms of partnership and participation. The preferred aim of the Government remained that of a fully devolved system, but Roy Mason accepted both the undesirability, if not impossibility, of imposing such a system on the Province and also the fact that the time had not yet been reached where such a system could be established by agreement. He continued:

> There are, therefore, two options open to us. One is to continue with direct rule. The other is to try to find an interim system of devolved government which will help us to make progress towards the aim of a fully developed administration and which in the meantime will bring a larger measure of participation back into the government of Northern Ireland.[44]

He specifically envisaged that the interim system of devolution would be temporary and would be located in a single chamber Assembly elected by proportional representation, with devolved administrative powers and a consultative role in relation to legislation. The system, he explained, would have the potential of progressing towards full legislative devolution but in the interim the devolved administrative powers would be exercised in a way that would safeguard the interests of the minority community. The Secretary of State concluded his letter by inviting all four parties to take part individually in more detailed talks with his officials in order to ascertain whether or not it was possible to establish a form of devolved government consistent with these general principles.

This general proposal for some form of administrative devolution with potential for developing into a fully-fledged system of devolved government did not at this stage bear fruit, although the Northern Ireland Act 1982, which will be considered in the next chapter, seems to draw much of its content from this idea. In early 1978 the OUP and the DUP both withdrew from the talks in the light of certain remarks made by the then Irish Prime Minister, Jack Lynch, on his Government's aspirations for a united Ireland. This sequence of Government initiatives within certain specified perimeters, exploratory talks, boycotts or withdrawals continued until the end of the decade and into the early 1980s. With hindsight, it would seem that at this stage the Irish dimension was finally removed from the context of an internal settlement of the Northern Ireland constitution and placed more directly in the context of London-Dublin relations. This and the deletion of the term, but not the substantive requirements, of "power-sharing" from the political vocabulary probably marked the only changes from the Government's position as formulated in 1972-73. Certainly when Humphrey Atkins, who had succeeded Roy Mason as Secretary of State after the May 1979 General Election, announced in September

1979 the Government's intention to convene a Conference of representatives of the main Northern Ireland political parties with the purpose of reintroducing a new system of devolved government, the White Paper[45] which set out the Government's objectives differed little from what had gone before, in most essential respects. The White Paper contained the following proposals. Westminster's overriding authority was to be preserved in and over any new devolved system and it would specifically retain responsibility for defence, foreign affairs (including European Community matters), the courts, electoral matters, law and order and taxation. To the Northern Ireland Assembly, it was hoped, would be transferred all the matters transferred under the Constitution Act 1973, although this need not be done in one devolution order but could be achieved progressively over a period of time (thus keeping open the option aired in the "Mason talks" of 1977).[46] "Reasonable and appropriate arrangements" to safeguard the interests of the minority would be required to be made: in the absence of the "power-sharing" requirements as such, these safeguards could be provided by, for example, a requirement of weighted majorities for certain categories of legislation, proportionate allocation of select committee chairmanships and membership, the enactment of a judicially enforceable Bill of Rights, the vesting of override powers in the Secretary of State, the establishment of an upper chamber (with the minority disproportionately over-represented there) possessing blocking powers—or any feasible combination of these. The Appendix to the White Paper contained illustrative models of systems of government which would meet the Government's main objectives and indeed for a constitutional lawyer they represent a fascinating range of options: a unicameral or bicameral system of government with legislative and executive powers; a system of government with legislative and executive powers operating on an executive committee basis; a system of government with executive but no legislative powers operating on a committee basis; a system of government with executive but no legislative powers based on the "Cabinet" system, but with advisory committees; and a system of government with executive, but no legislative, powers exercised by one or more local authorities. It has to be said, however, that the range of options and the questions to be discussed at the Conference, which met at Stormont under the chairmanship of the Secretary of State, proved less appealing to the political parties. The Official Unionist Party did not accept the invitation to the Conference,[47] which began on 7th January 1980, although it did submit a detailed paper to the Secretary of State. The representatives of the three other political parties—SDLP, Alliance and DUP—did meet with him for thirty-four half-day sessions from 7th January until 24th March, when the talks were adjourned with little evidence of any progress towards an agreed solution.

Meanwhile, as will be considered in chapter VII, the Government was moving relatively quietly towards the formalisation of the Anglo-Irish dimension, and having set its face against any improvement in the system of direct rule,[48] strove to maintain the impetus, if that is the right word, engendered by the Atkins Conference. In July 1980 the Secretary of State issued a further White Paper entitled, realistically if mundanely, "The Government of Northern Ireland: Proposals for Further Discussion".[49] On this occasion the models of systems of government were reduced to two: and the two options available concerned the formation of the Executive. On what the White Paper called "the outer framework" there was broad consensus: that a unicameral Assembly should be elected by the single transferable vote system of proportional representation; that to it should be transferred the legislative and executive responsibility for those matters transferred under the 1973 Constitution Act; that the Secretary of State should retain responsibility for reserved and excepted matters; that, whatever form the Executive would take, there would be instituted a system of Assembly departmental committees with scrutiny and advisory functions *vis-à-vis* the Executive; and that the existing anti-discrimination provisons should be maintained and, if need be, strengthened. A final feature of the White Paper with regard to the "outer framework" was the willingness of the Secretary of State to "convene under his Chairmanship representative leading members of the Assembly as an advisory council for consultation on those matters for which he will remain ministerially responsible and accountable to Parliament".[50]

The two models on the "inner framework" were (1) responsibility shared within the *Executive*, that is, in form if not in name, proportionate power-sharing, although not necessarily wrought in a way identical to that contained in section 2 of the Constitution Act 1973;[51] and (2) responsibility shared within the *Assembly*, that is, the creation of a single (majority) party Executive, the exercise of whose powers would be counter-balanced by certain institutional arrangements outside the Executive itself. The White Paper specified the possibility of creating a "novel institution in which powers may be vested in order to serve as a balance against those to be exercised by the Executive, but to do so in a way which would secure a constructive relationship and avoid deadlock."[52] The novel institution, labelled the "Council of the Assembly", would, it was suggested, be composed of the chairmen and deputy chairmen of the Assembly's departmental committees (which posts would be allocated *equally*, not proportionately, between Government and opposition), with a chairman drawn from its membership but with no additional voting power. Composed in this way its membership would thus "be equally divided between those Assembly members supporting and those opposing the Executive, and to be effective any proposition on which it had to decide would have to attract 50 per cent and 1 votes".[53] The White Paper did not elaborate fully on the Council's likely powers except to state that to be effective it would have to possess powers greater than the merely advisory, including, for example, a delaying power over legislative proposals, power to refer such proposals back to the Assembly, or, if considered discriminatory, to the courts, and possibly even a blocking power over legislative proposals, subject to an override power vested in the Secretary of State and to Westminster's scrutiny.[54]

The White Paper itself realistically countenanced the possibility that neither option would be universally acceptable, and indeed the former was rejected by the Unionists as involving power-sharing and the latter was rejected by the SDLP which would not contemplate a return to single-party majority rule. In the penultimate paragraph of the July 1980 White Paper the Government stated that in the absence of an agreed settlement, it would then "explore other ways of making the Government of Northern Ireland more responsive to the wishes of the people of Northern Ireland".[55] Such alternatives, it continued, could involve a reconsideration of the possibility mentioned in paragraph 6 of the original White Paper of November 1979. Paragraph 6 had provided that

> [t]he transfer of powers ... need not be completed in one operation. It may be appropriate and desirable to consider arrangements for a progressive transfer over a period of time.

In September 1981, near the end of a year which witnessed the Republican hunger-strikes in support of political status for Republican prisoners and no abatement in the violence, James Prior succeeded Humphrey Atkins[56] as Secretary of State and he rapidly settled on rolling devolution as a possible way out of the political impasse.

## NOTES

1 The Northern Ireland Constitution, Cmnd 5675, July 1974.

2 *Ibid*, paras 30-33. Emphasis provided. Other provisions of the Constitution Act 1973, for example sections 1 and 17-23, remained and remain in full force and effect.

3 *Ibid*, para 50. This is the wording also used in section 2(1) of the Northern Ireland Act 1974, which provided for the establishment of the Convention.

4 *Ibid*, paras 45-48.

5 The Unionist Party of Northern Ireland was formed by Brian Faulkner in September 1974 and consisted of those former members of the Official Unionists who had supported him after his resignation as party leader in January 1974. They had continued to support power-sharing, but were no longer committed to a Council of Ireland: "though the Council of Ireland was originally proposed by Unionists, we believe it is counter-productive to the development of friendly co-operation on social and economic matters between the Republic and Northern Ireland, and have discarded the concept." UPNI Manifesto to the Constitutional Convention. Quoted in HC 1 (November 1975), Report of the Convention Proceedings, p 53. See also text below. This Report also allocates only one (not two) Independent Unionists to the UUUC: see p 5. The UPNI was disbanded in 1981.

6 Flackes, *op cit*, p 275. As Flackes points out, the total turnout (of 65.8%) may have reflected a certain amount of election weariness. In just over two years there had been in 1973 the Border Poll, the District Council Elections and the Assembly Elections; then the two General Elections of February and October 1974, and finally the Convention elections in May 1975. The referendum on the continued membership of the UK in the EEC also took place the following month.

7 The 1974 Act, schedule 2, para 1(*a*). The White Paper, Cmnd 5675, para 53 spoke of the need for the Convention to have an independent chairman, "a person of high standing and impartiality from Northern Ireland ... [who] will not be a member of the Convention."

8 During 1975, the violence continued unabated: there were 247 deaths, 2398 injuries and 615 bomb attacks: Cmnd 7009, Table A, p 6.

9 Discussion Paper 3. HMSO 1975. The other two papers were on the "finance and the economy" and on the "Constitutional Convention: Procedure".

10 See Part 3 of the Discussion Paper, pp 10-15.

11 These are to be found in the Appendices to the Report on the Convention Proceedings: *op cit*.

12 The majority Convention Report "noted with approval that in the Northern Ireland Act 1974 the United Kingdom Parliament did not impose any constraints such as power-sharing in an executive or all-Ireland institutions." *Op cit*, p 41. Their conclusions therefore made no provision for either.

13 Those opposed to William Craig on the issue broke away and formed the United Ulster Unionist Movement (later Party) under Ernest Baird. In February 1978, the Vanguard Party ceased to exist as a political party and by 1983 the UUUP had also ceased to exist.

14 The 1974 Act, schedule 2, para 15(1): ..."the Convention shall be dissolved (*a*) on the date on which its final report is laid before Parliament; or (*b*) on the expiration of the period of six months beginning with the date on which it first meets, whichever is the earlier."

15 HC Debs 1975-76, vol 903, cols 51-162, at col 54.

16 *Ibid*, see especially col 56. Emphasis provided.

17 *Ibid*.

18 HC Debs 1975-76, vol 906, cols 1715-1727.

19 See schedule 2, para 15(4) and (5) for the procedure on reconvening and dissolution. Section 2 and schedule 2 of the 1974 Act were repealed by section 7(3) and schedule 3 of the Northern Ireland Act 1982: see chapter VI, below.

20 The Provisional Sinn Féin and PIRA split from the Official Sinn Féin (Republican Clubs, now the Workers Party) and Official IRA in late 1969-early 1970. Since the early 1980s PSF has contested Westminster, Assembly, and district council elections, but on an abstentionist ticket for the first two bodies. During the elections in the 1980s it received from 60,000 to 100,000 votes. In 1986, Republican Sinn Féin was created by former PSF members who protested at the decision of PSF to end abstention from the Dáil.

21 This system is in all legal respects the same as that which existed under the Northern Ireland (Temporary Provisions) Act 1972, except that the Northern Ireland Commission, which was established under schedule 1 of the 1972 Act for as long as section 1 of that Act had effect and the membership of which was discontinued once the Northern Ireland Assembly was elected, was not revived. There are, however, some differences between the Parliamentary and pre-parliamentary processes of the two phases of direct rule: see text. For the relevant HC Standing Orders and for a detailed breakdown of the facts and figures on direct rule (Phase II) from 1974, see Appendix 5.

22 Section 1(4) of the 1974 Act provides that: "The interim period shall be the period of one year beginning with the passing of this Act but the Secretary of State may by order direct that it shall continue until a date after the date on which it would otherwise expire." Section 1(6) provides that the power to make an order under subsection (4) is exercisable by statutory instrument, the draft of which is to be approved by each House of Parliament. Consequently, the 1974 Act is renewed annually each July by this procedure.

23 Section 5(7) provides that "for the purposes of this section a provision is ancillary to other provisions if it is a provision which is necessary or expedient for making those other provisions effective or which provides for the enforcement of those other provisions or which is otherwise incidental to, or consequential on, those provisions ...". See also section 5(4).

24 Section 38(1) of the 1973 Act (as amended by the Northern Ireland Act 1982) states: "Her Majesty may by Order in Council make provision with respect to the following matters (*a*) elections (but not the franchise) and boundaries in respect of local authorities in Northern Ireland; (*b*) any reserved matter." Subsections (5) and (6) lay down the Parliamentary procedure for such Orders in Council but under the Northern Ireland Act 1982, schedule 2, para 7(1), "No recommendation shall be made to Her Majesty to make an Order in Council under section 38(1)(*b*) of the Constitution Act during the interim period...".

25 It is possible for a Private Members' Bill to be enacted, applying only to Northern Ireland and dealing with a non-excepted matter; see, *eg*, the Education (NI) Act 1978 and the Chronically Sick and Disabled Persons (NI) Act 1978. This is, however, a very rare occurrence.

26 This is, clearly, a very simplified outline, but it encapsulates the principles necessary for comparing Acts of Parliament and delegated legislation. For fuller discussion of the points made here, see Hadfield, "Direct Rule, Delegated Legislation and the Role of

Parliament" in Hayes and O'Higgins (eds) *Lessons from Northern Ireland*. Papers from a Conference held at King's College, London, March 1989. Publication pending.

27 See Sixth Report of the Select Committee on Procedure, 1966-67. HC 539. Appendix 8. Mr Speaker's Counsel Memorandum, para 6.

28 For truly emergency Orders, the procedure provided for under schedule 1, para 1(4)(*b*) of the 1974 Act is used; see text.

29 Discussion document. HMSO. October 1972, p 21, para 44(*a*). See also Cmnd 5675 (the White Paper preceding the Northern Ireland Act 1974), para 31, quoted above: "To proceed with [a full legislative programme such as that devised by the Northern Ireland Executive] entirely by way of Bills in the United Kingdom Parliament is out of the question."

30 For a more detailed consideration of these points, see Hadfield, "Committees of the House of Commons and Northern Ireland Affairs" 1981 (32) *NILQ*, pp 199-235. See also Appendix 5.

31 The number was increased from twelve to seventeen under the HC Redistribution of Seats Act 1979.

32 In 1982, when the Northern Ireland Assembly began discharging *its* scrutiny powers, the Committee became almost superfluous; see chapter VI, below. Given the reaction of the Unionist MPs to the signing of the Anglo-Irish Agreement, there has been no real drive to revive it since the Assembly was dissolved. The Committee has not met, therefore, since 1985. See Appendix 5 for a full list of its meetings from its inception.

33 It is appreciated that the Westminster Select Committees which do possess these powers are not concerned with the legislative work of the departments which they shadow. The point is made, in the context of legislation for Northern Ireland, because of the lack of detailed scrutiny elsewhere within Parliament. See, also, the powers of the (albeit infrequently used) Special Standing Committees under 1988 HC SO 91(1): "A special standing committee to which a bill has been committed shall have power, during a period not exceeding 28 days ... from the committal of the bill, to send for persons, papers and records, and, for this purpose, to hold up to four morning sittings of not more than three hours each. At not more than three sittings oral evidence may be given and, unless the committee otherwise orders, all such evidence shall be given in public". See further chapter VIII.

34 The Committee was set up in February 1975, three months before the Constitutional Convention began its deliberations on the future form of government for the Province. At this time also, therefore, little attention was paid to providing a coherent pattern of Westminster scrutiny of Northern Ireland affairs.

35 Limited use has, however, been made of Merits Committees for Northern Ireland draft Orders: see Appendix 5 for details.

36 Since 1980, Consolidation Orders in Council have been considered by the Joint Committee on Consolidation and Statute Law Revision.

37 First Special Report from the Joint Committee on Statutory Instruments. 1977-78; HL 51, HC 169, para 6.

38 This question cannot be finely weighed, for much depends upon how strongly one believes that Parliament itself should be involved in the law-making process, however

much consultation may take place between the Government and "the people" (or at least interested and affected parties) directly.

39 See also section 4(5) of the 1973 Act: "It is hereby declared for the avoidance of doubt that a Measure is not invalid by reason of any failure to comply with the provisions of section 5, 6, 14, or 18(2), (5) or (6) [of the 1973 Act]; and no act or omission under any of those provisions shall be called in question in any legal proceedings." The whole tenor of the 1973 Act on this point was to provide for political rather than judicial control over the procedural acceptability/validity of Measures, other than with regard to section 17. Northern Ireland Orders in Council are, of course, subject to consideration by the European Court of Justice as is any other part of domestic law: see, *eg*, *Johnston* v *Chief Constable of the RUC* [1986] 3 All ER 135.

40 See, specifically, on a Ministerial order, *Minister of Health* v *R, ex p Jaffe* [1931] AC 494 and more generally *Anisminic* v *FCC* [1969] 2 AC 147.

41 After the 1987 General Election, when the Conservatives held relatively few Scottish seats, difficulty in forming the Scottish Select Committee was encountered and, at the time of writing, it remains unconstituted.

42 Palley, "Ways Forward. The Constitutional Options" in Watt (ed, 1981), *The Constitution of Northern Ireland, Problems and Prospects*, at p 189.

43 1976-1977, HC Debs vol 925, col 1644-5 (10th February 1977).

44 The full text of the letter is provided in HC Debs vol 941, cols 1839-40 (12th January 1978).

45 The Government of Northern Ireland: A Working Paper for a Conference. Cmnd 7763, November 1979.

46 The two elements in this should be kept distinct, and the November 1979 White Paper provided detailed consideration of both of these, namely the *range* of subjects to be transferred (agriculture, education, economic development etc) and the *extent* of the powers (legislative, executive or administrative) to be devolved over them.

47 The Conference differed from the round of talks instigated by Roy Mason in that he talked with each party separately. At the Atkins Conference, the parties were brought together for the first time officially for a number of years.

48 See Cmnd 7950, July 1980, para 14: "Though direct rule has performed a vital task over the past eight years and has achieved general acceptance in the province, it leaves no incentive for people in Northern Ireland to seek responsibility through politics and generally stifles local political initiative. Moreover for a part of the United Kingdom which has had a recent tradition of its own legislature and separate administration linked to it, it is only a second best and not a permanent answer." Given that successive Fianna Fail Governments in the Republic have also stressed their preference for a "British withdrawal" from Northern Ireland, direct rule also finds little support in the Republic.

49 Cmnd 7950. July 1980.

50 *Ibid*, para 29. See on this point, the White Paper preceding the 1973 Act, Cmnd 5259, para 69: "the Northern Ireland Executive will be invited to act as an advisory committee to the Secretary of State in relation to those responsibilities reserved to him." This was regarded as being of importance in providing for Northern Ireland involvement in, particularly, law and order matters.

51 The White Paper mentioned as possibilities either *direct* popular election, by a system of proportional representation, of the Executive, or election of the Executive by the Assembly members.

52 *Ibid*, para 56.

53 *Ibid*, para 57.

54 *Ibid*, para 58.

55 *Ibid*, para 64.

56 Earlier, in July 1981, he had proposed the creation of an Advisory Council, consisting of (around) fifty members. This proposal will be mentioned at the start of the next chapter, however, as it leads naturally into a consideration of rolling devolution.

# VI

# THE NORTHERN IRELAND ACT 1982

As was mentioned in the final note to the last chapter, in July 1981 Humphrey Atkins, aware that there would be some delay before there was sufficient agreement to establish a devolved assembly with legislative powers and anxious to proceed rather more rapidly to break the continuing stalemate, announced that he proposed

to proceed without legislation and to set up, by administrative act, a representative Northern Ireland Council which at least initially will be composed of [probably fifty] persons already elected by the voters of Northern Ireland to other representative bodies. ... I intend to invite people to serve after seeking nominations from the Northern Ireland political parties which have been shown in recent elections to have a substantial following in the Province. Each party will be asked for a specific number of nominations related to their electoral strength ... [The Council would not have legislative or executive functions but could] consider and report to me on the activities of the Northern Ireland Government Departments which cover the range of [transferred] matters ... Secondly, I shall invite the Council to consider proposals for legislation affecting Northern Ireland so that I and my colleagues can take account of it before laying draft legislation before Parliament ... Thirdly, I shall invite the Council to consider the future government of Northern Ireland and what proposals for the exercise of executive powers and legislative powers by elected representatives might prove to be acceptable to both parts of the community in the Province ... [In taking account of the Council's advice] I would attach, as Parliament would attach, special importance to advice that was unanimous or, failing that, commanded widespread support from representatives of both parts of the community ... but ... responsibility for all legislation would rest with Parliament and I would remain responsible to Parliament for the direction and control of the Northern Ireland Departments in the discharge of their executive functions.[1]

Two months later James Prior succeeded Humphrey Atkins as Secretary of State and with certain limited modifications he accepted, although not in as many words, the above plan as the basis of his scheme for "rolling devolution". In April 1982, yet another White Paper, this time entitled "Northern Ireland: A Framework for Devolution" was published.[2] In it the Government proposed the institution of a seventy-eight member unicameral Assembly, elected by the single transferable vote system of proportional representation, possessing, from its inception, "scrutinising, deliberative and consultative functions". It was further proposed that the Assembly would be asked to make recommendations to the Secretary of State as to "arrangements under which the whole or part of the range of legislative and executive responsibilities previously transferred under the Northern Ireland Constitution Act 1973 could be exercised by the Assembly and by a devolved administration answerable to it".[3] The scheme was to be implemented by Act of Parliament rather than by administrative decree and the relevant Bill, the Northern Ireland Bill 1982, after a somewhat fraught Parliamentary passage largely due to opposition from Government backbenchers and Official Unionist MPs, culminating eventually in the imposition of the "guillotine", received the Royal Assent on 23rd July 1982 and came into force on that day.

This Act must be read in conjunction with the 1973 and 1974 Acts and a general summary of its provisions may assist in a more detailed consideration of the work of the Assembly.[4] The 1982 Act was in essence primarily a facilitative Act, although it also contained provisions which were designed both to improve the processes and scrutiny of direct rule and also to lay the foundations for a future system of legislative and executive devolution. Sections 3 and 4 of the Act related to the functions which the Assembly possessed from its inception. First, it was required by section 4 to establish committees, known as the statutory committees, to which was entrusted the responsibility of monitoring each of the six Northern Ireland departments as they operated under the direct rule provisions of the 1974 Act. The membership of the committees, including also the offices of chairmen and deputy chairmen taken as a whole, was, as far as practicable, to reflect the balance of parties in the Assembly. The powers of these committees were much more limited than those possessed by Westminster's select committees, being circumscribed by the following statutory provision which was inserted by the 1982 Act into the Constitution Act 1973, section 26:[5]

Neither the Assembly nor its committees shall have power—

(*a*) to *require* any person to give evidence, or to produce any papers, relating to any matter other than one in respect of which the Assembly has power to pass a Measure not requiring the consent of the Secretary of State; or

(*b*) to *require* any person to give evidence, or to produce any papers, relating to any matter which is or has been within his responsibility as a Minister of the government of the United Kingdom or as an officer of a department under the control of any such Minister.

That is, the normal scrutiny power possessed by select committees, the power to require persons to give written and/or oral evidence, would only have been available to Assembly committees with regard to any transferred matter had there been a new subsequent system of legislative devolution. In the initial deliberative stages of the 1982 Assembly's existence and with regard to any aspect of direct rule (even had it come to an end) the power was simply one of invitation and the committees' effectiveness, therefore, depended upon the good graces of the Westminster Government Ministers and of local and public bodies in Northern Ireland.

Section 3 of the 1982 Act conferred two related powers on the Assembly at its inception. It was given a general deliberative function: on its own motion, it could debate any matter which was transferred or reserved[6] under the 1973 Act and it could debate any matter, including an excepted matter, referred to it by the Secretary of State. Secondly and more specifically, the Secretary of State was empowered, the discretion being his, to refer to the Assembly for its general consideration any *proposal* for a draft Order to be made under the 1974 Act.[7] It must be stressed that the Assembly at no stage possessed any legislative powers; these remained at all times with Westminster.

These are the only parts of the 1982 Act, other than section 5 which provided for the dissolution of the Assembly, which became fully operative. The long title of the Act, however, did refer to its provision for "the resumption of legislative and executive functions by the Northern Ireland Assembly and by persons responsible to it", and this aim is reflected in sections 1 and 2. They empowered the Assembly to submit to the Secretary of State proposals concerning the resumption of legislative and executive devolution but they also laid down the perimeters of acceptability as far as such proposals were concerned. They provided that, given the fulfilment of certain conditions relating to cross-community consensus, legislative and executive powers over one or more transferred matters (partial devolution) or over all transferred matters (full devolution) could have been devolved to the Assembly.[8] The provisions on cross-community consensus took various forms. Specifically, section 1(2) imposed the duty on the Assembly when making proposals for partial devolution to include in those proposals recommendations with regard to the appointment of the political head of the devolved department(s), and when making proposals for full devolution to include recommendations relating to the formation of a devolved Executive.[9] Section 1(4), however, contained the major requirement on cross-community consensus:

> The Assembly shall not submit any proposals under this section unless—
>
> (*a*) the proposals have the support of at least 70 per cent of the members of the Assembly; or
>
> (*b*) the proposals have the support of a majority of those members and the Secretary of State has notified the Assembly that he is satisfied that the substance of the proposals is likely to command widespread acceptance throughout the community.

Any proposals submitted to the Secretary of State were required by section 1(5) to be laid by him before Parliament. The wording in section 1(4)(*b*) was not of pristine clarity, nor was very much light cast upon it by the White Paper which preceded the 1982 Act. It stated that

> in forming a judgment on this the Government would only consider a proposal to command sufficiently widespread acceptance if it appeared to be acceptable to both sides of the community.[10]

Section 1(4)(*a*) superficially seemed more straightforward, but the Secretary of State stated during the Parliamentary debates that all that satisfaction of that criterion ensured was that the proposals would be debated in the Commons, and only if the cross-community consensus criterion were also satisfied would the Government have asked "Parliament to approve the Assembly's recommendations so that devolved Government could be restored".[11] This position was enshrined, after some debate on the matter, into the legislation through a Government amendment to clause 2, which became section 2(2):

> No recommendation shall be made to Her Majesty to make [a partial or full devolution Order] unless each House of Parliament has passed a resolution approving a draft of the Order, and stating that its provisions are, in the opinion of that House, likely to command widespread acceptance throughout the community.

Although, of the 1982 scheme, the provisions on "rolling devolution" probably made the most impact on the popular awareness, it was clear even before the elections to the Assembly were held that they would in fact remain completely unfulfilled. This was so for two reasons. First, the statutory requirements were themselves a strange amalgam of the precise (section 1(4)(*a*)) and the imprecise (sections 1(4)(*b*), and 2(2)) with the latter being dominant. Secondly, and anyway, the Nationalist parties fought the Assembly elections on an abstentionist ticket, to which they rigidly adhered for the duration of the Assembly,[12] thereby ensuring that the formulation of proposals attracting "cross-community consensus" would remain as distant a prospect as ever. The 1982 Act itself did not provide for the elections to the Assembly—they were still controlled by the provisions of the Northern Ireland Assembly Act 1973, which was amended by the 1982 Act in certain minor respects as to the numbers of members to be returned for each constituency. Although under the House of Commons (Redistribution of Seats) Act 1979, the number of Northern Ireland Westminster constituencies had risen for the next General Election, which as it transpired was in 1983, from twelve to seventeen, the constituencies for the Assembly elections held on 20th October 1982 were based on the pre-existing twelve constituencies. As a result of that election the seventy-eight member Assembly, which met at Stormont, was composed as follows:

| *Party* | *Seats* | *First preference votes* | *% of votes* |
|---|---|---|---|
| OUP | 26 (later 27)[13] | 188,277 | 29.7 |
| DUP | 21 | 145,528 | 23.0 |
| SDLP | 14 (later 13) | 118,891 | 18.8 |
| Sinn Féin | 5 | 64,191 | 10.1 |
| Alliance | 10 | 58,851 | 9.3 |
| Workers Party | 0 | 17,216 | 2.7 |
| Ulster Popular Unionists | 1[14] | 14,916 | 2.3 |
| UUUP | 0 | 11,550 | 1.8 |
| Independent Unionist | 1 | 9,502 | 1.6 |
| Others | 0 | 4,198 | 0.7 |
| | 78 | 633,120 | 100.00[15] |

The turnout was 61.7 per cent, a low figure by Northern Ireland voting standards. Given that both the SDLP and Sinn Féin, (who had contested such an election for the first time and in so doing had made considerable in-roads upon the position of the SDLP as the sole spokesmen for the minority community), were committed to boycotting the Assembly, it began its existence with an active membership of 60.[16]

Once its Presiding Officer/Speaker had been elected, this being the first task of the new Assembly, he was required to exercise his powers under section 4 of the 1982 Act, namely to make the appointments to the statutory committees, these appointments being required to reflect so far as practicable "the balance of parties in the Assembly". This phrase was interpreted, in the light of the boycott, as the "balance of the parties *actually* in the Assembly". Consequently, the chairmanships of the Economic Development, Finance and Personnel, and Health and Social Services Committees were given to the Official Unionists, Agriculture and Environment to the DUP, and Education to the Alliance Party. Subject to the limitations imposed by section 26(1A) of the 1973 Act, which was quoted above, these statutory committees[17] had the task of scrutinising all departmental functions, both legislative and executive, and also, under the Assembly's Standing Order 31, each department's "associated public bodies". Further, Standing Orders also gave them the power to adjourn from place to place, to sit during the adjournment of the Assembly and to appoint specialist advisers.[18] It was through the work of these committees that the Assembly performed its most effective and worthwhile work. The weaknesses of the system of direct rule have been mentioned in the previous chapter; they all relate to the essential fact that little time has been made available (or is available) for the consideration of Northern Ireland affairs at Westminster. The sterling contribution of the Assembly to the mitigation of the identified weaknesses of direct rule is best illustrated by the figures in Table 1.

TABLE 1

| | |
|---|---|
| Plenary meetings of the Assembly : | 229 |
| Meetings of the statutory committees: | 725 |

*Ministerial Attendances*

| | | |
|---|---|---|
| A | Plenary Sessions: | |
| | Secretary of State | 3 |
| | Ministers | 18 |
| B | Committees: | |
| | Agriculture | 11 |
| | Economic Development | 7 |
| | Education | 4 |
| | Environment | 5 |
| | Finance and Personnel | 3 |
| | Health and Social Services | 5 |

*Committee Reports adopted by the Assembly*

| | |
|---|---|
| Agriculture | 23 |
| Economic Development | 14 |
| Education | 19 |
| Environment | 27 |
| Finance and Personnel | 19 |
| Health and Social Services | 16 |
| **(Total:** | **118)** |

*Committee Reports by Category*

| | | |
|---|---|---|
| A | Reports on Proposals for draft Orders in Council | 28 |
| B | Reports on subordinate statutory instruments | 10 |
| C | Reports requested by the Secretary of State, Ministers or Departments, based on documents other than those in categories A and B | 32 |
| D | Reports prepared by Committees of their own volition | 48 |
| | **(Total:** | **118)**[19] |

These figures, impressive in themselves, require a certain amount of further elaboration. First, included in these statistics is a reference to Ministerial attendances at both the Assembly's plenary sessions and its committee meetings. The White Paper which preceded the 1982 Act stressed that the Assembly's existence did not diminish the doctrine of Ministerial responsibility to *Westminster*:

Ministers responsible to Parliament will not sit in the Assembly but the Assembly may invite a Minister to attend, for example to explain a Proposal for an Order in Council on which the Assembly is invited to comment. Similarly, the Assembly departmental [*ie* statutory] committees will be able to discuss departmental issues with Ministers who may be represented by officials, and to invite departments to provide information. Ministers and their departments will co-operate closely with the Assembly and its committees, although the Assembly will not have a formal power to summon Ministers responsible to Parliament, or their officials, or have access as of right to departmental papers.[20]

The United Kingdom Government never deviated from this position which is constitutionally strong—if not impregnable: Government Ministers drawn from the Westminster Parliament are answerable to it and to it alone. Other arguments are not as compelling, either way; and indeed, given the modern doctrine of ministerial answerability to the media of communication, a voluntary acceptance by Government Ministers of some form of Assembly question-time may not have gone too amiss. Be that as it may, however, while the Assembly's Standing Orders were still in draft form, James Prior warned the Assembly against trying to model itself too closely on Westminster and ruled out any possibility of an Assembly Ministerial Question-Time.[21] The Assembly, however, in a somewhat futile gesture pursued its own preference and by Standing Order 13(1) provided for questions to be asked in the Assembly not only of the committee chairmen but also "of the Minister of the Crown relating to public affairs with which his department is officially concerned or to any matter of administration for which he is responsible". Not surprisingly the Government view prevailed and Government Ministers attended the Assembly or its committees only for the purpose of leading the debate or conveying information. Although the burden of answering *questions*, therefore, rested squarely on others, it may be instructive to provide some substantive information to flesh out the figures on Ministerial attendances at the Assembly and its committees from November 1982 and this is done in Table 2.

TABLE 2

| *Ministerial Attendances* | *Matters for discussion* |
|---|---|
| A *Plenary Sessions* | |
| Secretary of State (3) | Security; Government Policy in NI (2) |
| Ministers (18) | Unemployment; Michelin's NI Operations; Proposal for a Housing Order; Public Expenditure (6); Economic Strategy; Rationalisation of Schools; Regional Strategic Plan for Health and Personal Social Services; Housing Finance; Dairy Produce Quota; Education Policy; Developments in Agriculture and Industry; Health and Personal Social Services—Level of Resources; and Transport |
| B *Committees* | |
| Agriculture (11) | Special Aid; Inland Fisheries; Less-favoured Areas; Pig, Poultry and Potato Sectors; Draft Fisheries (Amendment) Order 1983; General; EEC Common Agriculture Policy; Special Aids; EEC Farm Price Agreement; |

| | |
|---|---|
| | Conservation of Scallop Stocks in the Irish Sea; Milk Quotas |
| Economic Development (7) | Economic Strategy (2); Gas and Gas Industry, and Proposal for a draft Gas (NI) Order (3); Lear Fan and Enterprise Ulster ( 1 meeting); Lignite Technology |
| Education (4) | Rationalisation of Schools, Merger between the NUU and Ulster Polytechnic and Teacher Training (1 meeting); Special funding for Capital Projects; Merger between NUU and UP; Inspectorate Report on the Effects of Expenditure Policies on the Education System in NI |
| Environment (5) | Housing Rents, Housing Strategy, Integrated Operations, Planning, Vice Shops (1 meeting); Policy Statement on Departmental Issues (3); Proposal for a draft Local Government Change of District Name (Londonderry) Order NI |
| Finance and Personnel (3) | Public Expenditure Priorities; Implications of the Budget for NI; Anglo-Irish Discussions |
| Health and Social Services (5) | Review of Structure and Management of the Health and Personal Social Services; Proposed Reform of Housing Benefits; Regional Strategic Plan; Proposal for a draft Betting etc Order; Liquor Licensing |

The vast amount of the information provided to the committees, however, came from other bodies and the co-operation of the departmental civil servants, of the representatives of local and public bodies and of the voluntary agencies was also striking.[22] Although there were some refusals to respond positively to a committee invitation to submit written and/or oral evidence, O'Leary, Elliott and Wilford[23] provide an impressive list of witnesses who gave oral evidence at the committees' public evidence sessions (see Table 3).

TABLE 3

| *Committee* | *Number of appearances by civil servants* |
|---|---|
| Agriculture | 22[24] |
| Economic Development | 25 |
| Education | 10 |
| Environment | 27 |
| Health and Social Services | 17 |
| Finance and Personnel | 16 |

| *Committee* | *Significant number of appearances by other public body representatives* |
|---|---|
| Agriculture | NI Agricultural Producers' Association—13 |
| Economic Development | Industrial Development Board—12<br>NI Electricity Service—4<br>NI Committee of Irish Congress of Trade Unions—3 |
| Education | Western Education and Library Board (WELB)—4<br>Belfast ELB, North Eastern ELB, South Eastern ELB, Southern ELB—3 |
| Environment | NI Housing Executive—7<br>Belfast City Council—5 |
| Health and Soc Services | Eastern Health and Social Services Board- 4 |
| Finance and Personnel | Office of Law Reform—5 |

A considerable array of other bodies, pressure groups and interested individuals made at least one appearance to give evidence before the relevant committee, the overall total number of such appearances being 426.

The second matter of interest to note concerning the original set of figures presented in Table 1 concerns the division in the Assembly's time between matters referred to it by the Secretary of State (Categories A, B, and C) and matters which it itself chose to pursue (category D). The composite table has been provided above; the committee breakdown is provided in Table 4.

TABLE 4

| *Committee* | *Report Classification* | *Totals* |
|---|---|---|
| Agriculture | A | 2 |
| | B | 5 |
| | C | 4 |
| | D | 12 |
| | **(Total:** | **23)** |
| Economic Development | A | 5 |
| | B | 0 |
| | C | 3 |
| | D | 6 |
| | **(Total:** | **14)** |
| Education | A | 3 |
| | B | 0 |
| | C | 6 |
| | D | 10 |
| | **(Total:** | **19)** |
| Environment | A | 11 |
| | B | 5 |
| | C | 5 |
| | D | 6 |
| | **(Total:** | **27)** |
| Finance and Personnel | A | 5 |
| | B | 0 |
| | C | 7 |
| | D | 7 |
| | **(Total:** | **19)** |
| Health and Social Services | A | 2 |
| | B | 0 |
| | C | 7 |
| | D | 7 |
| | **(Total:** | **16)** |

In light of the identified weaknesses in the process of legislating for Northern Ireland under direct rule, specific consideration should be given to the figures on the reports falling in Category A, namely Reports on Proposals for draft Orders in Council. They belong to a more detailed set of figures on the scrutiny work of the Assembly over proposed legislation:

*Proposals for draft Orders in Council referred to the Assembly*

| | |
|---|---|
| Considered by Committee and Assembly | 29[25] |
| Considered by Assembly only | 3[26] |
| (This relates to December 1982, when the Committees had not yet been established) | |
| Considered by Committee only | 1 |
| Not considered | 4[27] |
| (This relates to the period from December 1985 to April 1986, when the Committees were not meeting) | |
| **(Total** | **37)** |

By Standing Orders 34 and 35, the Assembly provided that its non-statutory Business Committee should determine whether or not a proposal for a draft Order should be referred to the Assembly in its plenary capacity for an initial consideration of its general principles or be referred direct to the appropriate departmental committee. If the Assembly in its plenary form had first considered the proposal (as, for example, it did with regard to the proposal for the draft Housing Order, but this was very rare) then it automatically went next to the relevant committee unless the Assembly had resolved otherwise. The almost invariable procedure, however, was for the committee to consider the proposal first and then to report to the Assembly. The committees, in their consideration of the proposal, would, as with their other investigations, invite the submission of written and/or oral evidence from the department and from other interested bodies. This procedure should be contrasted with the direct rule scrutiny at Westminster of Northern Ireland draft Orders in Council. The Assembly, quite simply, gave a lengthier and a much more informed scrutiny to proposals for draft Orders than the pre-existing and subsequent system of what may be termed "unmitigated direct rule" ever achieved. It is granted that the Assembly's work related to the pre-parliamentary scrutiny of Northern Ireland Orders and left untouched the Parliamentary consideration given to them; nevertheless given the statutory requirement in subsections 3(3) and (4) of the 1982 Act, that the Assembly reports on such matters should go to the

Secretary of State and hence to Parliament, and given the whole purpose of the exercise, there can be no argument but that crucially the Government's final draft of the Order which was laid before Parliament, subject to brief Parliamentary consideration, had, at the least, been fully considered in the light of what an informed Northern Ireland Assembly had had to say on the matter. The following proposals were amongst those considered by an Assembly departmental committee and debated in the Assembly itself—Access to the Countryside; Housing; Housing Benefits; Family Law (Miscellaneous Provisions); Wildlife; Industrial Training; Road Traffic, Transport and Roads (Miscellaneous Provisions); University of Ulster; Betting, Gaming, Lotteries and Amusements; Recreation and Youth Service; Foreign Limitation Periods; Historic Churches; Credit Unions; Gas; Guardianship; and Mental Health. The width and the importance of the matters considered by the Assembly here clearly indicate the value of the contribution it made.

Only ten of the Assembly's Reports fell into category B—Reports on Subordinate Statutory Instruments. The Secretary of State requested all departments as from 1st January 1983 to refer to the Assembly for its comments the proof form of all statutory rules on transferred matters which were subject to either Westminster's negative scrutiny procedures for delegated legislation or to no Westminster scrutiny at all. This general requirement on the departments was subject to certain exceptions, namely, where uniformity was required throughout the whole United Kingdom (for example, where the primary legislation was the same or European Community Law was involved) or where speed was essential. Standing Order 43 dealt with the procedure for the Assembly's consideration of statutory rules—and much depended upon the committee chairman to whom the Speaker would forward the copy of the proposed rule. The chairman, after "reasonable consultation" with his committee members, was required to indicate within seven days whether or not he wanted his committee to consider the rule, and if he did, the rule had to be considered within three weeks of its receipt.

On category C reports there is little of significance to note. Of much more importance—as reflecting the committees' own interests and as enabling them to take the initiative rather than being merely responsive or reactive—are the category D Reports, the reports prepared by the committees of their own volition.

The committees as a whole spent approximately half their time on category D reports, the room for manoeuvre of each committee being to a certain extent dependent upon the legislative output of the shadow department, the Environment Committee particularly having a heavy programme of proposed legislation. The most notable or possibly illustrative of category D reports include:

| | |
|---|---|
| Agriculture | Proposed Extension of Less-favoured Areas in NI; Future Administration of the Salmon and Inland Fisheries of NI; Sea Fishing Industry; Portavogie Harbour Development; Kilkeel Harbour Development and Improvement Work; Specific Aspects of the EEC's Common Agricultural Policy (2 reports) |
| Economic Development | Industrial Incentives; Electricity Supply; Free Ports; Youth Training Programme |
| Education | Rationalisation of Schools; Youth Service; Educational Needs of Unemployed Adults; Public Library Service in NI; Education of Hearing-Impaired Children; Proposed changes in Student Awards Regulations; Museum Service in NI; Proposed Closure of the Department of Architecture at Queen's University, Belfast |
| Environment | Rent Structures and Levels; NI Housing Executive; Belfast Housing Renewal Strategy; Homelessness in NI; Private Hire Taxis |
| Finance and Personnel | Additionality of Receipts from European Funds; Investigation by the Fair Employment Agency into the Non-industrial NI Civil Service |
| Health and Social Services | Social Security Fraud; Social Security Parity; Homeopathy; Report of the Joint Review Team on Developing Hospital Services; Green Paper on Reform of Social Security |

It should be appreciated that *all* reports considered by the Assembly in categories C and D fell substantively into the category of matters transferred, not reserved or excepted, under the Constitution Act 1973, although some topics did impinge upon an excepted matter. Similarly, the Secretary of State exercised his discretion to refer to the Assembly proposals for draft Orders by referring virtually all[28] proposals dealing with transferred matters published during the active life of the Assembly. Proposals dealing with reserved matters, of which there were only four,[29] were not specifically referred to the Assembly, although all of them were made available and circulated to Assembly members. The Assembly then, had it so wished, could have used its own initiative to consider them, but it chose not to do so. Indeed the only non-transferred area in which the Assembly expressed a real and continuing interest was that of security.[30] One of its major substantive non-statutory committees was that on Security and Home Affairs,[31] the remit of which ran like an extract from schedule 3 to the Constitution Act 1973 on reserved matters—to report to the Assembly on law and order, including the criminal law, the creation of offences and penalties, the prevention and detection of crime, the treatment of offenders and the establishment and organisation of the RUC. The Secretary of State made it clear, however, that security being a reserved matter, and likely to remain so, even with devolution, for a not inconsiderable period of time, belonged to the purview of Westminster and Whitehall and that the Assembly's sole role was that of ventilating local public and political opinion. Neither the General Officer Commanding (the Armed Forces) Northern Ireland nor the Chief Constable of the RUC nor any other security personnel ever met with the Committee, which essentially became another forum for the expression of Unionist frustration at security policy in the Province. From 1972 onwards, the Unionists have regarded local control and influence over security policy as an essential element in any devolved scheme; successive Westminster Governments have insisted that for as long as "the Troubles" persist security remains a matter reserved to central government—and the establishment by the Assembly of a Security and Home Affairs Committee was never going to change anything.

Security apart, however, according to what criteria should one assess the overall contribution of the Assembly in the discharge of its functions under sections 3 and 4 of the 1982 Act? It must be borne in mind that these sections were designed to facilitate the exertion of influence on the Westminster Parliament and specifically on the Government and did not involve the transfer of *power* from Westminster to Stormont. Furthermore, the Northern Ireland Assembly was directing its influence at an Executive which was not drawn from it and which was not constitutionally responsible to it. This is one mark of distinction between the Assembly and the House of Commons, although in other respects there are similarities, the Commons having far fewer *powers* than is popularly appreciated. If the Assembly is assessed, however, in terms of the extent of its influence on the Government, how successful was it? The simplest way to answer this question is to provide the percentage acceptance rate of its recommendations. The figures given vary, but within a relatively narrow band. The Assembly itself produced a booklet entitled "Local Democracy at Work" in March 1984 and in it claimed a success rate of 64 per cent.[32] Later that year the Assembly set the figure at 69 per cent.[33] O'Leary, Elliott and Wilford, cautiously, provide the following information on the fate of committee recommendations:

> Overall the Committees generated a total of 998 recommendations; of these 417 (41.8 per cent) were accepted in full; 119 (11.9 per cent) were accepted either in part or in principle; 99 (9.9 per cent) were subjected to further consideration...; 61 (6.1 per cent) were rejected; 17 (1.7 per cent) required no change in the original proposals; and a further 29 (2.9 per cent) met some "other" fate (*i.e.* they were delegated by the target Department to another administrative body for comment, such as an Area Health Board). Thus on a rule of thumb basis the outcome of the Committees' labours resulted in an unweighted ratio of acceptances to rejections of approximately 2 to 1... Individual Committees varied in the extent to which they were able to influence their target Departments. As far as unqualified acceptances were concerned the least 'successful' was the Health and Social Services Committee: out of a total of eighty-seven recommendations only twenty-two (25.3 per cent) were accepted by the DHSS. At the other end of the scale, the most 'successful' was the Economic Development Committee: 112 of its 169 recommendations were accepted, a 'strike-rate' of 66.3 per cent. Yet such figures have to be put in context. In the case of the Economic Development Committee, the majority of its recommendations did not involve proposals to increase expenditure but rather were concerned to effect certain managerial and administrative changes which suited the temper and policy of the DED and the UK Government. By contrast, the Agriculture Committee devoted much of its time and effort in seeking to influence the European dimension of relevant policy, something that not only lay beyond the formal control of DANI but which, strictly speaking, lay beyond the Committee's remit. Moreover, where the Committees sought to vary national policy to the advantage of Northern Ireland they also came unstuck... [this was] particularly pronounced in the cases of Education, Environment and Health and Social Services. The hard-won lesson here is that Committee potential is enhanced where they seek either to work within the bounds of existing national policy or where the Government is genuinely seeking to clarify the terms of proposed action, and diminished where Committee proposals conflict with national policy, especially in the field of revenue-raising and preferred patterns of expenditure.[34]

A statistical assessment of the extent of the Assembly's contribution is in no wise an assessment of the substantive value or worth of the recommendations accepted or rejected, but such an evaluation is virtually impossible to make. There are no universally acceptable criteria by which to rank the importance of the various matters considered by the Assembly. For example, the Government rejected Assembly recommendations (not all unanimous) that the name of Londonderry City Council should not be changed to Derry City Council, that hare-coursing should be banned in Northern Ireland and that industrial and commercial consumers of gas should be fully, rather than only partially, compensated by the Government for the conversion costs engendered by the closure of the gas industry. On the other hand, it accepted Assembly recommendations that Housing Executive repair grants should be made available to tenants living in houses built before 1957, that the Department of Architecture at Queen's University, Belfast should not be closed and that Northern Ireland should have an "industrial incentives package" largely comparable with that in the Republic of Ireland. It would make an interesting exercise to require one hundred people chosen at random from the population of Northern Ireland to rank, in their own reasoned order of preference, these or any other six broadly selected topics. It would, therefore, be rather futile to attempt any assessment in these terms of the contribution of the Assembly: all that can be stated with certainty is that the Assembly had a not-insignificant influence upon the substantive and detailed content of policies for Northern Ireland. Its existence ensured that those policies were subjected to a more informed and more prolonged scrutiny than theretofore under direct rule or subsequently. Also, equally important, the Assembly in its power to choose for itself what matters to debate and to scrutinise was able to collect information on and provide publicity for issues it considered important. Power to take the initiative is an important power and is one largely denied the Northern Ireland Members at Westminster—adjournment debates and Northern Ireland Question-Time being largely discounted as valuable in this context.

It is undeniable that the Assembly discharged a worthwhile function. In the longer term, the work may not have been satisfying to the Assembly members themselves—pursuit of influence without prospect of power is not usually a politician's prime aspiration. The continued existence of the Assembly was jeopardised anyway from its inception by the boycott to which both the SDLP and Sinn Féin Assembly members were committed, and indeed also partly by the ambivalent attitude of the Official Unionists. Whilst the validity of the Assembly's scrutiny and deliberative functions has on occasion been questioned in the light of the Nationalist boycott and the consequential political imbalance in the Assembly, the boycott was far more crucial in terms of its guaranteeing that the Assembly would not itself produce rolling devolution recommendations acceptable to the Government under the statutory criteria of the 1982 Act. The Assembly operated successfully under sections 3 and 4 of the Act in terms of making direct rule more accountable. The exercise of those functions, however, may have constructed a platform, but a new devolved system was not going to be built on it.

## THE ASSEMBLY AND DEVOLUTION

The Assembly did in fact consider the question of devolution, with increasing rapidity as the Anglo-Irish discussions, to be considered in the next chapter, moved towards their culmination (as it transpired) in the Anglo-Irish Agreement of 1985. On 7th February 1984 the Assembly resolved to establish a non-statutory Devolution Report Committee, with the remit of examining "how the Assembly might be strengthened and progress made towards legislative and executive devolution". The Committee, composed of eleven Assembly members representing proportionately the participating parties in the Assembly, commenced its work in June 1984, the delay being due to an OUP boycott, and produced its first interim report in October 1984.[35] This Report published the initial submissions on devolution of the three parties active in the Assembly as a basis for further discussion, and, as an intermediate measure, provided a series of recommendations largely designed to enhance the efficiency and effectiveness of the scrutiny work of the Assembly. These recommendations included the following: that there should be regular scheduled business meetings between the chairman of each statutory committee and the responsible Minister, the frequency of such meetings to be related to the volume of business of each committee; that the chairman/Minister meeting should be the primary channel of communication between the department and the committee; that consideration should be given to the feasibility of extending the role of the Assembly's Finance and Personnel Committee to embrace a quasi-(Westminster) Public Accounts Committee function; that there should be more regular scheduled and structured attendances by Ministers in the Assembly; and that there should be introduced a system of Assembly Questions for *written* answer by the Secretary of State and the other Northern Ireland Ministers.[36] The Devolution Report Committee also recommended that there should be a Bill of Rights preferably for the United Kingdom as a whole but failing that for Northern Ireland specifically, based on the substantive rights set forth in the European Convention on Human Rights and to be introduced in order to ensure "that everything that can possibly be done by legal means to still any remaining fears and to remedy any genuine grievance" had been done.[37]

The three interim party papers on devolution published in the Report revealed an expected divergence, although all agreed on the need for a Bill of

Rights. In many ways they constituted an increasingly hollow exercise given the SDLP's reluctance to be involved in any way at all, having by this stage resolutely set its face in the direction of an all-Ireland dimension as an integral part of any future system of government for Northern Ireland. This was a dimension not considered by the three parties active in the Assembly as relevant to the creation of new political institutions for Northern Ireland. The OUP, in its paper entitled "The Way Forward", stated that, as there was no immediate prospect of executive and legislative devolution,[38] there should instead be introduced a system of what it termed "administrative devolution", designed to fill the gap created when a large number of traditional local government functions[39] were transferred to the Northern Ireland Parliament. When it was prorogued in 1972 and abolished in 1973, these functions were passed to civil and public servants and to nominated public bodies over which there was no local political control. The Official Unionists, therefore, proposed that

> those functions and powers transferred from the [pre-1970] County and County Borough Councils to Stormont should be devolved to the Northern Ireland Assembly as the nucleus of its responsibilities ... [In] broad terms, the proposal is that the ... Assembly would be an administrative body for the whole of Northern Ireland. It would not legislate nor would it exercise its powers through the medium of a cabinet government, but rather make its decisions within the areas of power granted to it by the enabling legislation and by such legislation as related to the services and functions being administered by it.[40]

The DUP, by contrast, took a much broader sweep, and recommended the transfer of "full Law and Order powers ... at an appropriate time in the future", (coupled with the hope that certain "non-security" aspects of the criminal law could be transferred immediately), the establishment of a Cabinet system of government, to be drawn from the largest party or group of parties in the Assembly and, as a way of providing a "meaningful role for minority groups", to be shadowed by a system of strong departmental committees with the chairmanships and composition reflecting the party-political complexion[41] of the Assembly. It was envisaged that these committees[42] would possess both executive and legislative functions, operating with extensive powers. The DUP also recommended that fuller consideration should be given to the second option detailed in the Government White Paper of July 1980[43] which followed the "Atkins Conference" and which option was in general terms not far removed from these DUP proposals. The second option assumed the creation of a *single-party* not power-sharing Executive and consequently suggested a system of balances, to counterpoise majority rule and to provide safeguards for the minority, including a Council of the Assembly. The DUP proposed certain modifications to the Government's delineation of the Council and if they were acceptable, then the party was "prepared to countenance a Council ... provided its powers are not such as to render meaningful government impossible or to turn democratic government into a farce".[44]

The Alliance Party, in its proposals, recommended first, a "committee system of partnership government based upon the principle of proportionality", which would be structured as follows. Once the Assembly had elected a Chief Executive from amongst its members by the "alternative vote" system,[45] it would proceed to elect, by the single transferable vote system, a panel of chairmen and committee members, the objective being to have every Assembly member involved in at least one committee. Each chairman would act as the Minister for the relevant department and the chairmen together would form a Finance Committee, under the chairmanship of the Chief Executive. The second element in the Alliance Party scheme was its recommended creation of what it termed "a political right of appeal," to supplement the legal protection to be afforded by a Bill of Rights. The essence of this proposal was that

> at the instance of a substantial minority of opinion in the [Assembly] (one-third plus one indicated by Petition to the Speaker) any issue ... can be appealed from the [Assembly] to [the] Westminster... Government ... subject to approval by Parliament.

"Any issue" would include actions in prospect both legislative and executive, legislation already made, any other action already taken and omissions to act.[46]

In the months which followed the publication of the Devolution Report Committee's first report, the three parties themselves sought both to refine their own positions in the hope of achieving some overall consensus and to involve the SDLP in some way in the process of formulating devolution proposals but they were unsuccessful on both counts. The second report of the Committee, published in February 1985, simply repeated the views of the three parties, republished their own papers and also published written proposals and advice submitted to the Committee by outside persons and bodies and witness evidence, but the Committee did not comment on this evidence beyond stating that the various ideas submitted "should not be construed as an indication of the Committee's mind on any such ideas and proposals."[47] The Committee both expressed its hope that publication of the evidence received by it would increase public awareness of the issues involved and expressed its willingness to entertain any further proposals.

What was substantively the Committee's final act came in October 1985, when it produced a third report,[48] explaining the outcome of the processes of deliberation and consultation which had taken place since the Spring of 1985. The Committee had by this stage invited Sir Frederick Catherwood MEP to act as "interlocutor and conciliator" between the various parties and his recommendations were endorsed by the three parties in the Devolution Report Committee's Third Report. The Catherwood Report, noting that the parties actually participating in the Assembly constituted over 70 per cent of the Assembly's membership, the percentage requirement for manifesting the consensus specified in section 1(4)(*a*) of the 1982 Act, and referring to the lack of input from the SDLP, recommended:

that the whole range of legislative and executive powers transferred under the Constitution Act 1973 should again be transferred to the Assembly and a devolved Executive answerable to it;[49]

that the initial administration in the new devolved Assembly should require a vote of confidence of two-thirds of the Assembly Members;[50]

that the Executive should be shadowed by a Committee system, proportionately reflecting party strengths in the Assembly;

that a Bill of Rights, enacted by Westminster, should be entrenched in the new constitution;[51]

and that, in order to strengthen the statutory safeguards for minority parties, 30% of the Assembly should be able to require the Secretary of State to exercise his powers under section 18 of the Constitution Act, that is, to request the Judicial Committee of the Privy Council to determine the compatibility of any proposed Assembly legislation with the anti-discrimination requirements of section 17 of the Act.[52]

Although these proposals were endorsed by the three Assembly parties as an agreed basis for further negotiations, the Alliance Party entered immediate caveats, namely that the SDLP must be involved in the subsequent discussions, that the talks should be solely concerned with political structures within Northern Ireland and that those talks should not be used to (attempt to) frustrate the then current Anglo-Irish negotiations.[53] The Catherwood Report, however, was a dead letter; the Government made no formal, immediate response to the Report; the Anglo-Irish Agreement was signed just over two weeks later on 15th November; and on 5th December the OUP and DUP Assembly members resolved, with the Alliance members dissenting, that the Assembly should stand adjourned and that all business should be suspended other than the sittings of the newly established "Committee on the Government of Northern

Ireland", sometimes called "the Grand Committee", which was established "to examine the implications of the Anglo-Irish Agreement for the government and future of Northern Ireland and the operation of the Northern Ireland Constitution Act 1973 and the Northern Ireland Act 1982".[54] The Alliance Assembly members immediately withdrew from the Assembly and took no part whatsoever in the proceedings of the Committee. In January 1986, the Unionists stated that

> the various schemes for devolution considered by the Devolution Report Committee, including the "Catherwood Plan" are withdrawn and are no longer operative while [the Anglo-Irish] Agreement subsists.[55]

This chapter began with devolution as its main focal point. The Northern Ireland Assembly was given two tasks by the Northern Ireland Act 1982: to scrutinise the operation of direct rule and to formulate "acceptable" plans for devolution. It succeeded in its first task, a task which was of prime legal and constitutional importance but which was politically clearly subordinate to the second. It failed in its second task but this was not solely due to factors over which the Assembly itself had any control. The refusal of the Unionists to espouse or support an institutionalised Irish dimension and the refusal of the SDLP to countenance devolution without such a dimension together leave little room for manoeuvre. The Irish dimension was scarcely referred to in the White Paper which preceded the 1982 Act and was not mentioned in the Act itself; but that which had been peripheral in the early 1980s had become dominant by the middle 1980s and the demise of the Assembly, of its scrutiny work and of its devolution plans can only be considered in the light of developments in and between London and Dublin.

## NOTES

1 1980-81, HC Debs, vol 7, cols 1029-1031 (2nd July 1981).

2 Cmnd 8541, April 1982.

3 See, *eg*, para 30.

4 For a more detailed consideration of the legislation itself, see Hadfield, "The Northern Ireland Act 1982—Do-it-yourself Devolution?" 1982 *NILQ* (vol 33), pp 301-325, Maguire, "The Northern Ireland Act 1982", Current Statutes Annotated, 38-1 to 38/schedule 3; and Gearty, "The Northern Ireland Act 1982", 1982 *Public Law*, pp 518-529.

5 Section 26(1A) of the Constitution Act 1973, which was inserted into the 1973 Act by schedule 2, para 3 of the 1982 Act. Emphasis provided.

6 Clause 3 (1)(*a*) of the 1982 Bill originally provided that the Assembly had power to

deliberate *suo motu* on "any matter affecting Northern Ireland which is not an excepted or reserved matter". The reason behind this original grant of power was that the Government wanted the Assembly to concentrate on those matters which would fall within its unrestricted legislative competence if there were to be devolution. The Government was, however, prevailed upon to enable the Assembly to debate of its own volition reserved matters (which, crucially, include many security matters) but it counter-balanced this concession by inserting a new provision into the Bill which became section 3(4) of the 1982 Act: "The Secretary of State shall lay before Parliament any report received by him under this section which relates to a transferred matter considered by the Assembly ... [Note the absence of the reference to a "*reserved*" matter also] or to a matter which has been referred to it ... by the Secretary of State."

7 The deliberative power of the Assembly over proposed legislation also referred to any other delegated legislation (subordinate statutory instruments) which would, but for direct rule, be subject to the Assembly's affirmative procedures but which, during direct rule, is subject to Westminster's negative procedures, or which would be subject to the Assembly's negative procedures but which, during direct rule, is subject to no Parliamentary scrutiny at all. See section 3(2)(*b*) of the 1982 Act, which refers to the Northern Ireland Act 1974, schedule 1, para 3. For a consideration of the work of the Examiner of Statutory Rules for Northern Ireland, see Maguire 1979 *NILQ* (vol 30), pp 306-318.

8 Had this happened, most of the provisions of sections 3 and 4 of the 1982 Act, which were tied to the direct rule status quo, would have ceased to operate, unless the Assembly had provided otherwise. Because the 1982 Act permitted devolution to take place in stages, the scheme was generally known as "rolling devolution".

9 Consequently, the 1982 Act made certain amendments to section 8 of the Constitution Act 1973. Section 8(4)(*b*) of the 1973 Act, as amended, provides that the appointment of members of the Executive "shall be such as will in the opinion of the Secretary of State command widespread acceptance throughout the community." This amended section, unlike its predecessor, requires neither that all political heads of departments should be in the Executive, nor indeed that there should be a Chief Executive member.

10 Para 42 of Cmnd 8541.

11 1981-82, HC Debs, vol 25, col 751-2, (15th June 1982).

12 The Constitution Act 1973, section 27, as amended by the 1982 Act, schedule 2, para 5, provided that the maximum life of the Assembly after an election was four years.

13 One of the SDLP members returned for the Armagh constituency, Seamus Mallon, was in December 1982 the subject of an Election Petition brought against him on the grounds that he was disqualified from membership of the Assembly under the Northern Ireland Assembly Disqualification Act 1975, section 1(1)(*e*), that is, that he was a member of the Irish Senate. His election was held by the Election Court to be void. At the ensuing by-election, in April 1983, contested only by the Official Unionist and Workers Party candidates, the OUP candidate was returned. See Graham, "The Armagh Election Petition", 1984 *NILQ* (vol 35), pp 76-85.

14 This was James Kilfedder, who became the Assembly's "presiding officer"—to use the requisite statutory phrase. The Assembly's Standing Orders preferred the title "Speaker".

15 Flackes, *op cit*, p 287. See also O'Leary, Elliott and Wilford, *The Northern Ireland Assembly 1982-86, A Constitutional Experiment* (1988), chapter 6.

16 The Official Unionists themselves were not altogether happy with the legislation: the OUP MPs had largely opposed the Bill at Westminster; and from December 1982 to February 1983 they refused to participate in the statutory committee system. Again from November 1983 until May 1984, the OUP boycotted the Assembly and its committees in protest at the Darkley massacre. Apart from these periods, however, from February 1983 until the signing of the Anglo-Irish Agreement in November 1985, the Assembly operated with all but the SDLP and Sinn Féin members present.

17 Section 4(4) of the 1982 Act gave the Assembly the power to establish "other committees to assist it in the discharge of its functions". These committees, the "non-statutory committees", included routine committees such as the Business Committee, the Committee on Procedure, the Committee of Privileges, and also more substantively important committees, most notably the Devolution Report Committee, the Security and Home Affairs Committee and the so-called Grand Committee, "the Committee on the Government of Northern Ireland", established after the signing of the Anglo-Irish Agreement.

18 For other considerations of the work of the Assembly, see O'Leary, Elliott and Wilford *supra*, especially chapters 7 and 8; Hadfield, "The Northern Ireland Assembly: The First Term Report", 1983 *Public Law*, pp 550-557; Smyth, "The Northern Ireland Assembly 1982-86: The Failure of an Experiment", 1987 *Parl Aff* (40) pp 482-500; and Alan Greer, "The Northern Ireland Assembly and Accountability of Government: The Statutory Committees", 1987 *Parl Aff* (40), pp 98-112.

19 Source: Northern Ireland Assembly Table Office, from which all subsequent unattributed statistical/factual information is also provided.

20 Cmnd 8541, para 36.

21 NIA Debs, vol 4, no 5, pp 132-4.

22 In terms of gathering information, the committees were also free to use specialist advisers (although for only 13 of the 118 reports were they actually used), and to meet outside Stormont for local assessment and investigation. All the committees held both public or open sessions and private evidence sessions.

23 *Op cit*, Appendix A, Table B, 8. The figures provided there for Ministerial attendances do not tally exactly with those given in Table 1 above.

24 This includes Ulster Farmers' Union representatives. It should be noted that the civil servants were subject to the same requirements as to the giving of evidence as civil servants giving evidence to the Westminster select committees.

25 The figure given in Table 1 for Category A reports is 28; here it is 29, because the latter includes the Health and Social Services Committee Reports on the proposal for a draft Betting, Gaming etc Order (which was originally not adopted by the Assembly) and the former table (and tables derived from it) do not.

26 On Rates Amendment, General Consumer Council and Licensing (International Airports).

27 On Road Races, Social Need, Rates Amendment and Industrial Relations. The

proposal on the draft Occupiers' Liability Order was held in Committee in November 1985 and not forwarded to the Assembly.

28 In the debate on the Northern Ireland Bill 1982 the Secretary of State indicated that he would not refer to the Assembly Consolidation Orders (which since 1980 have been considered by Westminster's Joint Committee on Consolidation and Statute Law Revision), Orders taken under the urgency procedure (which naturally have no consultation period at all) and Appropriation Orders.

29 Criminal Attempts and Conspiracy; Judgments Enforcement (Attachment of Debts); Fines and Penalties; Criminal Justice.

30 The first appearance of the Secretary of State before the plenary Assembly on 30th November 1982 was to discuss security.

31 Established on 2nd March 1983, it met for the last time in October 1985. See, O'Leary, Elliott and Wilford, *op cit*, pp 156-160.

32 At p 13: "... in every important area of departmental activity there is hard evidence to show that the Government is responding positively. The 138 recommendations which the Government has already accepted represents an acceptance rate of approximately 64%."

33 Greer, *op cit*, *supra*, p 106, quoting from the Assembly's own Official Report, vol 11, p 162, 9th October 1984. Greer, p 112, warned that "the tendency might be to inflate the figure in order to portray the Assembly as a success."

34 *Op cit*, pp 174-5, and see particularly Appendix B, Tables 6 and 7. See also p 167, on which the authors stressed the unanimity factor—a unanimous committee report had a greater chance of acceptance than a split committee report: "Where a body like a scrutiny Committee is seeking to influence government thinking and proposed legislation, the production of a report which divided on party lines invited dismissal by Ministers on the grounds that if the Committee cannot agree then the [Government] should not be expected to give the proposals serious consideration." The production of a unanimous report was not in itself, of course, a *guarantee* of success.

35 NIA 154, 2nd October 1984.

36 *Ibid*, paras 3.3, 4.1 and 7.

37 *Ibid*, paras 5.1-5.7. The Government accepted the detailed recommendations, but those relating to the Finance and Personnel Committee's functions, the possibility of a system of written Questions and Answers, and the Bill of Rights were all "put on the back-burner".

38 This was so, it was stated, because of the impossibility of reconciling the Official Unionists' opposition to sharing power with those whose political preferences included a United Ireland and the Government's (and SDLP's) insistence on the cross-community consensus criterion. " The present scheme for 'rolling devolution' under the 1982 Act fails to recognise the conflict and abdicates responsibility for government by stating to the contending communities that such power as there is agreement upon will be devolved, when patently agreement is the one thing that cannot be found"; page 2 of "The Way Forward".

39 These included education, public libraries, personal health, welfare and child care, planning, roads and traffic management, water, major sewerage systems, food compo-

sition, standards and labelling, criminal injuries compensation, major harbours, electricity, public road passenger transport and the fire service. This gap is often called "the Macrory gap" because the recommendations of the Review Body on Local Government in Northern Ireland, chaired by (Sir) Patrick Macrory, Cmd (NI) 546, June 1970, were that these regional or "upper tier" local government functions should be transferred to the Northern Ireland Parliament. The new twenty-six District Councils, which came into existence in 1973, consequently had and still have very limited powers, dealing with, for example, refuse collection, street cleaning, leisure centres and cemeteries. Housing was not transferred to the Northern Ireland Parliament but went directly to the NI Housing Executive in 1971. For a brief but useful summary of the history of local government in Northern Ireland, see O'Leary, Elliott and Wilford, *op cit*, pp 54-57, 62-63 and Palley, "The Evolution, Disintegration and Possible Reconstruction of the Northern Ireland Constitution" 1972, *op cit*, pp 404-406 and 427-433.

40 "The Way Forward", p 5.

41 The DUP paper did add: "However, if it was felt necessary, the [DUP] would not stand in the way of the membership of the Committees being drawn *equally* from Government and Opposition, with the Chairmanships similarly shared": para 30 of its submission to the Devolution Report Committee.

42 It also recommended that there should be established other "subject" committees to consider non-transferred matters of particular concern to Northern Ireland. These included a Security Subject Committee and an External Relations Subject Committee "to study, monitor and advise on EEC matters", with particular attention being given in this regard to relationships with the Irish Republic. The OUP's "The Way Forward" referred to an Irish dimension in these terms: "Moreover although resolutely opposed to an "Irish Dimension" in the form of a constitutional institution, unionists would not object to an "Irish Dimension" in the form of state recognition of the legitimacy of the fostering of distinctively Irish cultural activities in Northern Ireland nor to state funding of such activities in proportion to the degree of public participation or interest in them." In the Committee's Second Report, NIA 182-1, 19th February 1985, at para 3.17, the Alliance Party advocated "most strongly the development of a closer relationship between London and Dublin. The Party believes it is to the advantage of the people of Northern Ireland as a whole to have more and effective co-operation on social, economic and security matters, which in no way would impinge upon the constitutional integrity or the internal political affairs of Northern Ireland. To that end the Party would also welcome the establishment of a parliamentary tier to the Anglo-Irish Council."

43 Cmnd 7950, July 1980, paras 53-59. See paras 40-45 of the DUP paper for a detailed consideration of the White Paper proposals.

44 Para 40. The DUP was opposed, for example, to the Council possessing blanket blocking powers and to the involvement of the Secretary of State in the resolution of any conflicts between the Executive/Assembly majority and the Council. In the absence of agreement on full devolution, the DUP was prepared to consider an intermediate stage such as legislative devolution only.

45 This is not defined, but presumably refers to the system in which the voters list the candidates in order of preference. If on the first count, one candidate receives more than 50 per cent of the vote he is automatically elected. If no candidate receives 50 per cent

plus of the vote, the candidate with the lowest number of votes is removed and his votes are redistributed.

46 All three party papers are to be found in the Appendix to NIA 154, 2nd October 1984.

47 NIA 182-1, 19th February 1985, para 4.2.

48 NIA 225, 29th October 1985.

49 This was coupled with a request that negotiations should also start with the Secretary of State on the role of the Assembly in the field of law and order.

50 It was recommended that this figure should be reduced to 55 per cent for the establishment of the second administration, and thereafter to a simple majority.

51 It was also recommended that "because of the diverse nature of the Northern Ireland community, the separate systems of education and the desire for expression of different cultures, provision could usefully be written into the constitution to support recognition of these wishes".

52 Appendix to NIA 225.

53 O'Leary, Elliott and Wilford, *op cit*, p 155.

54 The Finance and Personnel Committee was permitted to conclude its investigations into the consequences for the Northern Ireland civil service of the Anglo-Irish Agreement.

55 First Report of the Committee on the Government of Northern Ireland, NIA 237-1, 29th January 1986, chapter 7, p 68. The Devolution Report Committee was dissolved in March 1986; see NIA 242, 13th March 1986 and Chapter VII below.

# VII

# THE IRISH DIMENSION AND THE ANGLO-IRISH AGREEMENT

## THE INTERGOVERNMENTAL COUNCIL

From the point of view of Anglo-Irish relations the formal introduction of the Irish dimension into Northern Ireland affairs can be dated from the communiqués which were issued after the meetings between the British and Irish Prime Ministers, then Margaret Thatcher and Charles Haughey, on 21st May 1980 in London and on 8th December 1980 in Dublin. It will be recalled that in the early months of 1980, from 7th January to 24th March, the "Atkins Conference" had held some thirty-four meetings, the aim of which was to achieve party political agreement on the future form of government for Northern Ireland. The OUP refused to participate in the talks, which were attended by the DUP, the Alliance Party and the SDLP, which was increasingly insistent upon a formal Irish dimension in any future settlement for Northern Ireland.[1] These talks proved inconclusive, and the two options or models put forward by the Government in July 1980 also proved unacceptable—the first, involving power-sharing, was rejected by the Unionists; the second, excluding power-sharing but incorporating a delicate pattern of checks and balances, was rejected by the SDLP as incompatible with their commitment to power-sharing.[2] It is hardly revelational to state that by this stage within Northern Ireland there was something of an impasse. One attempt to remove the deadlock was the creation of the Anglo-Irish Intergovernmental Council. The communiqué issued at the conclusion of the May 1980 Anglo-Irish summit meeting referred to the wish of both Margaret Thatcher and Charles Haughey "to develop new and closer political co-operation between their two governments" and with this purpose in mind to hold "regular meetings on a continuing basis".[3] The first such meeting was that held in December 1980, the communiqué from which reads as follows:

> The Taoiseach and the Prime Minister noted with satisfaction the useful exchanges at ministerial and official level since their last meeting, leading to new and closer co-operation in energy, transport, communications, cross-border economic development and security. They agreed that further improvements in these and other fields

should be pursued. The Taoiseach and the Prime Minister agreed that the economic, social and political interests of the peoples of the United Kingdom of Great Britain and Northern Ireland and the Republic are inextricably linked but that the full development of these links has been put under strain by division and dissent in Northern Ireland. In that context they accepted the need to bring forward policies and proposals to achieve peace, reconciliation and stability, and to improve relations between the peoples of the two countries. They considered that the best prospect of attaining these objectives was the further development of the unique relationship between the two countries.

They accordingly decided to devote their next meeting in London during the coming year to special consideration of the totality of relationships within these islands. For this purpose they have commissioned joint studies covering a range of issues including possible institutional structures, citizenship rights, security matters, economic co-operation and measures to encourage mutual understanding ...[4].

These joint studies were undertaken by senior officials of the two Governments and their reports were published in November 1981 under the title "Anglo-Irish Joint Studies: Joint Reports and Studies".[5] Whilst the other specific matters for the joint studies mentioned in the December 1980 communiqué were felt to require further consideration, the report of the Joint Study Group on Possible New Institutional Structures was immediately influential. Its terms of reference essentially required it to attempt to fulfil the two Governments' hopes as expressed in the December 1980 communiqué, namely the achievement of peace, reconciliation and stability and the improvement of relations between the peoples of the two countries. The Group "agreed" that the new institutional structures should be placed within the existing "factual"[6] constitutional position as far as the status of Northern Ireland within the United Kingdom was concerned. It further agreed, however, that subject to this,

no structure should be excluded which, in the view of either side, could contribute, over whatever timescale, to the objectives agreed by the Heads of Government. The Irish side reaffirmed the wish to secure the unity of Ireland by agreement and in peace.[7]

With these aims in mind, the Joint Study Group sought to devise institutional structures "flexible ... and resilient ... [with] a reasonable chance of proving to be durable ... and [having] the capacity to evolve".[8] What they proposed was the creation of an Anglo-Irish Intergovernmental Council (the Council) and at talks held in London on 6th November 1981 between the British and Irish Prime Ministers (Garrett Fitzgerald holding the office of Taoiseach from June 1981 until February 1982, when Charles Haughey replaced him) the establishment of the Council was announced, as a means "through which institutional expression can be given to [the unique] relationship between the two Governments".[9] In light of the general paucity of information, both then and subsequently, concerning the nature and operation of the Council, the definition of it provided by the Joint Study Group merits extensive quotation:

[The Council] should have flexible characteristics, permitting it to subsume many of the existing patterns of contact between the executive branches of Government, although informal contact between Ministers—and between officials—on a non-institutional basis should of course continue wherever appropriate. The body would meet at Head of Government, Ministerial or official level. Meetings at Head of Government level, at which Heads of Government would be accompanied by Ministerial colleagues as appropriate and as agreed for each occasion, would take place once or twice a year. At each such meeting Heads of Government would receive reports of the activities of the Council at other levels since their previous meeting. Different counterpart Ministers could meet in pairs or groups, with each such meeting constituting a meeting of the Council whenever both sides so agreed in advance. The framework of the Council would allow for discussion of matters of common interest and concern to the two Governments, including (where so agreed by both Governments) cross border co-operation and other matters of common interest between the two parts of Ireland. As in the past there would continue to be regular meetings between the Secretary of State for Northern Ireland and the Minister for Foreign Affairs, accompanied as appropriate by other Departmental Ministers concerned, to review North-South matters. A senior Official Committee of Ministers' Deputies might meet in a North-South or East-West configuration, as appropriate to prepare the work of the Ministers, or as otherwise necessary.

Other aspects of the character and functions of the Council will require further consideration to take account of the results of other studies. Within the framework of the Council there should be the closest bilateral consultation on matters relating to the achievement of peace, reconciliation and stability or the improvement of relations between the peoples of the two countries. Provision could also be made for emergency meetings to consider current problems of an urgent nature of concern to both Governments. There might also be provision for the establishment by the Council, subject to any necessary process of law, of ancillary bodies including corporate bodies, in particular areas of economic co-operation or areas concerned with the promotion of mutual understanding, where joint activity might be agreed to be desirable.

It would be possible to establish some form of Anglo-Irish Ministerial Council without legislation in either country, for example on the basis of statements in the respective Parliaments. A formal inter-governmental agreement in writing could (but need not) be used to establish it. If this were done, the agreement would have to be laid before the Dáil, and it would be normal to take similar action with the United Kingdom Parliament.[10]

In her notification to the House of Commons of the establishment of the Council, the Prime Minister said that "it involved no change whatever in the constitutional position" with regard to relations between the United Kingdom and the Republic of Ireland and added her own definition of the Council:

> [It] is an informal organisation which will not publish agendas. It is a framework against which many ministerial meetings and meetings of officials will take place. Some of those meetings already take place. Now they will perhaps take place more often against that general framework.[11]

The Joint Study Group had noted the following arrangements as already existing, in addition to European Community and diplomatic contacts: regular Prime Minister/Taoiseach meetings accompanied by other Ministers as appropriate; occasional meetings of the Joint Steering Group on Anglo-Irish Economic Co-operation,[12] and more frequent meetings of a number of sub-groups on North/South co-operation, communications, energy, customs etc; direct informal contacts between Government departments (both Dublin/Belfast and Dublin/London); and meetings of the Anglo-Irish Parliamentary Group every two years, alternately in Dublin and London.[13]

The Council thus was clearly only a part of a larger complex of already existing institutional arrangements, albeit with a cohesive role as far as they were concerned. It was also the general intention of the two Prime Ministers at that time that the governmental and official tier of the Anglo-Irish framework should be supplemented by both a parliamentary and an advisory tier. The communiqué from the summit meeting of 6th November 1981 stated that the two Prime Ministers

> agreed that it would be for the Parliaments concerned to consider at an appropriate time whether there should be an Anglo-Irish body at parliamentary level comprising members to be drawn from the British and Irish Parliaments, the European Parliament and any elected Assembly that may be established for Northern Ireland. They also agreed to work towards the establishment of an advisory committee associated with the ... Council on economic, social and cultural co-operation, with a wide membership.[14]

The Joint Study Group had regarded the creation of an interparliamentary body to complement the Council as a "natural and desirable development".[15] Further it had stated that the proposed Advisory Committee on economic, social and cultural co-operation "associated with the Council" should have the principal objective of promoting

> contact and exchanges across a wide front of economic activity and of society within these islands. [Therefore] the membership should be reasonably large and in composi-

tion should reflect vocational interests ... It can be envisaged that the Committee would advise the Council on economic and social matters referred to it, would be able to issue opinions on its own initiative in fields to be determined, and would present an annual report on the state of economic, social and cultural co-operation, including recommendations.[16]

As the Joint Study Group considered that it might take some time to assess how the Advisory Committee would fit into the new institutional structures for closer co-operation, it recommended as an interim measure the establishment of an "Anglo-Irish Encounter" organisation with the prime responsibility of arranging a "high-level" annual conference, bringing together trade unionists, agriculturalists, Irish/British residents in Britain/Ireland, industrialists, academics, journalists, church leaders, politicians and officials.[17]

Although the first meetings of the Council at Ministerial and official level took place in January 1982, the Council, certainly at the level of Heads of Government (Charles Haughey replaced Garrett Fitzgerald in the Spring of 1982), did not flourish during 1982. There were two main reasons for this. Relations between the two countries worsened during the Falklands War, particularly when in May 1982 the Republic of Ireland decided not to continue the sanctions against Argentina which had been agreed by the European Community the previous month. Further, and more crucially here, the Irish Foreign Minister, Gerard Collins, accused the British Government of "breaking the spirit and letter of the Anglo-Irish arrangements"[18] by introducing its plans for rolling devolution for Northern Ireland without first consulting the Irish Government. The fact that these plans did not have an Irish dimension was also a source of irritation to the Irish Government.[19] Consequently, in July 1982 a meeting took place between the Minister of State at the Foreign and Commonwealth Office, then Douglas Hurd, later to become Secretary of State for Northern Ireland, and the Irish Ambassador to the United Kingdom Eamon Kennedy, at which Douglas Hurd

made it perfectly clear to the Irish ambassador that no commitment exists for Her Majesty's Government to consult the Irish Government on matters affecting Northern Ireland. That has always been our position. We reiterate and emphasise it, so that everyone is clear about it.[20]

Simultaneously the Taoiseach, Charles Haughey, expressed his regret that "Britain has turned away from a course which undoubtedly contained the possibility for a long-term solution to the situation in the northern part of this island and, for reasons which are unclear, has taken an initiative which is almost certain to fail".[21]

## THE NEW IRELAND FORUM

The 1982 Assembly's chances of success were certainly not enhanced by the boycott of it by the SDLP, which in its pursuit of an Irish dimension had embarked upon an initiative which led to the establishment of the New Ireland Forum in Dublin in May 1983. Four political parties took part in the Forum "which was open to all democratic parties which reject violence and which have members elected or appointed"[22] to either House of the Oireachtas (the Irish Parliament) or to the Northern Ireland Assembly, the four participating parties being Fianna Fáil (nine members), Fine Gael (eight members) and Labour (five members) from the Republic and the SDLP (five members). The New Ireland Forum set itself the aim of finding the means by which "lasting peace and stability could be achieved in a new Ireland through the democratic process"— and, it stressed, through agreement.[23] It sat for one year, until May 1984, and in its report it set out three possible constitutional models by which, it believed, peace and stability could be achieved. Its own preferred or first solution was the establishment of a united and unitary Ireland:

> [T]he particular structure of political unity which the Forum would wish to see established is a unitary state, achieved by agreement and consent, embracing the whole island of Ireland and providing irrevocable guarantees for the protection and preservation of both the unionist and nationalist identities.[24]

The constitution of this unitary Ireland, which would be a "single unit under one government and one parliament elected by all the people of the island"[25] and with a single legal and judicial system, would contain the following protections for what would then be the Unionist/Protestant minority: the incorporation of the European Convention on Human Rights; weighted majorities in the Parliament on certain fundamental issues; a minimum number of reserved seats in the Senate which would be given certain blocking powers (there is no mention of power-sharing in government); and an integrated Irish civil service and police force. Joint citizenship would be permitted for those who qualified and who desired it and an Irish-British Council, with inter-governmental and inter-parliamentary structures, would in unspecified ways "provide expression of the long-established connections which unionists have with Britain". All cultural traditions within Ireland would be equally fostered and protected and the education system would "reflect the two main traditions on the island".[26] It was also stated that the "Irish language and culture would continue to be fostered by the state, and would be made more accessible to everyone in Ireland without any compulsion or imposition on any section".[27]

The next model dealt with by the Forum, after its favoured proposal for a unitary Ireland, was that of a two-province non-denominational federal or confederal state based on the two existing entities, North and South. The new constitution would provide safeguards for the different minorities within each province and within Ireland as a whole by, for example, the provision of a Bill of Rights and a Supreme Court possibly containing a non-Irish judge.[28] In both of these proposals, as in the first, there would be exclusive Irish sovereignty throughout the whole island, but the federal and confederal models differed from each other in terms of the extent of the powers to be concentrated centrally. In both, security and law and order were to be the responsibility of the central authorities, as also would be foreign affairs and currency and monetary policies, leaving education, health, housing and social welfare for the two provinces. In the federal model only, agriculture, industry, energy, transport, industrial promotion and marketing would also be located centrally; in the confederal model, they would be allocated to the provinces.[29]

The third model suggested by the New Ireland Forum bears the label "Joint Authority" and unlike the other proposals does not involve exclusive Irish sovereignty over Northern Ireland. This model, which is sketched only briefly in the Forum report itself,[30] deserves close scrutiny, not least with the benefit of a hindsight nurtured by the provisions of the Anglo-Irish Agreement. Joint Authority, as defined by the Forum sub-committee established to consider this model,[31] is "the equal sharing of responsibility and authority for all aspects of the government of Northern Ireland by the governments of Great Britain and Ireland,"[32] including external relations and diplomatic representation. At no stage is the term "Joint Sovereignty" employed. The sub-committee stated that it would be possible to envisage a Joint Sovereignty arrangement, but found a Joint Authority approach "simpler" in that

> it would avoid the conflict between the provisions of Articles 2 and 3 of the Irish Constitution[33] and section 1 of the Northern Ireland Constitution Act 1973, *while providing the essential elements of joint sovereignty, viz. responsibility for all aspects of government and international relations.*[34]

This "simpler" model of Joint Authority would have two main institutional elements:[35] an Executive Joint Authority (the Authority) and, appointed by the Authority, a Joint Authority Commission (the Commission) to run Northern Ireland. The powers of the Authority

> would derive from the agreement between the two governments. The fundamental principle would be an absolute commitment from both governments to work together

to implement Executive Joint Authority on the basis of a high level of understanding and trust. This would be reinforced by the careful construction of a stable and secure system of government and consultation and the setting out of the undertaking and obligations of both governments in a binding enforceable agreement or in a formal treaty which could be registered with the United Nations.

All powers and responsibility for Northern Ireland would be vested in [the Authority] for an unlimited period. ...[36]

This Executive Joint Authority refers as much to the overarching framework agreement between London and Dublin as to an actual system of government, although the Forum sub-committee report did state that "[t]he existing Anglo-Irish Intergovernmental Council could provide an initial framework for implementation".[37] The sub-committee delineated two possible forms of governmental infrastructure, based on the Commission which was to be composed of two Commissioners, appointed by the British and Irish Governments and assisted if necessary by deputy commissioners.[38] The first form of government was labelled "shared direct rule" in which the Commission would exercise *all* executive powers and legislation would be enacted by the British and Irish Parliaments by way of their own procedures for delegated legislation. Under the second model, it was proposed that the Authority could, on the advice of the Commission, allocate or devolve certain "transferred powers" to a locally elected Assembly. This enumeration of transferred powers comes very close in substance to those matters transferred to the Northern Ireland Assembly under the Constitution Act 1973: housing, the physical infrastructure, agriculture, education, commerce, health and social services and minor taxation powers. The basis on which the devolved Executive, that is, the Executive exercising the transferred powers, would be formed was not specified: majority rule, weighted majority rule (across the board or on certain sensitive issues), power-sharing and a rolling devolution model were all deemed possible.[39] It was envisaged, however, that subject to a formula for the resolution of disagreements, either Commissioner would have the power to refuse to assent to Assembly legislation and the power to veto any action proposed by the Assembly or the devolved Executive. Those matters not transferred to the Northern Ireland institutions would remain reserved to the Commission: international relations, defence and security,[40] police, the franchise and constituency arrangements, major taxation and the overall level of public expenditure, the courts and legal officers and public service appointments.[41] The Forum sub-committee itself preferred the "local option" or devolved model seeing in it the potential "for the evolution of ...

new political attitudes and positions" and the means of facilitating "local democratic legitimacy"[42] in government, but it stated that if that subordinate structure were to collapse then the "shared direct rule" model could take over with little difficulty—"in the event of the collapse of the Executive all transferred powers would return to the Joint Authority Commission".[43]

The Forum sub-committee report dealt only briefly with the administrative consequences of Joint Authority, although they would be potentially massive:

> A secretariat working under the general direction of the Joint Authority Commission would be appointed to provide back-up and to ensure the implementation of the decisions of the Joint Authority Commission and to liaise with Dublin, London and any local assembly. It would replace the Northern Ireland Office. It would be for discussion how far-reaching a programme of development and reform would be undertaken in order to ensure that the concept of Joint Authority, i.e. the equal standing and responsibility of both identities as established at the top tier of government, was adequately reflected through the public administrative, judicial and security services.[44]

The Forum sub-committee identified the following as being among the advantages which could be claimed for Joint Authority: "operational recognition throughout the whole of Ireland of the rights of the Nationalists to their Irish identity but without infringing the rights of Unionists to maintain and have operational expression of their identity"; diminution of the alienation of Nationalists in Northern Ireland from the existing structures;[45] the ability of the Joint Authorities to withstand non-violent opposition;[46] its potential for immediate implementation;[47] its capacity for evolution with [Unionist] consent; and its provision of an acceptable political superstructure for security.[48] The disadvantages to be attributed to Joint Authority were as follows: its incomplete realisation of Nationalist aspirations; the danger of a lack of identification (on the Nationalist side, with structures which maintained British involvement and on the Unionist side, with structures which introduced an Irish involvement); cumbersomeness; the risks of instability; security drawbacks; and an insufficient assurance of evolution, that is, towards the fulfilment of Nationalist aspirations.[49]

The Forum sub-committee finally listed the conditions which it believed had to be met if the perceived advantages were to be best exploited and the perceived disadvantages minimised:

> (1) A high level of trust and understanding between the Irish and British governments;
> (2) An absolute commitment from both governments and peoples in political resolution and in resources to maintain and uphold the system, even in the face of strong opposition;

(3) A comprehensive presentation of the concept with as much international backing as possible;
(4) A positive response from the Nationalist community in the North leading to a reduction in the level of violence; and
(5) A containable response from the Unionist community in the North.[50]

The Forum Report, without the sub-committee report fully incorporated or attached, was published in May 1984[51] with little immediate prospect of general acceptability, certainly within the Northern Ireland political spectrum. The three parties participating in the Northern Ireland Assembly clearly indicated in their submissions to the Devolution Report Committee then sitting that their own solutions to the Northern Ireland constitutional impasse did not embrace such an Irish dimension. More crucial to the success or failure of the Forum's recommendations, however, was the response of the British mainland political parties and most especially that of the Government. In a debate on the Forum Report, held in the House of Commons on 2nd July 1984, the then Secretary of State for Northern Ireland, James Prior, spelt out "five realities" which, when read with the Forum's perspectives, effectively provide the boundaries within which the Irish dimension specifically and developments within Northern Ireland generally will be contained. The first "overriding and abiding reality from which we cannot escape" is that consent is not forthcoming for any formulation that denies the Unionists their right not only to belong to the United Kingdom but to be apart from the Republic: "[t]hat consent must be free and cannot be coerced." The second reality is that, whatever the arguments concerning partition, Northern Ireland is a part of the United Kingdom and is internationally recognised as such. The third reality is that as long as Northern Ireland is a part of the United Kingdom, its government and administration must ultimately remain a matter for Parliament to decide, taking account of the wishes and principles of both the majority and minority communities within Northern Ireland and the values and standards of the people of the United Kingdom as a whole. The fourth reality is that the needs and responses of the people of Northern Ireland and the resources of the United Kingdom would be best served by a devolved administration which had the support of both sides of the community: "[w]hen it comes to the government and administration of Northern Ireland within the United Kingdom, there is no unionist veto, just as there is no nationalist veto." The fifth, and final, reality is that geography, as well as the fact that many people in Northern Ireland feel an allegiance to Dublin and the Irish state, calls for a close relationship between the United Kingdom Government and the Republic.[52]

These realities, particularly the first when coupled with the Westminster Government's insistence upon exclusive British sovereignty in Northern Ireland, precluded the acceptability to the Government of all of the Forum models, although they did not also preclude the strengthening of Anglo-Irish relationships. While the Forum was sitting from May 1983 to May 1984, the first summit meeting of the Anglo-Irish Intergovernmental Council took place at Chequers on 7th November 1983, between Margaret Thatcher and Garrett Fitzgerald, the former being briefed by the latter on the work of the Forum. The two Prime Ministers also considered a joint report reviewing co-operation between the two countries since 1981 on the matters considered by the original joint study groups, namely, institutional structures, citizenship rights, security matters, economic co-operation and measures to encourage mutual understanding. The communiqué of the summit meeting and the related documents[53] provide some insight into the working of the (by then) two operative tiers of the Council, namely the Ministerial and official on the one hand and the advisory on the other, the parliamentary tier still being under discussion. At the official level, the Council was already operating through both a Steering Committee and a Co-ordinating Committee, both of which were chaired by senior United Kingdom officials and their Irish Republic counterparts: the Council was not at this stage permanently staffed but drew on the relevant official expertise as appropriate. At the Ministerial level there had been by the time of the first summit meeting, twenty bilateral Ministerial meetings within the framework of the Council: six on Kinsale Gas, five (between the Secretary of State for Northern Ireland and the Republic's Foreign Minister) on Anglo-Irish relations, three on the language question and regional development, and one meeting each on the cross-border infrastructure, fisheries, EEC issues, oil production policy, local government and youth matters.[54] Further, as regards the advisory tier of the Council, following a meeting between the Secretary of State for Northern Ireland and the Republic's Foreign Minister in July 1983, the Anglo-Irish Encounter Organisation had been established,[55] as an independent non-governmental organisation[56] and has, since then, organised a series of biannual conferences, dealing with, for example, the improvement of work prospects in Great Britain and Ireland, the promotion amongst the young of a greater respect for religious and cultural diversity, the promotion of Irish studies in Britain, the role of the Churches in British-Irish relationships and the role of the media.

## THE ANGLO-IRISH AGREEMENT

In the year intervening between the first and second summit meetings of the Intergovernmental Council, the Forum Report was published. The communiqué of the second summit meeting, held at Chequers on 19th and 20th November 1984, records the agreement of the two Prime Ministers that "the identities of both the majority and minority communities in Northern Ireland should be recognised and respected, and reflected in the structures and processes of Northern Ireland in ways acceptable to both communities" and that there should be "close and continuing dialogue" on that matter between the two Governments over the coming months. The significance of this agreement was, however, overshadowed by the press conference which followed the conclusion of the summit meeting, at which Margaret Thatcher gave her concise response to the three Forum models:

> I have made it quite clear—and so did [James Prior] ... — that a unified Ireland was one solution that is out. A second solution was confederation of two states. That is out. A third solution was joint authority. That is out. That is a derogation from sovereignty.[57]

"Out-out-out" caught all the headlines, but what came in or at any rate continued were confidential Anglo-Irish negotiations which, amidst mounting concern amongst the Unionists,[58] culminated, somewhat later than the participants probably had expected, in the signing of the Anglo-Irish Agreement at Hillsborough on 15th November 1985. The extent of these negotiations was revealed by Garrett Fitzgerald to the Dáil (the Irish Government tending to be far more forthcoming or informative about Anglo-Irish relations than its Westminster counterpart):

> The Agreement is ... the outcome of ... negotiations which took place over a period of 18 months involving two summits between the British Prime Minister and myself; four informal meetings between us in the margin of the European Council meetings; three joint meetings between the Tánaiste [Deputy Prime Minister] and the Minister for Foreign Affairs on behalf of the Irish Government and the Secretaries of State for Foreign Affairs and Northern Ireland on behalf of the British Government; ten meetings between the Irish Minister for Foreign Affairs with the Foreign Secretary and/or the Secretary of State for Northern Ireland; and about 35 meetings of the negotiating group led by the secretaries of the two cabinets, convening often as frequently as every week, as well as many other meetings of officials in the margin of these structured encounters.[59]

The Agreement, the fruit of these negotiations, received a varied response from the political parties. It was welcomed virtually right across the mainland British political spectrum, as well as by the parties then represented in the Government of the Irish Republic (the Fine Gael and Labour parties), by the SDLP which, it is generally believed, had been kept informed by the Republic's Government of the progress of the negotiations, and, much more cautiously, by the Alliance and Workers' Parties. It aroused the hostility both of the OUP and the DUP, and of Sinn Féin and other Irish Nationalists (in, for example, the Fianna Fáil party) who perceived the Agreement as reinforcing partition and hence as weakening the prospects for a united Ireland.

What, therefore, are the provisions of the Agreement itself[60] which caused or reinforced such deep divisions in political opinion? Even the initial statements concerning the Agreement have to be expressed carefully. It was signed at Hillsborough by Margaret Thatcher on behalf of "the Government of the United Kingdom of Great Britain and Northern Ireland" and by Garrett Fitzgerald on behalf of "the Government of the Republic of Ireland". That, however, is the wording of the United Kingdom version of the Agreement; the Irish version refers to the Governments of "Ireland" and of "the United Kingdom". Once the Agreement had been signed it was approved by both the British and Irish Parliaments and an exchange of diplomatic notes on 29th November 1985 brought the Agreement, which has been lodged at the United Nations, into force. The Preamble to the Agreement itself in effect sets forth its aims as being to diminish the divisions in Northern Ireland and to achieve lasting peace and stability. Consequently, the two Governments committed themselves to a series of principles which were designed to satisfy both Nationalists and Unionists—or one should more accurately write "either" Nationalists "or" Unionists. These principles include the development of the "unique relationship" between the United Kingdom and the Republic, the need to attempt to reconcile and to acknowledge the "rights of the two major traditions that exist in Ireland", the need to respect the identities of the two communities in Northern Ireland, and the right of each to pursue its aspirations by peaceful and constitutional means. The two Governments committed themselves to "a society in Northern Ireland in which all may live in peace, free from discrimination and intolerance, and with the opportunity for both communities to participate fully in the structures and processes of government." The Preamble also records the Governments' total rejection "of any attempt to promote political objectives by violence or the threat of violence and their determination to work together to ensure that those who adopt or support such methods do not succeed."

If Article 1 of the Agreement was indeed designed to diminish the divisions in Northern Ireland, it has hardly succeeded in its task. It reads:

> The two Governments
>
> (*a*) affirm that any change in the status of Northern Ireland would only come about with the consent of a majority of the people of Northern Ireland;
>
> (*b*) recognise that the present wish of a majority of the people of Northern Ireland is for no change in the status of Northern Ireland;
>
> (*c*) declare that, if in the future a majority of the people of Northern Ireland clearly wish for and formally consent to the establishment of a united Ireland, they will introduce and support in the respective Parliaments legislation to give effect to that wish.

Looking at this Article from the point of view of the Unionists, it is hard to see its overall attractiveness. Article 1 of the Anglo-Irish Acts of Union 1800 proclaims the Union to last "for ever" and section 1 of the Constitution Act 1973 declares and affirms that Northern Ireland remains a part of the United Kingdom. Article 1 (*a*) of the Anglo-Irish Agreement by contrast *begins* with a reference to a change in the status of Northern Ireland, and in contrast with the United Kingdom's declaration in the parallel Article 5 of the Sunningdale Agreement,[61] that status is not even specified. This point is reinforced by the Agreement's unadorned reference to "Ireland" and "United Kingdom" in the Republic of Ireland's version already mentioned. Furthermore, the Irish Supreme Court had ruled in 1974 in *Boland* in a challenge to the Irish declaration in Article 5 of the Sunningdale Agreement that the phrase "status of Northern Ireland" could only refer to its *de facto* status, its *de jure* status under Irish constitutional law being controlled by Articles 2 and 3 of the Irish Constitution. The exceedingly influential report of the Joint Study Group on Possible New Institutional Structures stated that the work of any new structures, such as the Council and presumably also the Conference established by the Agreement, should take place within "a constitutional framework in which the *factual* position of Northern Ireland within the United Kingdom cannot be changed without the consent of a majority of the people of Northern Ireland and the agreement of Parliament at Westminster".[62] Also Article 1(*c*) of the Agreement, unlike section 1 of the Constitution Act 1973, expressly spells out the willingness of the respective Parliaments, more pertinently here Westminster, to enact legislation for a united Ireland if and when this becomes the wish of the majority of the people in Northern Ireland.[63] For the Unionists, the benefit which is stated to flow from Article 1 is the recognition by the Republic of Ireland in an international treaty of the current status of Northern Ireland. This, however, becomes a double-edged sword, because if it is such a recognition of its status *within the United Kingdom*, then in the words of Charles Haughey, at that time leader of the Opposition, in the Dáil debate on the Agreement:

> For the first time the legitimacy of Partition has been recognised by the Republic; the British guarantee to the Unionists has been reinforced by the Irish Government; and the Government are also endorsing the British military and political presence in Ireland. The Irish Government are saying to the world that Northern Ireland is legitimately part of the British State, that Northern Ireland is no longer part of the national territory.[64]

As has been seen, any such recognition would be unconstitutional as conflicting with Articles 2 and 3 of the Irish Constitution, and equally clearly Article 1 of the Agreement was drafted with Irish constitutional requirements and the *Boland* case[65] in mind in order to avoid judicial, although not political, apprehension of such a conflict. As it transpired, the constitutionality of the Agreement was challenged in the Irish courts not by an Irish Nationalist but by two Northern Ireland Official Unionists being, in Irish law, citizens of Ireland. In *McGimpsey* v *Ireland and An Taoiseach*[66] the main substantive argument[67] of the plaintiffs, that the Agreement violated Articles 2 and 3 of the Constitution, was rejected by the court. Barrington J held that whether the claims to national unity in Articles 2 and 3 were interpreted as either a part of the political or of the legal order, Article 1 of the Agreement was not unconstitutional, because in it

> the two Governments merely recognise the situation on the ground in Northern Ireland (paragraph (b)), form a political judgment about the likely course of future events (paragraph (a)) and state what their policy will be should events evolve in a particular way (paragraph (c)).[68]

If Article 1 of the Agreement, thus, reaped mainly opprobrium for its deliberate ambiguity rather than praise for its delicate tact, what of the provisions of the Agreement dealing with the new institutional structure? As has already been mentioned, Margaret Thatcher stated at the time of the institution of the Anglo-Irish Intergovernmental Council that *its* establishment did not involve any commitment on the part of the Westminster Government to consult with the Irish Government on matters affecting Northern Ireland. After the Agreement of 1985 this is no longer the case, although Article 2(*a*) does state that the Intergovernmental Conference (the Conference) which it establishes is established "within the framework" of the Council. According to Article 2(*a*), the function of the Conference, which meets at either Ministerial or official level and which is concerned with Northern Ireland and with relations between the two parts of the island of Ireland, is to deal on a regular basis[69] with (i) political matters, (ii) security and related matters, (iii) legal matters, including the administration of justice, and (iv) the promotion of cross-border co-operation. Article 2(*b*) states that the United Kingdom Government accepts that

> the Irish Government will put forward views and proposals on matters relating to Northern Ireland within the field of activity of the Conference in so far as those matters are not the responsibility of a devolved administration in Northern Ireland. In the interest of promoting peace and stability, determined efforts shall be made through the Conference to resolve any differences ... There is no derogation from the sovereignty of either the United Kingdom Government or the Irish Government, and each retains responsibility for the decisions and administration of government within its own jurisdiction.

Any assessment of the extent of the powers of the Conference has to attempt to balance the concluding sentence of Article 2(*b*) with its earlier phrase "determined efforts". Is the Conference merely a consultative or advisory body, for the Secretary of State for Northern Ireland and the United Kingdom Government generally, or does it have executive or decision-making powers? It is clear that while the actual forms of decision-making within Northern Ireland remain unaltered (Westminster Acts of Parliament, Orders in Council, departmental circulars, etc.)—and in this respect there is a marked departure from the Forum sub-committee's recommendations on Joint Authority—the decisions which those formal documents incorporate or implement will not necessarily be solely those of the Westminster Government and/or Parliament. This general point is specifically reinforced by Article 5(*c*), which states that if

> it should prove impossible to achieve and sustain devolution on a basis which secures widespread acceptance in Northern Ireland, the Conference shall be a framework within which the Irish Government may, where the interests of the minority community are significantly or especially affected, put forward views on proposals for major legislation and on major policy issues, which are within the purview of the Northern Ireland Departments and which remain the responsibility of the Secretary of State for Northern Ireland.

Article 6 further provides that the Conference "shall be" the framework within which the Irish Government may put forward views and proposals on the role and composition of, for example, the Standing Advisory Commission on Human Rights, the Fair Employment Agency, the Equal Opportunities Commission, the Police Authority for Northern Ireland and the (then) Police Complaints Board. In the opinion of Garrett Fitzgerald the function of the

Conference goes beyond "a consultative role but necessarily, because of the sovereignty issue, [falls] short of an executive role";[70] Margaret Thatcher was merely content to define it as not executive. Beyond that, it is impossible to be more conclusive, particularly in light of the secrecy surrounding the Conference's agenda and deliberations.

The precise fields of activity which lie within the remit of the Conference under Article 2(*a*) now fall for consideration. Political matters are specified in greater, although not great, detail in Articles 5 and 6, and under Article 5(*a*) they include

> measures to foster the cultural heritage of both traditions, changes in electoral arrangements, the use of flags and emblems,[71] the avoidance of economic and social discrimination and the advantages and disadvantages of a Bill of Rights in some form in Northern Ireland.

Security matters (Article 7) include not only security policy itself but also more specifically the relations between the security forces and the community, "with the object in particular of making the security forces more readily accepted by the nationalist community", and prisons policy including the consideration of individual cases.

Legal matters (Article 8) include the enforcement of the criminal law, the possibility of harmonising some areas of the criminal law applying in Northern Ireland and the Republic, public confidence in the administration of justice, including the possibility of mixed courts in both jurisdictions for the trial of certain offences, and the policy aspects of extradition and extra-territorial jurisdiction.

The final area within the Conference's remit, namely cross-border co-operation (Articles 9 and 10), is elaborated on only in so far as it is made clear that it involves both security and also economic, social and cultural matters. On the first of these the Agreement does stress that the Conference has no operational responsibilities: those remain with the respective heads of the two police forces and the Secretary of State for Northern Ireland and the Republic's Minister for Justice respectively. The remaining three areas remain undefined.

Although many parts of the Agreement are vague or expediently ambiguous, its general tenor expressed itself with sufficient clarity to outrage virtually the whole spectrum of Unionist opinion—the Irish dimension had crystallised into something totally unacceptable to them.[72] In 1973-1974, the Westminster Government had first created a local Assembly and then, through Sunningdale, sought to incorporate an Irish dimension in terms of relationships between Belfast and Dublin. It had failed to achieve its objectives. In 1985, mindful of past experience when loyalist anger had brought down the local Assembly, the Irish dimension was introduced *first* and on the east-west (Dublin-London) dimension, leaving room for the later return of devolved institutions within Northern Ireland should such a desire manifest itself. The Forum sub-committee on Joint Authority had earlier spelt out its "local option" or devolved model, in which the Joint Authority Commission would deal with, for example, defence and security, police, the franchise and constituency arrangements and major taxation, leaving "transferred" matters in the hands of a devolved Assembly and Executive. It had, however, emphasised that if the devolved structure were to collapse then the Commission could resume responsibility for the transferred matters with little difficulty. The Agreement, no doubt reflecting an awareness of this line of reasoning, sought to secure the top tier first so that whatever happened subsequently—devolution, no devolution or collapsed devolution—the Agreement would be left (the Governments hoped) impregnable.

One of the main grievances of the Unionists against the Agreement was that it excluded them from the decision-making processes for Northern Ireland. The counter-argument to this relies on Article 4(*b*) of the Agreement:

> it is the declared policy of the United Kingdom Government that responsibility in respect of certain matters within the powers of the Secretary of State for Northern Ireland should be devolved within Northern Ireland on a basis which would secure widespread acceptance throughout the community. The Irish Government support that policy.

So, the argument continues, if the Unionists could agree to a system of devolution on a power-sharing basis or an equivalent[73] they could effectively deprive the Conference of its powers, although this would still leave the Council intact. Article 2(*b*) of the Agreement provides that the Irish Government may put forward its views and proposals on matters affecting Northern Ireland in the field of its activity only "*in so far as*" those matters are not the responsibility of a devolved administration. Similarly, it is only where devolution is impossible to achieve or sustain that the Irish Government may put its views to the Conference on proposals for major legislation and major policy issues. The question which this argument begs is this: which of the matters within the fields of the Conference's activity are likely to be devolved to a new Northern Ireland Assembly? Article 4(*b*) above refers only to "certain matters" within the powers of the Secretary of State. Article 5(*c*) also, by implication at the very least, indicates that the matters likely to be devolved are those matters within the purview of the Northern Ireland departments, that is, the "transferred" departments which under direct rule are subject to the direction and control of the Secretary of State. One can only guess at the Government's intentions, but given that in effect the Northern Ireland Act 1982 retained the same three categories of legislative power as the 1973 Act, with the Government largely excluding reserved and excepted matters from that Assembly's deliberative powers, it seems likely that the 1973 Act's allocation of powers would remain virtually if not totally intact for any new Assembly. This would, consequently, even with devolution, leave within the powers of the Conference the appointment and removal of members of the judiciary, Parliamentary elections including the franchise, special powers and other provisions dealing with terrorism or subversion, many aspects of the criminal law including the creation of offences, prosecution and extradition, the establishment, organisation and control of the RUC and trade with any place outside the United Kingdom. Further, on the question of cross-border co-operation—if there were to be devolution again—the powers of the devolved Executive would be affected by Article 10(*c*) of the Agreement:

> if responsibility is devolved in respect of certain matters in the economic, social or cultural areas currently within the responsibility of the Secretary of State for Northern Ireland, machinery ***will need to be established*** by the responsible authorities in the North and South for practical co-operation in respect of cross-border aspects of these issues.

It would thus seem that if there were to be devolution operating largely under the 1973 Act scheme, certain modifications would have to be made to section 12 of the Act to ensure a North-South Irish dimension in these areas. Section 12(1) was mentioned in chapter IV, and it may be recalled that it provides that

> A Northern Ireland executive authority may—
>
> (*a*) consult on any matter with any authority of the Republic of Ireland;
>
> (*b*) enter into agreements or arrangements with any authority of the Republic of Ireland in respect of any transferred matter.

Presumably, then, in any area which could be considered "economic, social or cultural" this currently facilitative provision would be rendered mandatory in terms of Article 10(*c*) of the Agreement—or alternatively any failure by the devolved Assembly to comply with the spirit of section 12(1) and Article 10(*c*) would lead to these matters returning to or remaining with the Conference. There is nothing at all in the 1973 Act to require *all* non-excepted and non-reserved matters to be transferred—and some matters even once transferred may be recalled, under its section 3(1)(*b*), to the reserved category.

The Agreement's devolution "carrot" to the Unionists was not, therefore, as appetising as the Government may have believed it to be. Equally crucially, there was no bait in the Agreement to lure the SDLP into the Northern Ireland Assembly, which at that time was sitting with only consultative powers, or indeed into any devolved Assembly, even one with full, legislative powers. The provisions of Article 5(*c*), which made the Republic's Government the guarantor of the Northern Ireland minority community's rights and interests, and the (perceived) close links, in terms of a "ready ear", between that Government and the SDLP provided that party with at the least an attractive alternative to what may be an uneasy co-existence in a power-sharing or equivalent devolved executive within Northern Ireland.

## THE SEQUEL

Whatever the scope for devolution in the Agreement, however, the Agreement itself immediately sounded the death knell for the Northern Ireland Assembly then deliberating under sections 3 and 4 of the Northern Ireland Act 1982. Unionist wrath at the Agreement manifested itself in various ways but as far as the Assembly itself was concerned it resolved at a special adjournment debate held on 16th November 1985, the day after the Agreement was signed, by 44 votes to 10, the Alliance party Assembly members dissenting, to repudiate the Agreement as involving "an intolerable derogation of British sovereignty incompatible with the security of Northern Ireland's constitutional position" and demanded that the Government seek "forthwith" the consent of the Northern Ireland electorate to the Agreement. On 5th December it decided to set up the Committee on the Government of Northern Ireland, the "Grand Committee", in which the Alliance party took no part whatsoever and during the proceedings of which all other Assembly business was suspended. The work of the Assembly was now all but over. The Committee on the Government of Northern Ireland produced its first Report on 29th January 1986. Its own conclusions included these, that

> there is no prospect of devolution while the Agreement remains; that devolution is now in the effective gift of the SDLP and is unlikely to be offered on terms acceptable to unionists; that devolution will not eliminate the Intergovernmental Conference; [that] ... these events must lead to a radical reappraisal of the future of the Assembly and of proposals for the future of Northern Ireland; that the proposals considered in the Devolution Report Committee are nullified while this Agreement subsists; that a further report or reports should be made by the Committee on the Government of Northern

Ireland and that to aid such reports the departmental scrutiny committees of the Assembly should, for a limited period, carry out an urgent investigation into the interaction between the Northern Ireland Departments and the Intergovernmental Conference.[74]

The Assembly on 29th January 1986 accepted this last recommendation in the Committee's Report and instructed the six statutory committees to carry out those investigations. In consequence the committees wrote in the requisite terms to the permanent heads of the departments (that is, the senior civil servants) but on 6th February 1986 the Clerk to the Assembly was informed that as the Secretary of State believed that matters relating to the Agreement were of a political nature "it would be inappropriate for them to be subject to evidence by Departmental officials" and therefore the Committee's invitation was declined. The Secretary of State, however, expressed his own willingness to discuss with members of the Assembly, including specifically the chairmen of the six statutory committees, the "impact and implications of the Agreement", including the work of the Conference and its Secretariat. Finally, the Secretary of State drew the attention of the Assembly to the fact that it was not discharging its statutory duties under section 3 of the Northern Ireland Act 1982, and warned that "in the event that the Committees do not return in the near future to the proper discharge of their statutory duties, the position of [officials seconded from the Civil Service to the Assembly] will have to be a matter for urgent consideration and decision".[75]

The Committee on the Government of Northern Ireland in its second report "deprecated as blackmail" this warning from the Secretary of State, and was further of opinion that his communication effectively prevented the departmental committees from discharging their statutory functions by debarring them from considering matters germane to the operation of the Northern Ireland departments. The Committee believed that all this marked a "radical change of direction" in the departmental committees' scrutiny role and accused the Secretary of State of "wilfully [putting] his hand to the Assembly's destruction".[76] This report was followed by a spate of resignations from the departmental committees, whose work remained suspended. The rest of the Assembly's story may be dealt with briefly. On 13th March, the next time the Assembly met, the Committee published its third and final report. It spoke of the "destabilisation" in public affairs brought about by the Agreement and the questions which had been posed concerning the viability of the Assembly, and it made certain recommendations concerning the continuation of the Assembly's various functions. It resolved that the Devolution Report Committee should be discharged and its role subsumed within its own remit;[77] it so resolved because, it stated, after the Agreement devolution could no longer be "discussed in its own right but must be viewed in the wider context of political relations within these islands". It further argued that it would become a "meaningless exercise" to continue the Assembly's scrutiny function, in light of the decision which the Secretary of State had communicated to it in February and, therefore, recommended that that function be placed in abeyance. It recommended, however, that the Assembly's plenary sessions should continue, in the hope that they would discharge "the vitally important role ... of providing a platform for elected representatives to direct positive and co-ordinated opposition to the ... Agreement". The report continued: "it is only in the Assembly that the different strands of opposition can be brought together and forged into a single instrument of protest, and direction given as to its most effective use."[78] It was by now highly unlikely that the Government would permit the Assembly to continue in such an attenuated form, both in terms of functions and personnel—and it did not. Although the Assembly met in "plenary" session on twelve occasions after 13th March 1986 to voice its opposition to the Agreement, the Assembly was dissolved on 23rd June 1986.[79]

The Assembly was not the sole focal point for the Unionists' opposition to the Agreement. They also sought to challenge its validity in the English High Court and its political acceptability within Northern Ireland through the ballot box. In November 1985 (before the exchange of diplomatic notes brought the Agreement into force), in *ex parte Molyneaux and others*[80] the applicants, all members of the Ulster Unionist Council, sought leave to apply for judicial review by way of a declaration that it would be unlawful for the Government to implement the Agreement without the authority of an Act of Parliament. Specifically they argued that the implementation of the Agreement would

(1) fetter the exercise of the Secretary of State's various statutory discretionary powers;
(2) be contrary to Article 6 of the Anglo-Irish Acts of Union; and
(3) be in breach of section 12 of the Constitution Act 1973.

Mann J refused the application for leave on 20th November 1985 and the renewed application by oral hearing was rejected by Taylor J on 26th November. He rejected the applicants' first argument by holding that the Conference (which, he said, would have no legislative or "executive powers") would not operate as an unreasonable fetter on the Secretary of State's various discretionary powers because Article 2(*b*) of the Agreement specifically provided that the Agreement would involve no derogation from the United Kingdom's sovereignty. Further, he held that the Conference would not be a new standing body *in* the United Kingdom, as the applicants argued, but a body of an international nature and that it was not the function of a court to inquire into any exercise of the Prerogative power to make treaties or their proposed method of implementation.

The second argument was rejected through a consideration of the precise wording of Article 6 of the Anglo-Irish Acts of Union which in the part cited to the court provides[81]

> ... that in all treaties made by his Majesty, his heirs and successors, with any foreign powers, his Majesty's subjects of [Northern] Ireland shall have the same privileges, and be on the same footing, as his Majesty's subjects in Great Britain ... .

Taylor J held that as section 2(1) of the Ireland Act 1949 enacts that the Republic of Ireland is not to be regarded by the United Kingdom as a foreign country, it was, therefore, not a "foreign power" as required by Article 6. Also, and less persuasively it is submitted, he held that

> the fact that there is to be consultation on matters which may affect [the people of Northern Ireland] ... with the Government of the Irish Republic, does not, to my mind, deprive them of privileges or place them on a footing other than that of Her Majesty's subjects of Great Britain, who may also be affected by any decisions of policy to be made with regard to Northern Ireland.[82]

Whilst this statement is no doubt correct on, for example, security matters and the prevention of terrorism, there is no specific Great Britain equivalent of the Anglo-Irish Agreement which in Article 2(*a*) states that the Conference is to be concerned with Northern Ireland and relations between it and the Republic.

The applicants' third argument was based on section 12 of the 1973 Act which, as has been seen, enabled the Northern Ireland devolved Executive to enter into consultations and agreements with any authority of the Republic in respect of any transferred matter. They argued that this section had replaced the Royal Prerogative powers in the field of relations with the Republic and that in the absence of any specific reservation of such powers they had effectively been abrogated by section 12 and could not revive. Taylor J held that under section 12 a part of the Prerogative power had been *delegated* but that under the Northern Ireland Act 1974 it had returned to the Government, which, therefore, had the power to enter into agreements with the Republic. Assuming that section 12 is indeed dealing with a Royal Prerogative power, rather than with the creation of a specific statutory power vested in a body operating in only one part of the United Kingdom, the judge's conclusion is reinforced by section 7 of the 1973 Act, which was not mentioned by the judge;

it provides that (1) the "executive power in Northern Ireland shall continue to be vested in Her Majesty", that (2) in respect of transferred matters the Secretary of State shall exercise on the Queen's behalf such Prerogative and other powers as she may delegate to him, and that (3) the powers so delegated shall be exercised through the Northern Ireland departments.

A further manifestation of the Unionists' opposition to the Agreement was the resignation of the fifteen Unionist MPs at Westminster.[83] As the Government had refused the Assembly's request for a referendum on the matter, the Unionists sought to procure the submission of the Agreement to popular scrutiny another way. The fifteen MPs all resigned their Westminster seats on the same day and the fifteen by-elections were held on 23rd January 1986. The total Unionist vote was 418,230,[84] an expression of considerable opposition to the Agreement within Northern Ireland. As against that, the figure fell quite considerably short of the target of half a million "No" votes which the Unionists had (probably) hoped for and they also lost the seat of Newry and Armagh to Seamus Mallon of the SDLP. The fourteen MPs who were returned, with the exception of Enoch Powell, who later lost his seat to the SDLP in the June 1987 General Election, eventually embarked upon a boycott of Westminster in continued protest at the Agreement.

The protest against the Agreement had other manifestations—rallies were held throughout the Province; a "day of action" was called for 3rd March 1986; a (largely unsuccessful) campaign of civil disobedience, particularly the refusal to pay rates and car taxes, began; in loyalist areas banners proclaiming "[area name] says no" appeared in profusion; Unionist councillors refused to conduct normal district council business and their actions were judicially reviewed at the instigation of Alliance councillors; and a campaign was mounted in January 1987 to collect signatures petitioning the Queen to intervene in the matter. The Government, however, stood firm in its resolve to abide by the Agreement and at the time of writing the three-year review of the working of the Conference provided for by Article 11 of the Agreement is under way.

Has the working of the Agreement primarily fulfilled the SDLP's hopes or fuelled Unionist fears and anxieties? One real difficulty in answering this sort of question stems from the paucity of information concerning the agenda and deliberations of the Conference. There are, however, other related difficulties. The Unionists regard the existence of the Agreement generally and the Conference specifically as an affront, and the more the work of the Conference satisfies Nationalist aspirations the more it will alienate the Unionists. The less it satisfies Nationalist aspirations, the more alienated they will become. That being so, both the Westminster and Dublin Governments have to proceed cautiously in terms of their public presentation of the achievements or non-achievements of the Conference, and this only enhances the likelihood that both Nationalists and Unionists, for very different reasons, will become increasingly dissatisfied with the Agreement.

An assessment,[85] non-Governmental at the time it was made although not necessarily disinterested, was given in a letter to *The Times* on 7th October 1987 by Garrett Fitzgerald, who wrote that the "major fact" about the Agreement was that two years after its conclusion "greater progress has been made in convincing the nationalist minority that they and their children have a future in their own land than happened for decades previously". He then listed "only some outstanding examples" of the achievements of the Agreement: the ending of so-called "super-grass" trials; reform of emergency laws, including grounds for arrest; a major improvement in the confidence of Nationalists in the RUC, especially through the courageous display of even-handedness by the overwhelming (*sc* overwhelmingly?) Protestant police force in dealing with loyalist extremism; a significant reduction in complaints about harassment of the minority by the Ulster Defence Regiment and some progress in implementing the policy of having the UDR accompanied by the RUC on occasions when they meet the public; legislation (abolition of the Flags and Emblems Act (NI) 1954, improvement in the law on incitement to hatred, strengthening of the law on parades); housing (decisions to demolish and replace progressively Divis, Unity and Rossville flats, which had been sought for over a decade but not achieved); public bodies (improvements in representation of Roman Catholics on a range of appointed bodies); courts (improvements in administration involving a shortening of the period spent by prisoners on remand before trial); employment practices (new and improved guidelines for fair employment and commitment to new and strengthened legislation); prisons (improvement by the authorities in arrangements for parole and compassionate leave and sensitive handling of many individual cases, while maintaining fully the requirement of good order); Irish language (commitment to improve the status of the Irish language which should be implemented progressively over the coming months); and the International Fund (a fund for employment-creation of over 150 million dollars—the International Fund for Ireland).

Certain of these illustrations can be reinforced by a consideration of the Joint Statements issued after each meeting of the Conference, these Statements being virtually the sole source of information concerning its working. A Code of Conduct was issued to members of the RUC in October 1987 and in

September 1987 there was published a Guide to Effective Practice on religious equality of opportunity in employment.[86] Furthermore, the Public Order (NI) Order 1987, which dealt with all the public order matters mentioned above by Garrett Fitzgerald, constituted the culmination of, *inter alia*, Irish pressure in the Conference concerning the repeal of the Flags and Emblems Act (NI) 1954. As has been seen, Article 5(*a*) of the Agreement itself refers specifically to the legislation on flags and emblems, and the Joint Statement issued after the Conference meeting on 10th January 1986 states: "The Irish side also put forward *views and proposals* on legislation relating to flags and emblems in Northern Ireland and on the position of the Irish language in Northern Ireland". Parenthetically here the italicised phrase, which is also used again in later Statements, should be noted. Article 5(*c*) of the Agreement empowers the Irish Government to "put forward *views on proposals* for major legislation and on major policy issues...". This implies a rather more passive role for the Irish Government than the wording used not only in the Joint Statements but also, more importantly, in Articles 2(*b*), 4(*c*) and 6 of the Agreement.

There have so far been no specific changes with regard to the use of the Irish language in Northern Ireland, although the matter is under continuing review. The Joint Statement issued after the Conference meeting on 17th June 1986 indicated a number of areas for possible future development, with regard to dual language street names where the local community desires it, a precise assessment of the number of Irish speakers in Northern Ireland and financial support for Irish language-related cultural activities. The establishment of the International Fund for Ireland was agreed upon in September 1986 and this agreement was brought into force on 1st December 1986 by exchange of notifications of acceptance between the British and Irish Governments on that date.

The Conference, mindful of the provisions of Article 10 of the Agreement on the promotion of cross-border co-operation, has also kept under continuous review the wide variety of existing cross-border projects and activities and its most informative Joint Statement issued after the Conference meeting of 11th March 1986 shows the range of such matters. Its illustrative value merits it full quotation.

## CROSS-BORDER SOCIAL AND ECONOMIC CO-OPERATION

### 1. *Economic*

| | |
|---|---|
| Tourism | Regular contact on various projects |
| Youth training | Cross-border exchanges of trainees |
| EC-assisted joint training projects | Various projects supported by the European Social Fund |
| Industrial science co-operation | Joint compilation of directories of expertise and services, by Co-operation North |
| Marketing | Joint participation in industrial promotions/ exhibitions |
| Industrial relations | Mutual exchange of industrial relations experience |
| Employment equality | Regular contact on common issues |
| Petroleum exploration | Exchange of information on exploration in areas straddling the border |
| National Economic and Social Council/Northern Ireland Economic Council | Co-operation on matters of mutual interest |
| Industrial Design | Joint co-operation |

### 2. *Infrastructure and Services*

| | |
|---|---|
| Newry–Dundalk road | Joint consideration of improved road links |
| Water services | Reciprocal arrangements on water services in border areas |

### 3. *Transport*

| | |
|---|---|
| Freight haulage licensing | Licensing of cross-border hauliers |
| Motor vehicle administration | General liaison in relation to motor vehicle registration |
| Transport companies | Regular contacts on road and rail issues of mutual interest |
| Commissioners of Irish Lights | Maintenance of lights and navigational aids |

| | |
|---|---|
| Marine search and rescue | Operational liaison and co-operation |
| Road safety | Regular contacts |

*4. Agriculture and Fisheries*

| | |
|---|---|
| Trade in agricultural produce | Co-operation on trade and EC funds including abuses |
| Animal plant and fish health | Co-operation to maintain/ improve disease status |
| Drainage | Co-ordination of complementary programmes |
| Foyle Fisheries Commission | Joint administration of Foyle Salmon Fisheries |
| Sea fisheries | Discussions about fishing limits |
| Timber utilisation | Exchanges of information on marketing and development |
| Horse breeding and racing | Joint administration of breeding scheme and regulation of racing |

*5. Health and Social Security*

| | |
|---|---|
| Medicines and food | Co-operation on cross-border control |
| Availability of health services | Liaison in relation to the provision of health services |
| Medical self-certification of ESSP scheme | Exchange of information and experience |
| Social security reform and computerisation | Exchange of information and experience |
| Social security fraud | Co-operation to counter cross-border fraud |
| Health Board co-operation in North West | Cross-border liaison on health services |
| Nuclear radiation | Exchange of information and regular liaison |

| | |
|---|---|
| Infectious and contagious diseases | Exchange of information and concerted action |
| Medical and dental manpower | Exchange of information on mutual manpower problems |
| | 6. *Education* |
| School teachers and inspector exchanges | Regular exchanges |
| Higher education | Co-operation between Higher Education Institutions |
| Teacher qualifications | Consideration of reciprocal recognition |
| Museums, libraries and films | Regular exchanges |
| Youth affairs | Co-operation in youth exchanges |
| History seminars for teachers | Joint educational seminars |
| European Studies (Ireland) | Shared curriculum development |
| | 7. *Environmental* |
| Environmental protection | Joint meetings on pollution, water quality, etc. |
| Planning | Joint co-operation on issues straddling the border |
| Conservation | Joint ecological considerations |
| Historic monuments and buildings | Joint contact on archaeology and historic buildings |
| | 8. *Taxation* |
| Inland Revenue | Operational contacts |
| Enforcement of revenue | Operational contacts |
| Customs procedures and documentation | Operational contacts |
| | 9. *Joint Studies* |
| EC-assisted cross-border | Joint studies supported by the European Regional Development Fund |

| | |
|---|---|
| Lough Melvin Study | Joint consideration of environmental study |
| North/West Study | Joint consideration of proposals by an independent study group |

*10. Arts, Sport & Cultural*

| | |
|---|---|
| Sport | Development of cross-border co-operation on sporting activities |
| Voluntary organisations in community relations | Wide range of bodies supported by both Governments |
| Arts Councils co-operation | Frequent exchanges and practical co-operation |
| Public records | Links at official and university levels on historical record matters |

*11. Miscellaneous*

| | |
|---|---|
| District council contacts | Regular contacts on matters of mutual interest in border areas |
| Fire and emergency services | Operational liaison in cross-border areas |
| Natural disaster contingency planning | Exchange of information |
| Ordnance Surveys | Contacts on mutual survey problems and joint publication |
| Meteorological Service | Operational liaison |
| General Register Office | Liaison in relation to registration of births, deaths and marriages and other census matters |
| Irish Soldiers and Sailors Land Trust | Co-operation on the Trust and its future |
| Training conferences | Joint conferences/visits between public service training centres |

Cross-border co-operation on security matters under Article 9 of the Agreement has tended to dominate both the headlines and the Joint Statements themselves, along with the handling of such potentially divisive issues as the

British Government's decision not to initiate prosecutions after the Stalker/Sampson inquiry into an alleged shoot-to-kill policy on the part of the RUC, and the Irish Government's attitude to the question of extradition. Indeed the dominance of these issues is most clearly encapsulated in the statement sometimes made that the Conference is only concerned with "crisis-management". Security matters are, however, but one, albeit a massively important, aspect of a far wider panoply of cross-border co-operation which is being spread out under the auspices or the scrutiny of the Anglo-Irish Intergovernmental Conference.

Even assuming it to be possible, it is too early to assess the achievements of the Conference in terms of all the aims set forth in the Preamble to the Agreement. All that can be stated with any certainty is that the Agreement has not—not yet at any rate—brought lasting peace and stability to Northern Ireland, but then it is surely fifty years too late for anyone to believe that simply clutching pieces of paper can guarantee peace for our time.

## NOTES

1 In November 1979, John Hume had succeeded Gerry Fitt as leader of the SDLP. Gerry Fitt had resigned in protest at the party's initial refusal to take part in the Atkins Conference. This refusal was prompted by the lack of an Irish dimension in the November 1979 White Paper. In order to secure the participation of the SDLP in the Conference, parallel talks took place between the Secretary of State and the SDLP on the question of an Irish dimension.

2 "Moreover (the SDLP's) insistence on an 'Irish dimension' had hardened into a demand for, in Mr Hume's words, 'A Federal Irish State'": Jenkins, *Political Constraints: London* in *The Constitution of Northern Ireland, Problems and Prospects* (ed Watt, 1981), p 163.

3 These communiqués are only occasionally issued as Command Papers. They are, however, otherwise lodged in the Library of the House of Commons. This quotation is taken from the communiqué as reported in *Keesing's Contemporary Archives* (1980) 30603A.

4 *Ibid*, 30878A.

5 Cmnd 8414, November 1981. It published the joint studies on possible new institutional structures, citizenship rights, economic co-operation and the encouragement of mutual understanding. The outcome of the joint study on security was not published.

6 Its own adjective—p 9, para 5. The Republic's constitutional provisions allow a *de facto* but not a *de jure* recognition of Northern Ireland as a part of the United Kingdom. See, *eg*, *Boland* v *An Taoiseach* [1974] IR 338, mentioned in chapter IV, note 67 and further below.

7 Cmnd 8414, p 9, para 5.

8 *Ibid*, p 8, para 4.

9 *Keesing's Contemporary Archives* (1982) 31578B-31579A. The *Council* should not be confused with the Anglo-Irish *Conference* established in 1985 by the Anglo-Irish Agreement, on which see below.

10 Cmnd 8414, p 10, paras 9-11.

11 1981-82, HC Debs (6th) vol 12,cols 422 and 426 (10th November 1981).

12 "...a Committee of senior officials set up following agreement between the then Prime Minister and the then Taoiseach in September 1977": Cmnd 8414, p 24, para 4. See generally also the Report of the Joint Study Group on Economic Co-operation, *ibid*, pp 24-32. Its work was in fact taken over by the Council.

13 *Ibid*, p 9, para 6. The Anglo-Irish Parliamentary Group, which comes under the auspices of the Inter-Parliamentary Union, is an all-party group with, at Westminster, a chairman, vice-chairman, treasurer and secretary; its membership is open to any backbencher.

14 *Keesing's Contemporary Archives* (1982) 31579A.

15 Cmnd 8414, p 11, para 14. For a fuller exposition of the respective British and Irish positions, see paras 15-18 and chapter VIII below.

16 *Ibid*, p 12, para 19.

17 *Ibid*, pp 12-13, para 20. It was envisaged that the ideas generated by this conference should be considered at an appropriate meeting of the Council, and that the annual conferences could be supplemented by smaller occasional seminars on specialised themes.

18 15th July 1982. Quoted in *Keesing's Contemporary Archives* (1982) 31790 B.

19 The White Paper preceding the Northern Ireland Act 1982, Cmnd 8541, at para 23 simply stated that "the first meetings of the Council have taken place and the Government is confident that these new arrangements will enhance close, friendly and practical co-operation in the interests of all the people of the United Kingdom."

20 *Per* the Prime Minister, Margaret Thatcher, in response to a question in the House of Commons from Enoch Powell on the nature of the intimation made by Douglas Hurd: 1981-82, HC Debs (6th), vol 28, cols 1225-6 (29th July 1982).

21 Quoted in the first report of the Assembly's Committee on the Government of Northern Ireland, January 1986, NIA 237-1, p 17. For a general consideration of party political attitudes within Northern Ireland on the issues which arose from 1982, see P.D.H. Smyth, "The Northern Ireland Assembly 1982-86: The Failure of an Experiment", vol 40 *Parl Aff* (1987) pp 482-500.

22 New Ireland Forum Report, 2nd May 1984, para 1.2. The Chairman of the Forum was the President of University College, Galway, Colm Ó hEocha. The Forum held twenty-eight private and thirteen public sessions, and received 317 submissions from the Republic and Northern Ireland, Great Britain, the USA, Belgium, France and Canada. In addition there were oral presentations from thirty-one individuals and groups.

23 Para 5.2(3) of the Forum Report defines "agreement" as follows: "Agreement means that the political arrangements for a new and sovereign Ireland would have to be freely negotiated and agreed to by the people of the North and the people of the South."

24 *Ibid*, para 5.7.

25 *Ibid*, para 6.1

26 See *ibid*, chapter 6.

27 *Ibid*, para 6.7.

28 There would also be certain other protective devices, for example, a requirement for weighted majorities in the federal Parliament on certain fundamental issues, an office of President/Head of State alternating between persons representative of the Northern and Southern states, and (where desired) parallel British citizenship.

29 "Federalism" and "confederalism" are terms often used loosely, indeed at times they are even regarded as interchangeable. Technically, in a federal state for example, Australia, Canada (even though referred to as a confederation) and the United States of America, the central and provincial authorities are of co-ordinate status with exclusive areas of competence, deriving their powers from a written constitution which cannot be unilaterally amended. In a confederal constitution, the central authorities are subordinate to the regional authorities which hold the residue of power. This contrasts with a unitary devolved state (such as the United Kingdom, during the life of the Northern Ireland Parliament) where the regional authorities are subordinate to the central authorities.

30 Chapter 8 of the Forum Report. The details here are taken from a Forum sub-committee report which was reproduced as an Appendix to the independent inquiry chaired by Lord Kilbrandon and set up by the British Irish Association. Its report was published in November 1984. The sub-committee report was also published unofficially in *The Irish Times* on 9th May 1984.

31 It is not publicly known why the Forum sub-committee report was not published as a part of the final report, nor is it known if all the details to be found in the sub-committee report were acceptable to the full Forum.

32 As quoted in the Kilbrandon Report, Appendix A, para 1. Power over all matters relating to Northern Ireland would be vested in and exercised by an Executive Joint Authority of the two Governments. The Forum Report, chapter 8, deals with Joint Authority, under which "the London and Dublin governments would have equal responsibility for all aspects of the government of Northern Ireland ...[it] would involve shared rule by the British and Irish Governments." Paras 8.1 and 8.3.

33 Article 2: "The national territory consists of the whole island of Ireland, its islands and the territorial sea."

Article 3: "Pending the re-integration of the national territory, and without prejudi
the right of the Parliament and Government established by this Constitution
jurisdiction over the whole of that territory, the laws enacted by that P
have the like area and extent of application as the laws of the Sa
like extra-territorial effect." One of the debates surroundin
is whether it confers on Northern Ireland the double
United Kingdom and not being a part of the Re
former.

34 As quoted in the Kilbrandon I
Chapter 8 of the Forum Rep

35 "Parallel to the establishment of Joint Authority a comprehensive and enforceable Bill of Rights would be promulgated ensuring the protection of both individual and communal rights and freedoms." *Ibid*, para 7. There would also be joint citizenship and equal status for the two flags: paras 25 and 26.

36 *Ibid*, para 3, and the beginning of para 4.

37 *Ibid*, para 41.

38 "Under the first model, the British and Irish Governments would appoint two Commissioners with equal responsibility for all matters dealing with Northern Ireland. The Commissioners... could appoint "Deputy Commissioners" to help in the task. The Commissioners and Deputy Commissioners could be drawn from the Irish or British Parliaments or from locally elected representatives from Northern Ireland ... Each power ... could be jointly exercised or there could be an agreed division of powers within the framework of collective responsibility...": *ibid*, para 9. It was envisaged that the two Prime Ministers would meet regularly to review the operation of the Authority.

39 *Ibid*, para 13.

40 "Joint responsibility for internal security and for a criminal justice regime would be a central component of Joint Authority. All security operations would be under control of the Joint Authority Commission. The emphasis in internal security policy would be on (i) the immediate establishment of a new police force (based on secondment from existing police forces in Great Britain and Ireland) with a new command structure and (ii) the establishment at as early a date as possible of a new police service throughout Northern Ireland responsive and loyal to the Joint Authority Commission ... The establishment of a new enlarged police service representative of the whole community of a sufficient size and with a high level of training and equipment should remove the present necessity for the permanent presence of a military back-up. In the event of such a back-up being required at any time its constitution would be for determination by the two sovereign governments." *Ibid*, paras 21-23.

41 It was hoped that the Commissioners in the exercise of their reserved powers would be advised by Assembly Committees: *ibid*, para 16.

42 *Ibid*, paras 17 and 18.

43 *Ibid*, para 14. See also para 40, under the heading of "Advantage: Capacity of Joint Authorities to implement and resilience": "If both Governments were fully committed, it would not be possible for Unionists or Nationalists to block implementation of the basic necessary structures ... There need be no weak link, exposed to pressures, (such as the vulnerability of the Faulkner Unionists to the Loyalist strike in 1974). If any subordinate structures collapsed, the joint authorities could simply carry on joint direct rule." See, further, text below.

44 *Ibid*, para 35.

45 In the context of the Joint Authority or Joint Sovereignty issue, the wording of para [illegible] be noted: "The arrangement would involve a major extension of the authority [illegible] institutions and would thus provide structures with which the [illegible] ould identify...".

[illegible] Anglo-Irish Intergovernmental Council

was mentioned.

48 As quoted in the Kilbrandon Inquiry Report, paras 37-43.

49 *Ibid*, paras 46-55.

50 *Ibid*, unnumbered para following para 55.

51 The Kilbrandon Inquiry Report was published in November 1984 and it saw *some* potential in the Joint Authority scheme, although it made it clear that it regarded any Joint Sovereignty scheme as unacceptable. See further on this, chapter VIII, below. For comments on the Report, see Hadfield, "More Reports on Northern Ireland: Panaceas or Pandora's Box" 1985 *Public Law*, pp 240-250; and Kenny, *The Road to Hillsborough: The shaping of the Anglo-Irish Agreement* (1986), chapter 13. Dr Anthony Kenny, Master of Balliol College, Oxford, was the Deputy Chairman of the Kilbrandon Report. His book also contains several chapters on the New Ireland Forum Report. For an "EEC" consideration of the situation, see the Report of the European Parliament's Political Affairs Committee: "Preliminary Draft Report on The Situation in Northern Ireland". Rapporteur: Mr Neils Haagerup. December 1983. The Report was discussed and adopted by the European Parliament in March 1984.

52 1983-84, HC Debs (6th) vol 63, cols 25-28 (2nd July 1984)

53 Cmnd 9094, November 1983.

54 *Ibid*, pp 9-10. Although, subsequently, information on the number of Ministerial meetings has been given, the topics under discussion do not appear to have been included. For example, a Commons' Written Answer of 1st April 1985 lists ten meetings from November 1984 to March 1985, providing the names of the participants but not the topics under discussion: 1984-85, HC Debs (6th) vol 76, *WA* cols 409-10.

55 See text above, including n 17.

56 Cmnd 9094, p 11, para 1.3: "The main activity of Encounter will be to hold periodic conferences and seminars, with a wide range of representation, on economic, social, cultural and other matters of common interest with a view to promoting mutual understanding, useful co-operation and good relations... The Organisation is independent of government control. The Irish and British Governments are providing a measure of financial control." This paragraph referred to the earlier Joint Studies Report which had envisaged the Encounter Organisation "as an interim measure, pending the eventual creation of an Advisory Committee on economic, social and cultural co-operation...".

57 Quoted in Kenny, *op cit*, p 82.

58 See the correspondence between the two Unionist Party leaders and the Prime Minister, 28th August-30th September 1985, reprinted in Appendix C to NIA 237-1, the first report of the [Assembly's] Committee on the Government of Northern Ireland, volume 1. It should be remembered that only the OUP and DUP were members of this Committee. Essentially the Unionists sought to stress that United Kingdom sovereignty in Northern Ireland "precludes any British/Irish machinery dealing only with Northern Ireland rather than with United Kingdom/Republic of Ireland relations as a whole." The Prime Minister replied that sovereignty means "first that Northern Ireland will remain part of the United Kingdom for as long as the majority in the Province so wish; and secondly that whatever may emerge from our discussions with the Irish authorities,

responsibility for the government of Northern Ireland will remain with UK Ministers accountable to Parliament."

59 Dáil Debates, 19th November 1985, cols 2573-4. Quoted in NIA 237-1 n 58, *supra*, chapter 3, p 24.

60 Cmnd 9657 (with communiqué) and also Cmnd 9690, November 1985. For further consideration of the Agreement, see, for example, Kenny, *The Road to Hillsborough*, *op cit*; Connolly and Loughlin, "Reflections on the Anglo-Irish Agreement", *Government and Opposition*, (1986) vol 21, pp 146-160; Cox, "Managing Northern Ireland Intergovernmentally: An Appraisal of the Anglo-Irish Agreement", *(1987) Parl Aff*, vol 40, pp 80-97; Hadfield, "The Anglo-Irish Agreement 1985—Blue Print or Green Print?" *NILQ* (1986) vol 37, pp 1-28. Also generally in terms of understanding fully both the New Ireland Forum Report and the Anglo-Irish Agreement, see Boyle and Hadden, *Ireland: A Positive Proposal* (1985) and, by the same authors, *The Anglo-Irish Agreement: Commentary, Text and Official Review* (publication pending).

61 See chapter IV *supra*. In Article 5, the Irish Government "fully accepted and solemnly declared", while in Article 1 of the 1985 Agreement it "affirms", and in Article 5 the word "could" [be no change] becomes "would" in Article 1(*a*) of the 1985 Agreement.

62 Cmnd 8414, November 1981, p 9, para 5. Emphasis supplied.

63 See also the Forum sub-committee report on Joint Authority, para 53: "It is possible that if and when the nationalists became a majority, the British would wish to end their involvement, following the provisions of section 1 of the ... Constitution Act 1973, and would enact legislation declaring that Northern Ireland had ceased to be a part of the United Kingdom. Indeed, nationalists might hope that the operation of Joint Authority and the gradual development of confidence and trust would lead unionists to accept movement towards some model of Irish unity, long before nationalists became a majority in the North."

64 Quoted in Kenny, *op cit,* p 107.

65 In *Boland*, the Irish Supreme Court was considering the compatibility of the Sunningdale communiqué with the Irish Constitution. In *McGimpsey*, see text below,the Irish High Court had to consider for the first time the constitutionality of a "Treaty in respect of which all formalities had been completed". In an earlier case of *Crotty* v *An Taoiseach* [1987] ILRM 400 the Court had to consider whether the Government should or should not, given the provisions of the Constitution, *ratify* the Single European Act.

66 The Irish High Court, July 1988 [1989] ILRM 209. Judgment given by Barrington J. In August 1988, the plaintiffs stated their intention to appeal to the Irish Supreme Court.

67 The plaintiffs were held to have the requisite standing to challenge the Agreement; *per* Barrington J: "... it appears to me that the plaintiffs are patently sincere and serious people who have raised an important constitutional issue which affects them and thousands of others on both sides of the border...".

68 *Ibid*, at p 224.

69 When it meets at Ministerial level, the Secretary of State for Northern Ireland and

an Irish Minister, designated the Permanent Irish Ministerial Representative who is (usually) the Foreign Affairs Minister, are the co-chairmen. The Conference has a permanent joint secretariat based at Maryfield, near Belfast.

70 Quoted in Kenny, *op cit,* p 105.

71 The Flags and Emblems Act (NI) 1954 was subsequently repealed by article 27 of the Public Order (NI) Order 1987. For a note on these provisions, see Hadfield "Order in the Law of Public Order" *NILQ* 1987 (vol 38) p 86 at pp 93-96. The Elected Authorities (NI) Act 1989, which was in operation in time for the district council elections in May 1989, brought the NI local election franchise broadly into line with that for Parliamentary elections. That is, by section 1 the Act abolishes the so-called "I-voter" category, consisting of some 11,000 persons born outside NI, entitling them to vote in district council elections. The Government's intention to change the law in this respect was announced after a meeting of the Conference on 17th June 1986. The 1989 Act, by section 3, also requires candidates at district council elections to make a "declaration against terrorism". Section 5, which is not yet in force, makes similar provision for NI Assembly elections. Note that as this involves an excepted matter (see the Constitution Act 1973, schedule 2, para 11, for example) it had to be legislated on by Act of Parliament rather than by Order in Council.

72 Article 12 of the Agreement indicates that no movement had been made from 1981 to 1985 on the establishment of an Anglo-Irish parliamentary body: "It will be for Parliamentary decision in Westminster and Dublin whether to establish an Anglo-Irish Parliamentary body of the kind adumbrated [in the Joint Study Report]...[T]he two Governments agree that they would give support as appropriate to such a body if it were to be established." In February 1989, however, some movement on the likely establishment of the interparliamentary body seemed imminent: see chapter VIII.

73 Article 4(*c*) provides that: "Both Governments recognise that devolution can be achieved only with the co-operation of constitutional representatives within Northern Ireland of both traditions there" and Article 5(*c*) refers to a "basis which secures widespread acceptance in Northern Ireland."

74 First Report of the Committee on the Government of Northern Ireland, NIA 237-1 p 73, paras 10 and 12.

75 Quoted in the Second Report of the Committee, 11th February 1986, NIA 239, para 3.

76 *Ibid,* paras 4 *et seq.*

77 In its fourth and final report, NIA 242, 13th March 1986, the Devolution Report Committee resolved to publish those of its proceedings and papers as it deemed appropriate and to give its unpublished material to the Committee on the Government of Northern Ireland, for it to use as it thought fit.

78 NIA 240, Third Report of the Committee on the Government of Northern Ireland, 13th March 1986. The Committee did recommend the institution of a new Assembly committee to "investigate allegations of discriminatory conduct and victimisation by employers and others against those who seek to exercise the democratic right of demonstrating their political opinion in opposition to the Agreement" and to make recommendations. The Committee on Victimisation in Employment reported on 28th May 1986: NIA 244. It was unable clearly to establish from the evidence and submis-

sions it received any cases "where direct and overt victimisation or discrimination had been practised against an employee." The Committee's inquiry had been prompted by allegations that some employees had been intimidated into working on the "day of action"/"day of political protest"/"(general) strike" which the loyalists had called on 3rd March 1986 as a protest against the Agreement.

79 Northern Ireland Assembly (Dissolution) Order 1986 SI 1986/1036.

80 [1986] 1 WLR 331.

81 The immediately preceding words of Article 6 are: "That ... his Majesty's subjects of Great Britain and Ireland shall from and after [1st January 1801] be entitled to the same privileges and be on the same footing, as to encouragements and bounties on the like articles, being the growth, produce or manufacture of either country respectively, and generally in respect of trade and navigation in all ports and places in the United Kingdom and its dependencies; and that in all treaties etc ..." (as in text). It could thus be argued, although the point is not made in the case, that the phrase "all treaties" has to be understood in the context of trade and navigation.

82 [1986] 1 WLR 331, 334.

83 See Hadfield, "The Anglo-Irish Agreement 1985—Blue Print or Green Print?" 1986 *NILQ* (vol 37) 1, at pp 26-28 and Boulton, "The Almost-General Election in Northern Ireland, 1986", 1986 *Public Law* 211-213.

84 This is the number of votes received by the OUP, DUP and UPUP. "Others", including the Alliance Party, the SDLP, PSF and the Workers' Party, received 159,981 votes.

85 See also Kenny, *op cit,* chapters 19 and 20.

86 The new Fair Employment Bill was published a year later and received the Royal Assent in July 1989.

# VIII

# CONCLUSIONS

Anyone who isn't confused here doesn't really understand what is going on.[1]

One of the criticisms levelled against the Home Rule Bills of 1893 and 1912-14 was that "they attempted to solve a problem in political sovereignty by a proposal for better government. They provide an object lesson in confused thinking."[2] This confusion is most clearly illustrated by the long title of the Government of Ireland Act 1920: it was "an Act to provide for the better government of Ireland". The issues ultimately in 1920, however, had nothing to do with better government and had everything to do with national status, that of Ireland and that of Ulster. Paradoxically, that Act and concomitant developments put these issues largely into abeyance for nearly fifty years but they returned with some force in 1968-70. Events which initially stemmed from concern about the quality of government were very rapidly replaced by events, in one forum or form or another, concerning the constitutional status of Northern Ireland. This has remained the dominant issue. From that time, the acceptability or unacceptability of virtually every proposal made depends not primarily upon its propensity to enhance the quality of the government of the Province, but rather upon its perceived impact, or lack of impact, upon Northern Ireland's constitutional status. This is seen most obviously with regard to any proposed system which either contains or lacks an Irish dimension, but it may also be seen in other respects. For example, recommendations may be made concerning the improvement of direct rule. These recommendations may be regarded as unacceptable on the ground that devolution is the preferred option of a wide spectrum of political opinion within Northern Ireland and, almost certainly, of the Westminster Government and, therefore, the argument goes, there is little merit in tinkering with a system which by a common consensus should be replaced. Rejection of the recommendations on this ground does relate at one level to the question of what constitutes the good or better government of Northern Ireland. It does, however, beg the question of why Northern Ireland should be treated differently on the devolution issue from any other region of the United Kingdom. Further, what is the thrust of the argument which labels recommendations for the improvement of direct rule as "integrationist", that is, as tending to bolster the position of Northern Ireland within Westminster's structures and processes and hence as militating against the diminution or termination of British rule in Northern Ireland? What is the thrust of the related argument which rejects the continuation of direct rule, improved or unimproved, on the ground that it is unacceptable to the Government of the Republic of Ireland?

The fact that constitutional status and form of government are so closely related can be coped with in one of two main ways by the constitutional lawyer. The first is to rehearse, but not necessarily to choose between, the whole range of constitutional options which have been proposed for Northern Ireland. The list is neither short nor lacking in variety.[3] There are those options revolving on the Irish axis: a united unitary or federal or confederal Ireland. There is the option of an independent Ulster. There are those options which involve the retention of British sovereignty in one form or another: direct rule, total integration, legislative and/or executive devolution in a multiplicity of forms, reform of local government. There are those options which involve both Great Britain and the Republic of Ireland: joint sovereignty/condominium or joint authority. There is the option of a federation between the United Kingdom and the Republic of Ireland, the constituent provinces being variously defined. There are much more specific options, such as the redrawing of the border between Northern Ireland and the Irish Republic. The likelihood of any option coming into existence or staying in existence depends upon a complex set of political, economic and security factors, local, national and international. However, although some options seem to be less likely than others, for example, the redrawing of the border, total integration or a federated British Isles, given the course of past events caution in prognostication seems sensible and recommendation is undesirable. Montgomery Hyde in 1972 commented that "No Englishman from Strongbow to Whitelaw has been able to solve the Irish problem".[4] The list of names is now longer and the present writer, being English, heeds the warning.

The second way of responding to the closeness of the two themes of national status and form of government is to work within the perimeters created by it, and to provide a critique of the status quo within its own terms. Such an approach, which will be adopted here, may then point the way towards a certain amount of incremental change. This will not satisfy those who seek the "Grand Design" but a century of developments and specifically twenty years of "the Troubles" teach that it is facile to assume that such a solution is within reach. From this more restricted stance, the two current elements in the Northern

Ireland constitution which seem to require comment are direct rule and the Anglo-Irish Agreement. Consideration of these leads into a brief consideration of the question of the redevolution of legislative and/or executive powers to locally-elected bodies within Northern Ireland.

## DIRECT RULE

The continuation of unreformed direct rule is patently unacceptable by any constitutional criterion. In the legislative sphere what exists is a pre-parliamentary mishmash of the not invariable consultation with the public by way of the circulation of a proposal for a draft Order; consideration of the "views and proposals" of the Irish Government through the medium of the Anglo-Irish Conference; and the very occasional sending of a proposal to the Northern Ireland (Standing) Committee, a committee of limited powers which has in fact not sat since 1985. At the Parliamentary level, Northern Ireland draft Orders in Council cannot be amended, are debated for a limited amount of time and, apart from Consolidation Orders, are subject to no technical scrutiny; there is an increasing tendency to subject these Orders to the negative resolution procedure; and the Merits Committees have a very limited role to play. In terms of the scrutiny of executive decision-making, no special Parliamentary provision is made to cater for the fact that the Secretary of State has extensive powers over the whole gamut of Northern Ireland affairs; there is no Select Committee on Northern Ireland affairs and the departmental select committees make only an occasional foray into the field; traditional local government powers are dissipated; and the work of both the Anglo-Irish Council and the Conference is secret and, at the time of writing, subject to no national Parliamentary scrutiny.

In order to ameliorate the situation, the following recommendations are made for the "interim period", whether or not devolution is an immediate prospect. It has become increasingly unacceptable permanently to treat direct rule as a temporary expedient.

(1) Reserved matters should be equated with excepted matters and legislated on by Act of Parliament. Given their substantive importance, resort to the Order in Council procedure is undesirable. Indeed it is recommended that this should be the practice for as long as the reserved matters remain undevolved. This would involve at the time of writing the amendment of the Northern Ireland Act 1974, schedule 1, paragraph 1*(b)* to exclude reserved matters from the Order in Council procedure. On devolution, implementation of this recommendation would involve the total repeal of section 38(1)*(b)* of

the 1973 Constitution Act, as amended by the 1982 Northern Ireland Act, which enables "any reserved matter" to be legislated on by Order in Council other than during the interim period.

(2) With regard to any proposed legislation for Northern Ireland in a transferred area involving major changes to the law,[5] either (a) provision should be made for amendment at the Parliamentary stage of the draft, or (b) greater use should be made of the special standing committee concept. The former would not be entirely without precedent. The Emergency Powers Act 1920, by section 2(4) provides that regulations made during a declared state of emergency "shall have effect as if enacted in this Act, but may be added to, *altered*, or revoked by resolution of both Houses of Parliament...". Given the width of the matters which may be dealt with by such regulations, however, and given the likely gravity of the situation then confronting the nation,[6] it would be distorting to insist on the persuasive value of this precedent. Indeed so widely is the 1920 Act regarded as an exceptional case, that the statement that "delegated legislation is unamendable by Parliament" is usually made without qualification.[7] It is, therefore, probably more realistic to confine suggestions for a better amending formula to the pre-parliamentary or proposal stage of Northern Ireland draft Orders. In this case, consideration should be given to the possibility of conferring upon the Northern Ireland Committee when deliberating on a substantively important proposal for a draft Order special standing committee powers. This would mean that it, retaining its current composition, would possess for up to four meetings the select committee powers of sending for persons, papers and records. In this way its subsequent detailed consideration of the proposal would be better informed and, therefore, the whole exercise should be more worthwhile.[8]

It is accepted that this procedure should be used for a very limited number of transferred matter proposals and that the simpler and quicker procedure would be used for the vast majority of the remaining proposals, although subject to recommendations (3) and (4).

(3) There should always be a *proposal* stage for all draft Orders in Council, other than Consolidation Orders, Appropriation Orders and Orders made under the urgency procedure of the 1974 Act. This recommendation speaks for itself, in that it is hard to present any counter-argument to it other than one based on expediency.

(4) Use of the negative resolution procedure for Northern Ireland draft Orders should be discontinued. If the desire is to have the law on any given matter the same throughout the United Kingdom, then let Parliament legislate by one Act accordingly. The argument on the "integrity of the Northern Ireland

statute book" has little merit. A uniform Act in its application to Northern Ireland could by so providing be subject to the Interpretation Act (NI) 1954 rather than the Interpretation Act 1978 if that was deemed desirable. Alternatively, Northern Ireland should be legislated for on the matter according to the original conception of the 1974 Act, namely an Order in Council laid subject to the affirmative procedure.[9]

To suggest improvements with regard to the scrutiny of executive decision-making is not as easy. The most obvious improvement would be the institution of a Select Committee on Northern Ireland affairs, but this seems to be a remote possibility. Departmental select committees have the remit of examining "the expenditure, administration and policy" of the principal government departments and of their associated public bodies. All these committees have Government party majorities although approximately half are chaired by an opposition Member of Parliament. These committees also all have a membership of eleven, bar the Scottish Affairs Select Committee which has thirteen members. Since the June 1987 General Election, however, the Scottish Affairs Select Committee has not yet been set up because of difficulties concerning its composition. Given the limited number of Scottish Conservative Members of Parliament a significant proportion of them is needed to be a part of the Government and is, therefore, precluded from select committee membership. It is virtually impossible, therefore, for the Scottish Affairs Select Committee now to retain both its regional composition and nature and also a Conservative majority, as had been possible prior to 1987. This difficulty has always been present with regard to any proposed Select Committee on Northern Ireland affairs, but the non-establishment of the Scottish Affairs Select Committee since 1987 confirms that this difficulty is virtually insuperable, certainly as far as Northern Ireland is concerned. To convert the existing Northern Ireland (Standing) Committee, with its potential membership of forty-two, into a select committee seems immensely impracticable. The Committee would be much too large to discharge select committee functions and it would not possess even a dominant, let alone exclusive, Northern Ireland "flavour". In this light, it is, therefore, to be hoped that, at least pending devolution, the existing departmental select committees remain ever mindful of their power to examine the relevant responsibilities of the Secretary of State for Northern Ireland. For understandable reasons, this power lay quiescent during the life of the Northern Ireland Assembly from 1982 until 1986. These reasons no longer apply.

Furthermore, there should be greater flexibility in and frequency of Northern Ireland Question-Time in the House of Commons. Given the extensive powers of the Secretary of State, Northern Ireland Question-Time should take place on a fortnightly but preferably on a weekly basis and there should be some greater willingness to net Northern Ireland's public bodies under this procedure. Given that this would entail a breach of the hallowed principle that a Minister only answers questions on matters for which he is directly responsible, however, such flexibility is unlikely to be manifested.

Undoubtedly greater use needs to be made of the Northern Ireland (Standing) Committee, although this involves co-operation on all sides, and one possibility would be to give it the main responsibility of shadowing Northern Ireland's public bodies. As was seen in Chapter VII, under Article 6 of the Anglo-Irish Agreement, the Irish Government may put forward into the Conference its views and proposals on "the role and composition" of bodies appointed by the Secretary of State, including the Standing Advisory Commission on Human Rights, the Fair Employment Agency, the Equal Opportunities Commission and the Police Authority for Northern Ireland.[10] There seems no reason why a committee of the Westminster Parliament should not also be involved in a consideration of their role and composition, and that of the Area Health and Social Services Boards and Education and Library Boards too. Given the composition of the Northern Ireland (Standing) Committee such a responsibility might involve the mutual broadening of horizons, those of both the Great Britain and also the Northern Ireland Members.

Finally, some way needs to be found of enabling the Northern Ireland Members of Parliament to take the initiative, certainly on transferred matters, in terms of their consideration or "airing" at Westminster. Under House of Commons' Standing Order 13(1) it is provided that, as a general rule, government business has precedence at every sitting. This is then qualified by Standing Order 13(2) and (3):

> Twenty days shall be allotted in each session for proceedings on opposition business, seventeen of which shall be at the disposal of the Leader of the Opposition and three of which shall be at the disposal of the leader of the second largest opposition party; and matters selected on those days shall have precedence over government business. For the purposes of this order "the second largest opposition party" shall be that party, of those not represented in ... [the Government], which has the second largest number of members elected to the House as members of that party.

Obtaining time and the freedom to dictate what shall be debated are precious and hard-won benefits for any opposition party at Westminster. Magnanimity on the part of either the Government or the larger opposition parties towards the Northern Ireland Members in terms of making time available to them is not realistically to be expected. If the Northern Ireland political parties, however, are to be expected on devolution to share power together, or something akin to that, then the Westminster Government and opposition parties should allocate one "Government" day and one "Opposition" day to the Northern Ireland Members for the whole House to debate at prime debating time a list of transferred matter topics agreed amongst the various Northern Ireland parties represented and at any given time active at Westminster. The idea is deliberately confined to "transferred matters". If excepted matters and, largely, reserved matters are matters of national importance or matters which should not be within the exclusive control of the representatives of the Northern Ireland electorate, then Government time should automatically be used for the full consideration of such issues. If there is ever a new devolved system, then this recommendation on transferred matters would cease to operate or apply.

## THE ANGLO-IRISH AGREEMENT

With the review of the working of the Conference under way at the time of writing,[11] caution here seems particularly advisable. A limited number of recommendations, however, do appear to be generally pertinent. First, the respective powers and responsibilities of both the Council and the Conference require clearer delineation. The Council now presumably exists essentially to deal with east-west/London-Dublin relations, whereas the Conference has been established to deal with *both* the North-South Irish dimension *and* the consideration of internal Northern Ireland affairs. This is not immediately apparent from the wording of Article 2(*b*) of the Agreement. It provides that

> *[t]he Conference will be mainly concerned with Northern Ireland*; but some of the matters under consideration will involve co-operative action in both parts of the island of Ireland, and possibly also in Great Britain. Some of the proposals considered in respect of Northern Ireland may also be found to have application by the Irish Government.

This rather general element on North-South reciprocity is dealt with more specifically in some of the later Articles of the Agreement. Article 4 (*a*) (ii) is particularly important here:

> In relation to matters coming within its field of activity, the Conference shall be a framework within which the United Kingdom Government and the Irish Government work together ... for peace, stability and prosperity throughout the island of Ireland by

promoting reconciliation, respect for human rights, co-operation against terrorism and the development of economic, social and cultural co-operation.

Articles 5(*b*) on political matters, 7(*c*) on security matters, 8 on legal matters and 10 on economic and social cross-border co-operation all refer to or include the possibility of action being taken by the Irish Government within its own jurisdiction.

In any reforms this element of reciprocity should be more clearly defined. Given the aims of the Agreement and given that the two Governments were of opinion in 1985 that the Conference is "not executive" (even if it is "more than consultative") there seems little reason why the Conference should not more explicitly be the framework into which suggestions for reform of the law in the Irish Republic also may be put in order to ensure that the aims of the Agreement and Article 4(*a*)(ii) particularly are fulfilled.[12] Consequently, in the light of these two dimensions along which the Conference operates, some thought should be given to reforming the composition of the Conference, although Unionist co-operation in its working is hardly likely to be forthcoming. The role of the Irish Government in the Conference is both to consider the North-South Irish dimension and also, on internal Northern Ireland matters, effectively to represent the interests of the minority community in Northern Ireland. The presence of the Secretary of State for Northern Ireland in the Conference clearly ensures the representation of the interests of the Westminster Government, but unless one equates those interests with the interests of the majority community in Northern Ireland those latter interests currently go unrepresented. One possibility for reform of membership would be to include three additional members in the Conference—all three to be elected by the Northern Ireland electorate, voting as one constituency by a system of proportional representation. If the elections to the European Assembly, now Parliament, are relied upon as a guide, this would mean that two Unionists and one SDLP representative would be elected to the Conference.[13] This possibility is in outline very similar to a suggestion made by the majority of the British Irish Association's Independent Inquiry chaired by Lord Kilbrandon. It reported in November 1984 and devoted a not inconsiderable amount of its time to a consideration of the New Ireland Forum Report and particularly the report of its sub-committee on Joint Authority. The Kilbrandon Committee saw some significant potential for future developments in Joint Authority, although it was unanimously of the opinion that co-operation between London and Dublin should not infringe either British sovereignty or section 1 of the Constitution Act 1973. It also emphasised the value of, if not the need for, devolution to a locally-elected Assembly in Belfast, coupled with the close involvement of the minority community in the administration of Northern Ireland and the "invited co-operation of Dublin in encouraging and developing such involvement".[14] The Kilbrandon Committee, however, split on the degree of the Dublin involvement which there should be in both law enforcement and the administration of Northern Ireland. The majority, favouring greater involvement for Dublin, adopted an approach labelled "co-operative devolution". One salient feature of this model was the creation of a five-member top tier of government, consisting of

> the Secretary of State for Northern Ireland or his deputy, the Minister for Foreign Affairs of the Republic of Ireland or his deputy, and three members elected by the voters of Northern Ireland, in such a way that two of them were representative of the majority community and one of them was representative of the minority...
>
> Within the executive, a simple majority vote would provide an effective decision-making procedure ... If all the local members boycotted the executive, the default position would in effect be joint direct rule, with decisions being taken by the London-Dublin members ... There would be little incentive for just one side to boycott the executive whilst the others take their places ... [because a] party which boycotted a co-operative devolution executive would forfeit its share of power and leave all local power in the hands of its opponents.[15]

The Kilbrandon Committee majority report envisaged that the members of this top-tier executive would not themselves be the "Ministers" in charge of the devolved departments but would instead make those appointments. Both the devolved Executive and the top-tier of government would be answerable to a devolved Assembly. In the plenitude of its powers, the top-tier of government would both supervise the exercise by the devolved Executive of all the transferred matters and itself exercise some of the matters reserved in terms of the Constitution Act 1973 classification of powers.

The Kilbrandon Committee envisaged a system of devolution in existence, as the Anglo-Irish Agreement does, and an unequivocal declaration of British sovereignty,[16] which the Agreement does not, but by and large a five-member rather than a two-member Conference would seem to be one reform to which consideration should be given. Indeed Article 2 itself probably envisaged such a development. It actually provides on the composition of the Conference that membership

> shall be small and flexible. When the Conference meets at Ministerial level the Secretary of State ... and [the] Irish Minister ... shall be joint Chairmen.

They are thus not the sole members and presumably a membership of five would still meet the criterion on size.

Two other related reforms may be suggested, with regard to the Anglo-Irish Agreement. First, the proceedings of the Conference should be handled with less secrecy, other than on security matters. Secondly, there should be some parliamentary scrutiny of its work, either at Westminster or via the full implementation of Article 12 of the Agreement on the institution of an Anglo-Irish Parliamentary body. The Joint Study Group on Possible New Institutional Structures stated in 1981 that there was agreement that

> it would be a natural and desirable development for the establishment of a new inter-governmental body to be complemented at an appropriate moment by the development of an inter-parliamentary body.[17]

The subsequent paragraphs clearly indicate that on the British side there was no firmly held opinion on the likely composition and functions of such a body:

> In the British view, this should be further considered in the light of experience and of opinions which might over time be expressed by members of either or both of the two national Parliaments (or by British or Irish members of any other relevant parliamentary body, such as the European Parliament or any Assembly which might be established locally in Northern Ireland). In the meantime, efforts should be made to deepen and broaden the activities and composition of the existing Anglo-Irish Parliamentary Group.[18]

The Irish side, however, had much clearer ideas on the nature and importance of such a body, in terms of its composition, ambit and purposes. In the Irish view,

> the parliamentary element could initially be constituted through an Anglo-Irish parliamentary committee as a natural development of the existing, rather loosely structured Anglo-Irish Parliamentary Group. The objectives would be to widen the composition of the existing Group, to provide a more regular and systematic pattern of inter-parliamentary exchanges and to deepen and broaden the activities undertaken by focusing them on a more structured agenda related to the work of the inter-governmental body. The proceedings would be to promote constructive discussion which would subsequently facilitate the transforming of the consultative committee into a constituent part of the Anglo-Irish Institution ... [In terms of the appropriate composition of the body, the Irish] considered that the guiding principle should be equitable representation of the various political interests and traditions within these islands. Apart from the obvious benefits of parliamentary exchanges, the Irish side saw the committee as providing a forum for the participation of representatives from Northern Ireland in the

new institutional structures. They considered that ... the Northern Ireland membership should be composed in proportion to the size of the different parts of the community there and should be a significant component of the committee. In the absence of an elected Assembly in Northern Ireland representatives could be chosen on the basis of appointment by the Secretary of State on the nomination of, or after consultation with, leaders of political parties ... The Irish side saw the ambit and purposes of the committee as corresponding to those of the inter-governmental body. Its functions would essentially be consultative, advisory and review in nature. It could discuss the activities of the inter-governmental body and review the work of ancillary bodies, on the basis—but not exclusively so—of an annual report on co-operation from the inter-governmental body.[19]

Article 12 of the Anglo-Irish Agreement states that it is for the London and Dublin Parliaments to decide "whether to establish an Anglo-Irish Parliamentary body of the kind *adumbrated*" in the Joint Studies Report. "Adumbrated" is complimentary to the British outline provided above and misleading as far as the far sharper and fuller opinions of the Irish side are concerned. At the time of writing, Spring 1989, movement on the institution of an inter-parliamentary body may be imminent.[20] It is important that in whatever emerges there will be these two elements: provision for significant representation from Northern Ireland and a remit which includes close scrutiny of, and the facilities for close scrutiny of, the work of the Anglo-Irish Conference. Scrutiny of the work of the Anglo-Irish Council, given that it is concerned with east-west relations, should be mainly exercised in and through the Westminster and Dublin Parliaments.

## THE ANGLO-IRISH AGREEMENT — A POSTSCRIPT

The details of the three-year review of the working of the Conference were published on 24th May 1989. In the review document, both Governments "reaffirm their full commitment to all of the provisions of the Agreement" including its Preamble. They state that the Conference, which had then met on twenty-seven occasions since November 1985, had provided

a valuable forum to address in a regular and organised way the full range of matters covered in the Agreement, mainly affecting Northern Ireland, and to promote cooperative action in both parts of Ireland. Through the Conference, the Irish Government have put forward views and proposals on these issues for consideration by the British side. Thus, in the development of measures relating to Northern Ireland the Conference has played an important role ... .[21]

Both Governments agreed that future meetings of the Conference should be organised on a regular pattern of ten each year, supplemented by at least one annual "informal ministerial meeting" in order to ensure the fullest possible consideration of longer-term issues. They further agreed in principle, with relation to Article 3 of the Agreement, that future Conference meetings should provide for "widened Ministerial participation … to encourage more structured discussion of a greater range of issues of common interest to both parts of Ireland." Both Governments also welcomed the progress which had been made towards the establishment of a British-Irish Interparliamentary Body "of the kind envisaged" in the Joint Studies Report of November 1981, "which would provide a valuable independent forum for interparliamentary contacts." Finally, both Governments accepted the need for the public to be made "fully aware of the contribution which the work of the Conference is making" and they intend to meet this desideratum in their future communiqués and press conferences.

The remainder of the review document considers the various substantive matters covered by the Agreement and the changes, actual or proposed, in these respects. So, for example, the document repeats the policy of both Governments to encourage progress towards "devolution of responsibility for certain powers to elected representatives in Northern Ireland as set out in Article 4 of the Agreement". It refers to various changes in the law in such fields as public order and fair employment, to the need for the proper protection of human rights and to the importance of the Irish language in the education system, and both Governments undertook "to support efforts to enhance awareness and appreciation of this particular strand of the cultural heritage." The Governments further undertook to reinforce the principle that "public bodies in Northern Ireland should be so constituted as to enjoy the widest possible respect and acceptance throughout the community", by considering how "to remedy imbalances arising from the use by others of their existing nominating powers without due regard to fairness or balance."[22]

The review document is also concerned with confidence in the security forces and the system of justice, and cross-border security and economic co-operation. The former encompasses, for example, the systematic monitoring of complaints made by members of the public about the behaviour of members of the security forces, the need for a police presence in all operations involving direct contact between the armed forces and the community, and the publication of a guide to the operation of the Emergency Provisions and Prevention of Terrorism Acts. The document records a difference of opinion between the British and Irish Governments on the desirability of three-judge "Diplock" courts.

Finally, the review document refers to the establishment in September 1986 of the International Fund for Ireland, with the financial support of the United States, Canada, New Zealand and, from 1989, the European Community and records that from its foundation the Fund has committed over £50 million to projects in Northern Ireland and the border counties in the Republic.

As can be seen and as the review document itself acknowledges, no fundamental change has been made to the working of the Conference. The document concludes, however, by stating:

If in future it were to appear that the objectives of the Agreement could be more effectively served by changes in the scope and nature of the working of the Conference, consistent with the basic provisions and spirit of the Agreement, the two Governments would be ready in principle to consider such changes.

## DEVOLUTION

As has been seen throughout the last few chapters, there is little room for manoeuvre on the devolution issue. Virtually all interested parties have as their first preference some form of devolution within Northern Ireland. All statements made by the Westminster Government since 1972 have been to the effect that (1) in any devolved system there must be an Irish dimension, and that (2) there will be no return to the pre-1972 system of unmitigated majority rule. Article 4(*b*) of the Anglo-Irish Agreement repeats that

the declared policy of the United Kingdom Government [is] that responsibility in respect of certain matters within the powers of the Secretary of State for Northern Ireland should be devolved within Northern Ireland on a basis which would secure widespread acceptance throughout the community. The Irish Government support that policy.

Article 4(*c*), recognising that devolution can only come about with the co-operation of the "constitutional representatives" of both "traditions" within Northern Ireland, states that the Conference is the framework within which

the Irish Government may put forward views and proposals on the modalities of bringing about devolution in Northern Ireland, in so far as they relate to the interests of the minority community.

What those "modalities" will be cannot be precisely forecast, but on the general level they will undoubtedly involve either power-sharing or a close equivalent. Similarly, it is exceedingly probable that the substantive powers devolved will fall almost completely, if not completely, within the list of matters transferred under the Constitution Act 1973.

It is for the political parties themselves to decide whether or not they will co-operate in any new system of devolution operating within these principles.[23] Minority interests can—and should—be protected. The environment within which a devolutionary system would operate now is very different from that prevailing in 1920. The existence of the European Economic Community and of the European Convention on Human Rights, with the facility for an individual to petition the European Commission of Human Rights with regard to alleged State infringements of the Convention's Articles, involve a considerable amount of external control and scrutiny over a wide range of issues. In 1920 Westminster's attitude was marked by a desire to extricate itself from Northern Ireland affairs; there is now an unequivocal determination to retain and use political scrutiny and override powers even over the matters to be devolved, and in the enlarged area of anti-discrimination provisions, to use the courts. The withholding from a future Assembly of the excepted and reserved categories of power ensures that such matters cannot be controlled at all by the representatives of the majority community in Northern Ireland. The Irish dimension has been established through the Conference and through the Council. If there is to be devolution, against this probably immovable background, then consideration must be given not only to minority but also to majority rights. If devolution is to work effectively, a government has to be able to govern and there must be mutual respect within Northern Ireland for the concerns of both traditions. The new devolutionary scheme must not only provide for the prevention or frustration of abuse of majority power, or more positively provide for the development of minority interests, it must also facilitate the legitimate exercise of majority power within the transferred areas. The nature of the composition of the devolved executive will undoubtedly continue to be the hardest hurdle to surmount in terms of the formulation of a generally acceptable devolutionary scheme.

The general tenor of this chapter, in spite of its heading, has been both tentative and inconclusive. In terms of Northern Ireland's constitutional history, however, the major difficulty has come not in identifying what needs to be rectified but in being able to provide widely acceptable solutions. This is as true now as it has ever been. Let Horace have the last words:

> *Omne* tulit punctum qui miscuit utile dulci.[24]

## NOTES

1 A Belfast citizen, 1970, quoted by Hunter, *An Analysis of the Conflict in Northern Ireland* in *Political Co-operation in Divided Societies* (ed Rea, 1982), p 9.

2 Mansergh, *The Government of Northern Ireland* (1936), p 16. Quoted in Palley, "The Evolution, Disintegration and Possible Reconstruction of the Northern Ireland Constitution" (1972), p 375, n 23.

3 See, *eg*, Palley, *Ways Forward: The Constitutional Options* in *The Constitution of Northern Ireland* (ed Watt, 1981), pp 183-206. For one specific model, the consociational democracy and its limits, see Lijphart, *Democracy in Plural Societies* (1977), especially chapters 2 and 3 and pp 134-141. The four elements of such a democracy are (a) a grand coalition of the political leaders of all significant segments of the plural society, (b) the mutual veto or "concurrent majority" rule, (c) proportionality as the principal standard of political representation, civil service appointments and allocation of public funds, and (d) a high degree of autonomy for each segment to run its own internal affairs. See more briefly Lijphart, *Consociation: The Model and its application in divided societies*, chapter 6 in *Rea* ed, *op cit, supra.*

4 Quoted in Palley 1972, *op cit, supra*, at p 476.

5 This could include, where relevant, parity legislation mentioned under recommendation (4) below, if that recommendation is not acceptable. For major changes made by Act, applying throughout the UK, to the law of Northern Ireland in the "transferred" field, see the Consumer Safety Act 1978 and the Sale of Goods Act 1979. These should be compared procedurally with the Consumer Protection (NI) Order 1987, which was made under the negative procedure in accordance with section 49 of the Consumer Protection Act 1987 and which implements parts of the 1987 Act in Northern Ireland. Other parts of the Act, however, apply directly to Northern Ireland.

6 Section 1 of the Act lays down the conditions under which a state of emergency may be declared. Section 2(1) then enacts that: "where a proclamation of emergency has been made, and so long as the proclamation is in force it shall be lawful for His Majesty in Council, by Order, to make regulations for securing the essentials of life to the community, and those regulations may confer or impose on a Secretary of State (etc) ... such powers and duties as His Majesty may deem necessary for the preservation of the peace, for securing and regulating the supply and distribution of food, water, fuel, light and other necessities, for maintaining the means of transit or locomotion, and for any other purposes essential to the public safety and the life of the community ...". The 1920 Act did not extend to Ireland; for a state of emergency in Northern Ireland specifically, see the Emergency Powers Act (NI) 1926, passed in consequence of the General Strike in 1926. This Act created powers quite distinct from those contained in the Civil Authorities (Special Powers) Act (NI) 1922.

7 Bradley in Wade and Bradley's *Constitutional and Administrative Law* (10th ed, 1985) at p 618, n 44 also cites the Census Act 1920, section 1(2) as being an exception to the rule.

8 These Committees, first established in October 1980 in order to enhance the Commons' consideration of Bills, have been used very infrequently. Only five Bills so far have been considered by them: Criminal Attempts, Education and Deep Sea Mining

(all in 1980-81), Mental Health (Amendment) (1981-82) and Matrimonial and Family Proceedings (1983-84). See Benyon, "The House of Commons' Experiment with Special Standing Committees" 1982 *Public Law*, pp 193-198 and the Second Report from the Select Committee on Procedure (1984-85) HC 49-1, paras 11-13.

9 This recommendation is to be read in conjunction with recommendation (2) and see n 5 above.

10 See below, under the heading "The Anglo-Irish Agreement—a Postscript", a change in the operation of Article 6, stemming from the three-year review of the Conference.

11 It should be stressed that under Article 11 of the Agreement the three-year review is a review of the working of the Conference "to see whether any changes in the scope and nature of its activities are desirable" and is not a review of the Agreement itself.

12 Given that Article 2(*b*) also refers to Great Britain, the role of the Conference with regard to Great Britain and specifically issues affecting Irish citizens there should also be clarified.

13 Under the European Assembly Elections Act 1978 (as amended) the first-past-the-post or simple majority system is used in Great Britain, but in Northern Ireland the single transferable vote system of proportional representation is used. Northern Ireland is treated as one constituency and it returns three MEPs, currently one OUP, one DUP and one SDLP.

14 Para 6.4.

15 See paras 12.11-12.15.

16 The Committee also proposed the repeal of Articles 2 and 3 of the Irish Constitution and their replacement with these words: "The Irish nation hereby proclaims its firm will that its national territory be reunited in harmony and brotherly affection between all Irishmen." See para 1.14. Although a strong argument can be mounted that the Agreement itself should be reworded so that it is unequivocal one way or the other on both the sovereignty issue and on the status of Northern Ireland, such a suggestion is not being made here because it is accepted that the Agreement is deliberately vague and ambiguous in order to try to satisfy two conflicting political ends.

17 Cmnd 8414, November 1981, para 14, p 11. At that time, the new intergovernmental body referred to was the Council. The institution of the Conference has strengthened the arguments on the need for some form of parliamentary scrutiny.

18 *Ibid*, para 15, p 11. See chapter VII, note 13.

19 *Ibid*, paras 16-18, pp 11-12.

20 The Interparliamentary Body will be composed of twenty-five members each from the Westminster and Dublin Parliaments, with government party majorities for each delegation; it will meet twice yearly in London and Dublin and its first meeting is expected to be in London in February 1990. The British co-chairman will be Peter Temple-Morris (Conservative MP for Leominster) who was for three years chairman of the British branch of the Inter-Parliamentary Union. The Irish co-chairman will be James Tunney, the Leas-Cheann Comhairle (Deputy Speaker) of the Dáil. On the Westminster side two seats have been reserved for the Unionists, who are unlikely to participate in the new body, and one for the SDLP.

21 This wording casts no further light on the debate concerning the executive/consultative nature of the Conference.

22 This possibly widens the reach of Article 6.

23 As was adverted to in chapter VI, text and note 55, since the signing of the Anglo-Irish Agreement and during its subsistence, the Unionist leaders have not been prepared to contemplate formal negotiations concerning any future devolutionary scheme for Northern Ireland. They have insisted that a condition precedent to such talks is the suspension of the Agreement. The SDLP, on the other hand, is equally insistent that there should be no such suspension and that any discussions should take place "outside" the Agreement. Informal talks were held in October 1988 at Duisburg in West Germany between members of the OUP, Alliance, SDLP and DUP over the possibility of inter-party talks. The fact that these talks had taken place was disclosed in Spring 1989 but at the time of writing they do not appear to have produced a formula which would facilitate more formal talks.

24 "He has carried *every* vote (or point in an argument) who has combined the useful with the pleasing." The quotation then actually continues:

lectorem delectando pariterque monendo

("by delighting the reader as well as instructing him").

# APPENDIX 1

## CHRONOLOGY OF EVENTS

| DATE | EVENTS |
|---|---|
| 1800 (The Union was effective from 1st January 1801) | Acts of Union. (Technically the plural form should be used as legislation was passed by both the British and Irish Parliaments: Union with Ireland Act 1800 and Act of Union 1800 (Ir)). |
| 1886 | First Home Rule—Irish Government—Bill. |
| 1893 | Second Home Rule—Irish Government—Bill. |
| 1914 | Government of Ireland Act.<br>Suspensory Act.<br>(Both Acts received the Royal Assent on the same day, 18th September 1914, the Suspensory Act (chapter 88) actually preceding the Government of Ireland Act (chapter 90) onto the statute book). |
| 1920 | Government of Ireland Act.<br>(The Act received the Royal Assent on 23rd December 1920 and came into force on various appointed days in 1921 and 1922, the main appointed day being 3rd May 1921). |
| 1921 | Articles of Agreement for a Treaty between Great Britain and Ireland on 6th December. |
| 1922 | Irish Free State (Agreement) Act (which gave the force of law to the Articles of Agreement). |
| | Irish Free State Constitution Act (Session 2). Section 5 declared the date, 5th December 1922, from which the "Ulster Month" ran. |
| | Irish Free State (Consequential Provisions) Act. (It became law on the same day, 5th December 1922, as the above Act providing for the IFS Constitution, and it made such provisions as were consequential on or incidental to the establishment of the Irish Free State). |
| 1924 | Irish Free State (Confirmation of Agreement) Act (confirming the Agreement between GB and the IFS con- |

| | |
|---|---|
| | cerning Article 12 of the Articles of Agreement and the composition of the Boundary Commission). |
| 1925 | Ireland (Confirmation of Agreement) Act (which gave the force of law to the Agreement between GB and the IFS concluded on 3rd December 1925 amending and supplementing the Articles of Agreement). |
| 1949 | Ireland Act (declaring and affirming Northern Ireland's constitutional status). |
| 1968 | Start of major civil unrest—"the Troubles". |
| 1972 | Northern Ireland (Temporary Provisions) Act on 30th March 1972 prorogued the Parliament of Northern Ireland and suspended the Northern Ireland Government. The Act introduced "Direct Rule—Phase I".<br>October: the Government's discussion document on "The Future of Northern Ireland" is published. |
| 1973 | March: Border Poll held.<br>Northern Ireland Assembly Act.<br>Northern Ireland Constitution Act.<br>Sunningdale Agreement. |
| 1974 | January: the Northern Ireland Assembly and Executive start operating under the transferred powers.<br>February: the General Election is held.<br>May: Ulster Workers' Council Strike - Collapse of the Executive - Assembly prorogued and NI Office Ministers take over the functions of the Executive.<br>July: Northern Ireland Act introduces "Direct Rule—Phase II". |
| 1975 | May: elections are held to the Northern Ireland Constitutional Convention. Its report is published in November. |
| 1976 | February–March: the Convention is reconvened and then closed. |
| 1979 | House of Commons Redistribution of Seats Act: Northern Ireland representation at Westminster is increased from 12 to 17. (See now the Parliamentary Constituencies Act 1986). |

| | |
|---|---|
| | November: publication of a White Paper: "A working paper for a Conference". |
| 1980 | January–March—"the Atkins Conference". |
| | July: publication of a White Paper: "Proposals for Further Discussion." |
| | May and December: summit meetings between the British and Irish Prime Ministers. |
| 1981 | November: the Anglo-Irish Intergovernmental Council is established. |
| 1982 | Northern Ireland Act (rolling devolution). |
| | October: Assembly elections are held. |
| 1983 | May: the New Ireland Forum begins its deliberations. |
| 1984 | May: the New Ireland Forum Report is published. |
| 1985 | November: the Anglo-Irish Agreement is signed, and later approved by both Parliaments. The Anglo-Irish Intergovernmental Conference is established. |
| 1986 | June: the Assembly is dissolved. |
| 1988 | November: the review of the working of the Anglo-Irish Intergovernmental Conference begins. |

# APPENDIX 2

## STATISTICS ON THE VIOLENCE

The following figures make for sombre reading. They starkly provide the background against which the events mentioned in chapters IV to VII have taken place.

| | DEATHS | INJURIES |
|---|---|---|
| 1969 | 13 | 765 |
| 1970 | 25 | 1,056 |
| 1971 | 174 | 2,543 |
| 1972 | 467 | 4,876 |
| 1973 | 250 | 2,651 |
| 1974 | 216 | 2,398 |
| 1975 | 247 | 2,474 |
| 1976 | 297 | 2,729 |
| 1977 | 112 | 1,398 |
| 1978 | 81 | 985 |
| 1979 | 113 | 875 |
| 1980 | 75 | 801 |
| 1981 | 101 | 1,350 |
| 1982 | 97 | 525 |
| 1983 | 77 | 510 |
| 1984 | 64 | 866 |
| 1985 | 54 | 916 |
| 1986 | 61 | 1,450 |
| 1987 | 93 | 1,130 |
| 1988 | 93 | 1,047 |

*Source : The Northern Ireland Office*

My thanks are due to Mrs P. Smyth for assistance in the acquisition of this information.

# APPENDIX 3

# THE STATUS OF NORTHERN IRELAND

## UNION WITH IRELAND ACT 1800/ACT OF UNION 1800 (IR)

ARTICLE FIRST

*Great Britain and Ireland united into one Kingdom.* That it be the First Article of the Union of the Kingdoms of Great Britain and Ireland, that the said Kingdoms of Great Britain and Ireland shall, upon the first day of January which shall be in the year of Our Lord one thousand eight hundred and one, and for ever after, be united into one Kingdom, by the name of the United Kingdom of Great Britain and Ireland, and that the royal style and titles appertaining to the imperial crown of the said United Kingdom and its dependencies, and also the ensigns, armorial flags and banners thereof, shall be such as his Majesty, by his royal proclamation under the great seal of the United Kingdom, shall be pleased to appoint.

## GOVERNMENT OF IRELAND ACT 1920

SECTION 1(2)

For the purposes of this Act, Northern Ireland shall consist of the parliamentary counties of Antrim, Armagh, Down, Fermanagh, Londonderry and Tyrone, and the parliamentary boroughs of Belfast and Londonderry.

## IRISH FREE STATE (AGREEMENT) ACT 1922

*(This gave the force of law to the "Articles of Agreement for a Treaty between Great Britain and Ireland", dated 6th December 1921.)*

SCHEDULE, Article 1

Ireland shall have the same constitutional status in the Community of Nations known as the British Empire as the Dominion of Canada, the Commonwealth of Australia, the Dominion of New Zealand, and the Union of South Africa, with a Parliament having powers to make laws for the peace order and good government of Ireland and an Executive responsible to that Parliament, and shall be styled and known as the Irish Free State.

SCHEDULE, Article 11

Until the expiration of one month from the passing of the Act of Parliament for the ratification of this instrument, the powers of the Parliament and the Government of the Irish Free State shall not be exercisable as respects Northern Ireland, and the provisions of the Government of Ireland Act 1920, shall, so far as they relate to Northern Ireland, remain of full force and effect, and no election shall be held for the return of members to serve in the Parliament of the Irish Free State for constituencies in Northern Ireland, unless a resolution is passed by both Houses of the Parliament of Northern Ireland in favour of the holding of such elections before the end of the said month.

SCHEDULE, Article 12

If before the expiration of the said month, an address is presented to his Majesty by both Houses of the Parliament of Northern Ireland to that effect, the powers of the Parliament and Government of the Irish Free State shall no longer extend to Northern Ireland, and the provisions of the Government of Ireland Act 1920 ... shall, so far as they relate to Northern Ireland, continue to be of full force and effect, and this instrument shall have effect subject to the necessary modifications.

(The proviso to Article 12 required the establishment of a Boundary Commission, should such an address be presented).

(Note: The Irish Free State (Agreement) Act 1922 received the Royal Assent on 31st March 1922, but section 1(5) of the Act provided that: "This Act shall not be deemed to be the Act of Parliament for the ratification of the said Articles of Agreement as from the passing whereof the month mentioned in Article 11 of the said Articles is to run." The Irish Free State Constitution Act 1922 (Session 2), section 5 provided that: "This Act ... shall be deemed to be the Act of Parliament for the ratification of the said Articles of Agreement as from the passing whereof the month mentioned in Article eleven of the said Articles is to run.")

## IRELAND (CONFIRMATION OF AGREEMENT) ACT 1925

SCHEDULE

Agreement amending and supplementing the Articles of Agreement for a Treaty between Great Britain and Ireland to which the force of law was given by the Irish Free State (Agreement) Act 1922 and by the Constitution of the Irish Free State (Saorstat Eireann) Act 1922.

Whereas on the sixth day of December, nineteen hundred and twenty-one, Articles of Agreement for a Treaty between Great Britain and Ireland were entered into: And whereas the said Articles of Agreement were duly ratified and given the force of law by the Irish Free State (Agreement) Act 1922, and by the Constitution of the Irish Free State (Saorstat Eireann) Act 1922: And whereas the progress of events and the improved relations now subsisting between the British Government, the Government of the Irish Free State, and the Government of Northern Ireland, and their respective peoples, make it desirable to amend and supplement the said Articles of Agreement, so as to avoid any causes of friction which might mar or retard the further growth of friendly relations between the said governments and peoples: And whereas the British Government and the Government of the Irish Free State being united in amity in this undertaking with the Government of Northern Ireland, and being resolved mutually to aid one another in a spirit of neighbourly comradeship, hereby agree as follows:

1. The powers conferred by the proviso to Article 12 of the said Articles of Agreement on the Commission therein mentioned are hereby revoked, and the extent of Northern Ireland for the purposes of the Government of Ireland Act 1920, and of the said Articles of Agreement, shall be such as was fixed by subsection (2) of section one of that Act.

6. This Agreement is subject to confirmation by the British Parliament and by the Oireachtas of the Irish Free State... (Both Parliaments subsequently ratified this Agreement and on 9th December 1925 both Houses of the Northern Ireland Parliament adopted resolutions approving the terms of this Agreement).

## IRELAND ACT 1949

An Act to recognise and declare the constitutional position as to the part of Ireland heretofore known as Eire, and to make provision as to the name by which it may be known and the manner in which the law is to apply in relation to it; [and] to declare and affirm the constitutional position and the territorial integrity of Northern Ireland...

SECTION 1

(1) It is hereby recognised and declared that the part of Ireland heretofore known as Eire ceased, as from the eighteenth day of April, nineteen hundred and forty-nine, to be part of His Majesty's dominions.

(2) It is hereby declared that Northern Ireland remains part of His Majesty's dominions and of the United Kingdom and it is hereby affirmed that in no event will Northern Ireland or any part thereof cease to be part of His Majesty's dominions and of the United Kingdom without the consent of the Parliament of Northern Ireland.

## NORTHERN IRELAND (TEMPORARY PROVISIONS) ACT 1972

SECTION 1(3)

So long as this section has effect, the Parliament of Northern Ireland shall stand prorogued... and Her Majesty shall have power by Order in Council to make laws for any purpose for which the Parliament of Northern Ireland has power to make laws...

SECTION 2

Nothing in this Act shall derogate or authorise anything to be done in derogation from the status of Northern Ireland as part of the United Kingdom.

SCHEDULE, paragraph 4(5)

Where under any enactment or instrument it is a condition for the taking of any step... or for the coming of anything into operation that a resolution or motion has been passed or address presented by one or both of the Houses of the Parliament of Northern Ireland, then so long as section 1 of this Act has effect the step may be taken or the thing shall come into operation without any such resolution, motion or address; but this sub-paragraph shall have no application to the consent required under subsection (2) of section 1 of the Ireland Act 1949...

## NORTHERN IRELAND CONSTITUTION ACT 1973

*(Note that by section 31(1) of this Act: "The Parliament of Northern Ireland shall cease to exist".)*

SECTION 1

It is hereby declared that Northern Ireland remains part of Her Majesty's dominions and of the United Kingdom, and it is hereby affirmed that in no event will Northern Ireland or any part of it cease to be part of Her Majesty's dominions and of the United Kingdom without the consent of the majority of the people of Northern Ireland voting in a poll held for the purposes of this section...

SECTION 43(1)

"Northern Ireland" has the same meaning as for the purposes of the Government of Ireland Act 1920.

*(Note: All the above provisions are taken from United Kingdom statute*

*law. The position in Irish Constitutional law is currently to be found in Articles 2 and 3 of the Bunreacht na hEireann/Irish Constitution 1937. Cf the position in 1922-5, referred to above.)*

## BUNREACHT NA hEIREANN

ARTICLE 2

The national territory consists of the whole island of Ireland, its islands and the territorial sea.

ARTICLE 3

Pending the re-integration of the national territory, and without prejudice to the right of the Parliament and Government established by this Constitution to exercise jurisdiction over the whole of that territory, the laws enacted by that Parliament shall have the like area and extent of application as the laws of the Saorstat Eireann and the like extra-territorial effect.

## AGREED COMMUNIQUÉ ISSUED FOLLOWING THE CONFERENCE BETWEEN THE IRISH AND BRITISH GOVERNMENTS AND THE PARTIES INVOLVED IN THE NORTHERN IRELAND EXECUTIVE (DESIGNATE) ON 6th,7th, 8th AND 9th DECEMBER 1973

**(The Sunningdale Agreement)**

ARTICLE 5

The Irish Government fully accepted and solemnly declared that there could be no change in the status of Northern Ireland until a majority of the people of Northern Ireland desired a change in that status.

The British Government solemnly declared that it was, and would remain, their policy to support the wishes of the majority of the people of Northern Ireland. The present status of Northern Ireland is that it is part of the United Kingdom. If in the future the majority of the people of Northern Ireland should indicate a wish to become part of a united Ireland, the British Government would support that wish.

## THE ANGLO-IRISH AGREEMENT 1985
### Status of Northern Ireland

ARTICLE 1

The two Governments

(*a*) affirm that any change in the status of Northern Ireland would only come about with the consent of a majority of the people of Northern Ireland;

(*b*) recognise that the present wish of a majority of the people of Northern Ireland is for no change in the status of Northern Ireland;

(*c*) declare that, if in the future a majority of the people of Northern Ireland clearly wish for and formally consent to the establishment of a united Ireland, they will introduce and support in the respective Parliaments legislation to give effect to that wish.

# APPENDIX 4

# ANTI-DISCRIMINATION PROVISIONS

*(The following provisions relate to the exercise of, first, legislative and then executive powers.)*

## IRISH GOVERNMENT BILL 1886

CLAUSE 4

The Irish Legislature shall not make any law—

(1) Respecting the establishment or endowment of religion, or prohibiting the free exercise thereof; or

(2) Imposing any disability, or conferring any privilege, on account of religious belief; or

(3) Abrogating or derogating from the right to establish or maintain any place of denominational education or any denominational institution or charity; or

(4) Prejudicially affecting the right of any child to attend a school receiving public money without attending the religious instruction at that school... .

## IRISH GOVERNMENT BILL 1893

CLAUSE 4

The powers of the Irish Legislature shall not extend to the making of any law—

(1) Respecting the establishment or endowment of religion, or prohibiting the free exercise thereof; or

(2) Imposing any disability, or conferring any privilege, on account of religious belief; or

(3) Abrogating or prejudicially affecting the right to establish or maintain any place of denominational education or any denominational institution or charity; or

(4) Prejudicially affecting the right of any child to attend a school receiving public money, without attending the religious instruction at that school; or

(5) Whereby any person may be deprived of life, liberty, or property without due process of law, or may be denied the equal protection of the laws, or whereby private property may be taken without just compensation... .

Any law made in contravention of this section shall be void.

## GOVERNMENT OF IRELAND ACT 1914

SECTION 3

In the exercise of their power to make laws under this Act the Irish Parliament shall not make a law so as either directly or indirectly to establish or endow any religion, or prohibit or restrict the free exercise thereof, or give a preference, privilege, or advantage, or impose any disability or disadvantage, on account of religious belief or religious or ecclesiastical status, or make any religious belief or religious ceremony a condition of the validity of any marriage, or affect prejudicially the right of any child to attend a school receiving public money without attending the religious instruction at that school, or alter the constitution of any religious body except where the alteration is approved on behalf of the religious body by the governing body thereof, or divest from any religious denomination the fabric of cathedral churches or, except for the purpose of roads, railways, lighting, water or drainage works, or other works of public utility upon payment of compensation, any other property.

Any law made in contravention of the restrictions imposed by this section shall, so far as it contravenes those restrictions, be void.

## GOVERNMENT OF IRELAND ACT 1920

SECTION 5

(1) In the exercise of their power to make laws under this Act (neither the Parliament of Southern Ireland) nor the Parliament of Northern Ireland shall make a law so as either directly or indirectly to establish or endow any religion, or prohibit or restrict the free exercise thereof, or give a preference, privilege, or advantage, or impose any disability or disadvantage, on account of religious belief or religious or ecclesiastical status, or make any religious belief or religious ceremony a condition of the validity of any marriage, or affect prejudicially the right of any child to attend a school receiving public money without attending the religious instruction at that school, or alter the constitution of any religious body except where the alteration is approved on behalf of the religious body by the governing body thereof, or divest from any religious denomination the fabric of cathedral churches or, except for the purpose of roads, railways, lighting, water or drainage works, or other works of public utility upon payment of compensation, any other property or take any property without compensation.

Any law made in contravention of the restrictions imposed by this subsection shall, so far as it contravenes those restrictions, be void.

(2) Any existing enactment by which any penalty, disadvantage, or disability is imposed on account of religious belief or on a member of any religious order as such shall, as from the appointed day [3rd May 1921], cease to have effect in (Northern) Ireland.

## IRISH FREE STATE (AGREEMENT) ACT 1922

*(This gave the force of law to the "Articles of Agreement for a Treaty between Great Britain and Ireland" dated 6th December 1921).*

SCHEDULE, ARTICLE 16

Neither the Parliament of the Irish Free State nor the Parliament of Northern Ireland shall make any law so as either directly or indirectly to endow any religion or prohibit or restrict the free exercise thereof or give any preference or impose any disability on account of religious belief or religious status or affect prejudicially the right of any child to attend a school receiving public money without attending the religious instruction at the school or make any discrimination as respects State aid between schools under the management of different religious denominations or divest from any religious denomination or any educational institution any of its property except for public utility purposes and on payment of compensation.

Note that Quekett, *The Constitution of Northern Ireland*, 1933, part II p13 states:

"It is doubtful, having regard to the main object of the Articles of Agreement, whether it was intended that Article 16 should apply to Northern Ireland in the event of her voting herself out of the Irish Free State under Article 12 and thus remaining under the Government of Ireland Act 1920 (including section 5). Nevertheless, Article 16 appears to be unconditionally applicable to Northern Ireland as to the Irish Free State. ... As regards Northern Ireland, the substantial prohibitions added by Article 16 are—

(a) against making any discrimination as respects State aid between schools under the management of different religious denominations; and

(b) against diverting from any educational institution any of its property, except for public utility purposes and on payment of compensation."

## NORTHERN IRELAND CONSTITUTION ACT 1973

*(By section 41(1) and schedule 6, the 1973 Act repealed section 5 of the Government of Ireland Act 1920. Note: The Northern Ireland (Modification of Enactments—No1) Order 1973, SI 1973/2163, by schedule 5, paragraph 12 provided: "Article 16 of the Articles of Agreement for a Treaty between Great Britain and Ireland set out in the Schedule to the Irish Free State (Agreement) Act 1922 shall not apply to a (Assembly) Measure".)*

SECTION 17

(1) Any Measure, any Act of the Parliament of Northern Ireland and any relevant subordinate instrument shall, to the extent that it discriminates against any person or class of persons on the ground of religious belief or political opinion, be void.

(2) In this section "relevant subordinate instrument" means an instrument of a legislative character (including a byelaw) made (whether before or after the coming into force of this section) under any Act of the Parliament of the United Kingdom or the Parliament of Northern Ireland or under any Measure and extending only to Northern Ireland or a part of Northern Ireland.

SECTION 23

(1) For the purposes of this part of this Act a Measure, an Act of the Parliament of Northern Ireland or any other instrument discriminates against any person or class of persons if it treats that person or that class less favourably in any circumstances than other persons are treated in those circumstances by the law for the time being in force in Northern Ireland.

(2) For those purposes a person discriminates against another person or a class of persons if he treats that other person or that class less favourably in any circumstances than he treats or would treat other persons in those circumstances.

(3) No Measure, Act of the Parliament of Northern Ireland or other instrument and no act done by any person shall be treated for the purposes of this Act as discriminating if the instrument has the effect, or, as the case may be, the act is done for the purpose, of safeguarding national security or protecting public safety or public order.

(4) A certificate purporting to be signed by or on behalf of the Secretary of State and certifying that an act specified in the certificate was done for the purpose of safeguarding national security shall be conclusive evidence that it was done for that purpose.

(6) No provision of this part of this Act shall render unlawful anything

required or authorised to be done by any Act of the Parliament of the United Kingdom, whenever passed.

*(Note: Section 4(3) of the 1973 Act provides: "Subject to section 17 below, a Measure shall have the same force and effect as an Act of the Parliament of the United Kingdom" and the Northern Ireland Act 1974, schedule 1, paragraph 1(7) provides: "References to Measures in any enactment or instrument (whether passed or made before or after the passing of this Act) shall, so far as the context permits, be deemed to include references to Orders in Council under this paragraph".)*

## GOVERNMENT OF IRELAND ACT 1914

SECTION 4 (on Executive power)

(6) In the exercise of powers delegated [by the Crown] to the Lord Lieutenant in pursuance of this section (such powers being exercised through the Irish devolved departments) no preference, privilege or advantage shall be given to, nor shall any disability or disadvantage be imposed on, any person on account of religious belief, except where the nature of the case in which the power is exercised itself involves the giving of such preference, privilege, or advantage, or the imposing of such a disability or disadvantage.

## GOVERNMENT OF IRELAND ACT 1920

SECTION 8

(6) In the exercise of power delegated [by the Crown] to the Lord Lieutenant [i.e. the Governor of Northern Ireland] in pursuance of this section (such powers being exercised through the Northern Ireland devolved departments/Ministries), no preference, privilege, or advantage shall be given to, nor shall any disability or disadvantage be imposed on, any person on account of religious belief, except where the nature of the case in which the power is exercised itself involves the giving of such preference, privilege, or advantage, or the imposing of such a disability or disadvantage.

## NORTHERN IRELAND CONSTITUTION ACT 1973

SECTION 19 (as amended by the Fair Employment (NI) Act 1976)

(1) Subject to subsection (4) below it shall be unlawful for a Minister of the Crown, a member of the Northern Ireland Executive or other person

appointed under section 8 [of the 1973 Act], the Post Office and any authority or body listed in Schedule 2 to the Parliamentary Commissioner Act 1967, Schedule 1 to the Parliamentary Commissioner Act (NI) 1969 or Schedule 1 to the Commissioner for Complaints Act (NI) 1969 to discriminate, or aid, induce or incite another to discriminate, in the discharge of functions relating to Northern Ireland against any person or class of persons on the ground of religious belief or political opinion.

(The subsection effectively covers, for example, Westminster Government Departments "in the discharge of functions relating to Northern Ireland", the Northern Ireland departments, district councils and other public bodies, such as the Education and Library Boards, the Health and Social Services Boards, and the NI Housing Executive).

(2) The obligation to comply with subsection (1) above is a duty owed to any person who may be adversely affected by a contravention of that subsection, and any breach of that duty is actionable in Northern Ireland accordingly.

(3) Without prejudice to the right of any person apart from this subsection to claim an injunction restraining another from continuing or repeating any act which is unlawful by virtue of subsection (1) above, the plaintiff may in an action in respect of an act alleged to be unlawful as aforesaid claim any such injunction as is mentioned below on the grounds—

(*a*) that the act was done by the defendant and was unlawful as aforesaid;

(*b*) that the defendant had previously done such unlawful acts of the same kind as, or of a similar kind to, that act; and

(*c*) that he is likely, unless restrained by order of the court, to do further acts of the same or of a similar kind;

and the court may, if satisfied as to those grounds and whether or not damages are awarded, grant such injunction as appears to the court to be proper in all the circumstances, being an injunction restraining the defendant from doing, or causing or permitting others to do, further acts of the same or a similar kind.

(4) This section does not apply to any act or omission which is unlawful by virtue of the Fair Employment (NI) Act 1976 or would be unlawful but for some exception made by virtue of Part V of that Act.

# APPENDIX 5

# INFORMATION ON DIRECT RULE

## [A] House of Commons Standing Orders 1988 (1988-89 HC 1, 22nd November 1988) on Commons Committees and Northern Ireland matters.

(i) THE NORTHERN IRELAND COMMITTEE

*SO 99*—(1) There shall be a Standing Committee to be called the Northern Ireland Committee which shall consider such specified matters relating exclusively to Northern Ireland as may be referred to it and shall consist of all Members sitting for constituencies in Northern Ireland together with not more than twenty-five other Members to be nominated by the Committee of Selection, which shall have power from time to time to discharge the Members so nominated by it and to appoint others in substitution of those discharged.

(2) A motion may be made by a Minister of the Crown at the commencement of public business to the effect that a specified matter or matters relating exclusively to Northern Ireland be referred to the Northern Ireland Committee for its consideration and the question thereon shall be put forthwith.

(3) If such a motion be agreed to, the Committee shall consider the matter or matters referred to it and shall report only that it has considered the said matter or matters.

(ii) STANDING COMMITTEES ON STATUTORY INSTRUMENTS ("MERITS" COMMITTEES)

*SO 101*—(1) There shall be one or more standing committees, to be called Standing Committees on Statutory Instruments etc, for the consideration of statutory instruments or draft statutory instruments referred to them.

(3) Where—

(i) a Member has given notice of a motion for a humble address to Her Majesty praying that a statutory instrument be annulled, or of a motion that a draft of an Order in Council be not submitted to Her Majesty in Council, or that a statutory instrument be not made, or that the House takes note of a statutory instrument, or

(ii) a Minister of the Crown has given notice of a motion to the effect that a statutory instrument or draft statutory instrument be approved,

a motion may be made by a Minister of the Crown at the commencement of public business, that the said instrument or draft instrument be referred to such a committee, and the question thereupon shall be put forthwith; and if, on the question being put, not fewer than twenty Members rise in their places and signify their objection thereto, Mr Speaker shall declare that the noes have it.

(4) Each Committee shall consider each instrument or draft instrument referred to it on a motion, "That the committee has considered the instrument (or draft instrument)"; and the chairman shall put any question necessary to dispose of the proceedings on such a motion, if not previously concluded, when the committee shall have sat for one and a half hours (or, in the case of an instrument or draft instrument relating exclusively to Northern Ireland, two and a half hours) after the commencement of those proceedings; and the committee shall thereupon report the instrument or draft instrument to the House without any further question being put.

(5) If any motion is made in the House of the kind specified in paragraph (3)(i) or (3)(ii) of this order, in relation to any instrument or draft instrument reported to the House in accordance with paragraph (4) of this order, Mr Speaker shall put forthwith the question thereon and proceedings in pursuance of this paragraph, though opposed, may be decided after the expiration of the time for opposed business.

(iii) THE SELECT COMMITTEE ON STATUTORY INSTRUMENTS (THE "SCRUTINY" COMMITTEE)

*SO 124*—(1) A Select Committee shall be appointed to join with a committee appointed by the Lords to consider—

(A) every instrument which is laid before each House of Parliament and upon which proceedings may be or might have been taken in either House of Parliament in pursuance of an Act of Parliament, being—

(*a*) a statutory instrument, or a draft statutory instrument...

but excluding any Order in Council or draft Order in Council made or proposed to be made under paragraph 1 of Schedule 1 to the Northern Ireland Act 1974 .... .

(iv) DEPARTMENTAL SELECT COMMITTEES

*SO 130*—(1) Select Committees shall be appointed to examine the expenditure, administration and policy of the principal government departments ... and associated public bodies, and similar matters within the responsibilities of the Secretary of State for Northern Ireland.... .

(v) THE JOINT COMMITTEE ON CONSOLIDATION etc BILLS

*SO 123*—(1) There shall be a select committee, to consist of twelve members, to join with the committee appointed by the Lords as the Joint Committee on Consolidation etc Bills, to consider ...

(*f*) any Order in Council laid or laid in draft before the House where an affirmative resolution is required before it is made, or is a condition of its continuance in operation, and which but for the provisions of the Northern Ireland Act 1974 would, in the opinion of the Committee, have been enacted by a consolidation bill, whether public or private, or by a Statute Law Revision Bill.

(vi) THE SELECT COMMITTEE ON THE PARLIAMENTARY COMMISSIONER FOR ADMINISTRATION

*SO 126*—(1) There shall be a select committee to examine the reports of the Parliamentary Commissioner for Administration... and of the Parliamentary Commissioner for Administration for Northern Ireland, which are laid before this House, and matters in connection therewith.

*(Note: Under the Parliamentary Commissioner Act 1967, schedule 2 (as amended), the departments and authorities subject to the investigation of the UK "Ombudsman" include the Northern Ireland Office and the Northern Ireland Court Service. See now the Parliamentary and Health Service Commissioners Act 1987, section 1 and schedule 1.)*

**[B] House of Commons Standing Orders 1988 (1988-89, HC 1, 22nd November 1988) on sittings of the House.**

*(Note: SO 13(1) provides that "save as provided in this order, government business shall have precedence at every sitting".)*

*SO 9*—(3) At ten o'clock on Mondays, Tuesdays, Wednesdays and Thursdays, the proceedings on any business then under consideration, shall ... be interrupted ...

(6) After the business under consideration at ten o'clock has been disposed of, no opposed business shall be taken, save as provided in Standing Order No 14 (exempted business).

*SO 14*—(1) The following business may be proceeded with at any hour though opposed, shall not, save for the purpose of moving a motion pursuant to paragraph (2) of this order, be interrupted at ten o'clock, and if under discussion when business is postponed under the provisions of any standing order may be resumed, though opposed, after the interruption of business:...

(*b*) proceedings in pursuance of any Act of Parliament, save in so far as Standing Order No 15 .... otherwise provides ... but Mr Speaker shall put any question necessary to dispose of such proceedings not later than half-past eleven o'clock or one and a half hours after the commencement of those proceedings, whichever is the later:

Provided that, if Mr Speaker shall be of opinion that, because of the importance of the subject matter of the motion, the time for debate has not been adequate, he shall, instead of putting the question as aforesaid, interrupt the business, and the debate shall stand adjourned till the next sitting (other than a Friday)....

*SO 15 (which relates to prayers against statutory instruments, that is, the negative procedure)*

(1) No proceedings on a motion to which this order applies shall be entered upon at or after half-past eleven o'clock.

(2) If such a motion is under consideration at half-past eleven o'clock, Mr Speaker shall forthwith put any question which may be requisite to bring to a decision any question already proposed from the chair:

Provided that, if he shall be of opinion that—

(*a*) owing to the lateness of the hour at which consideration of the motion was entered upon, or

(*b*) because of the importance of the subject matter of the motion, the time for debate has not been adequate, he shall interrupt the business and the debate shall stand adjourned till the next sitting (other than a Friday)...

*(See further in this context, SO 101 in section (A) above. It should also be noted with regard to affirmative resolution Orders in Council that the Government must secure the approval of the House and if needs be, therefore, must allocate time for the discussion of the resolution from within the time set aside for Government business.)*

**[C] The number of Orders in Council made under the Northern Ireland Act 1974 (passed in July 1974).**

| Procedure | (a) | (b) | (c) | (d) | |
|---|---|---|---|---|---|
| Year | Urgent | Negative resolution | Shortened *ie* no proposal | Proposal | Total Orders in Council |
| 1974 | 3 | - | 3 | 1 | 7 |
| 1975 | 3 | - | 6 | 12 | 21 |
| 1976 | 4 | - | 7 | 17 | 28 |
| 1977 | 2 | - | 5 | 21 | 28 |
| 1978 | 1 | 4 | 6 | 17 | 28 |
| 1979 | - | 1 | 4 | 14 | 19 |
| 1980 | 2 | 2 | 4 | 9 | 17 |
| 1981 | 1 | 3 | 8 | 16 | 28 |
| 1982 | - | 6 | 7 | 10 | 23 |
| 1983 | - | 4 | 8 | 9 | 21* |
| 1984 | - | 1 | 5 | 9 | 15 |
| 1985 | - | 6 | 3 | 10 | 19 |
| 1986 | 1 | 5 | 9 | 10 | 25 |
| 1987 | - | 5 | 3 | 15 | 23 |
| 1988 | - | 13 | 3 | 8 | 24 |
| (Total) | 17 | 50 | 81 | 178 | 326 |

* No. 16 not allocated

(This table is, as far as can be ascertained, accurate; it is not, however, presented as being "definitive".)

**[D] Meetings of the Northern Ireland Committee (which has not sat since June 1985).**

| | |
|---|---|
| 9th July 1975 | Northern Ireland Economy |
| 21st January 1976 | Housing in Northern Ireland |
| 22nd January 1976 | Housing in Northern Ireland |
| 3rd March 1976 | Health and Social Services in NI |
| 10th March 1976 | Health and Social Services in NI |
| 16th December 1976 | Proposal for a Draft Transport (NI) Order and other road and rail matters in NI |

| | |
|---|---|
| 16th February 1977 | Proposal for a Draft Criminal Injuries (Compensation) Order |
| 2nd March 1977 | Proposal for a Draft Criminal Injuries (Compensation) Order |
| 22nd June 1977 | Proposal for a Draft Criminal Damage (Compensation) Order |
| 6th July 1977 | Northern Ireland Gas Industry |
| 20th July 1977 | 7th Report of the Examiner of Statutory Rules and NI Electricity Industry |
| 9th March 1978 | Reorganisation of the Housing Executive |
| 17th May 1978 | Proposal for a Draft Rent (NI) Order |
| 24th May 1978 | Proposal for a Draft Rent (NI) Order |
| 26th July 1978 | 8th and 9th Reports of the Examiner of Statutory Rules and Reorganisation of the Housing Executive (resumed debate) |
| 28th March 1979 | Rates and Rating in Northern Ireland |
| 12th March 1980 | Review of Policy in the Private Rented Housing Sector in Northern Ireland |
| 11th May 1980 | 3rd Annual Report of the Fair Employment Agency |
| 11th June 1980 | 3rd Annual Report of the Fair Employment Agency |
| 9th July 1980 | 3rd Annual Report of the Fair Employment Agency |
| 16th July 1980 | Proposal to establish an Enterprise Zone in Belfast |
| 21st January 1981 | Proposal to establish an Enterprise Zone in Belfast |
| 10th June 1981 | Housing conditions in Northern Ireland, Grants for Improvement (Intermediate and Repair), and proposal for a draft Housing (No 2) (NI) Order |
| 24th June 1981 | Housing conditions in Northern Ireland, Grants for Improvement (Intermediate and Repair), and proposal for a draft Housing (No 2) (NI) Order |
| 31st March 1982 | Industrial Development Board |
| 5th May 1982 | Industrial Development Board |

| | |
|---|---|
| 24th November 1982 | Proposal for a Draft Dogs (NI) Order |
| 23rd February 1983 | Proposal for a Draft Housing (NI) Order |
| 20th July 1983 | Future Policy for the administration of salmon and inland fisheries in Northern Ireland |
| 7th December 1983 | Matters arising from the Energy Discussion Document issued by the Department of Economic Development in July 1983 |
| 18th January 1984 | Matters arising from the Energy Discussion Document issued by the Department of Economic Development in July 1983 |
| 11th April 1984 | Draft Agriculture (Miscellaneous Provisions) (NI) Order 1984* |
| 26th June 1985 | Proposal for a Draft Gas (NI) Order |

* On the motion that "the matter of the draft ... Order be referred to the Northern Ireland Committee for its consideration". Proposals are referred to the Committee on the Order of the House "that the proposal for a draft ... Order be referred to the Northern Ireland Committee for its consideration".

*(Source: Northern Ireland Office)*

**[E] The Merits Committees.**

It would appear that little use has been made of Standing Committees on Statutory Instruments for Northern Ireland Orders in Council. According to the Public Information Office of the House of Commons, the following (draft) Orders were referred to a Merits Committee in the period from the beginning of the 1979 Parliamentary Session to the end of 1983:

| | |
|---|---|
| 14th November 1979 | Administration of Estates |
| 14th November 1979 | Building Regulations |
| 14th November 1979 | Industrial Assurance |
| 14th November 1979 | Legal Aid, Advice and Assistance |
| 4th May 1983 | Property (Discharge of Mortgage by Receipt) |
| 4th May 1983 | Rates (Amendment) No 2 |
| 16th November 1983 | Access to the Countryside |

(For a list of the draft Orders referred to a Merits Committee in the earlier part of direct rule, see Hadfield, "Committees of the House of Commons and Northern Ireland Affairs", 1981 *NILQ* (32), 199, at p 211, note 70.)

The House of Commons Sessional Information Digests yield the following information:

| | |
|---|---|
| 1984-1985 (p 33) | ——— |
| 1985-1986 (pp 34-35) | Mental Health |
| | Mental Health (Consequential Amendments) |
| | Road Races |
| | Social Need |
| 1986-1987 (pp 33-34) | Agriculture and Fisheries (Financial Assistance) |
| | Audit |
| | Enterprise Ulster (Continuation of Functions) |
| | Recreation and Youth Service |
| 1987-1988 (pp 38-39) | Adoption |
| | Corneal Tissue |
| | Minors' Contracts |
| | Statistics of Trade and Employment |

# APPENDIX 6

## GOVERNORS AND PRIME MINISTERS OF NORTHERN IRELAND

**Governors**

| | |
|---|---|
| Duke of Abercorn | 1922-1945 |
| Earl Granville | 1945-1952 |
| Lord Wakehurst | 1952-1964 |
| Lord Erskine | 1964-1968 |
| Lord Grey | 1968-1973 |

Viscount FitzAlan was Lord Lieutenant from April 1921 to December 1922.

*(Section 37(1) of the Government of Ireland Act 1920 provided that "no subject of His Majesty shall be disqualified from holding the office of [Lord Lieutenant] Governor on account of his religious belief.")*

**Prime Ministers**

| | |
|---|---|
| James Craig (Viscount Craigavon) | June 1921–November 1940 |
| John Miller Andrews | November 1940–May 1943 |
| Basil Brooke (Viscount Brookeborough) | May 1943–March 1963 |
| Terence O'Neill (Lord O'Neill of the Maine) | March 1963–April 1969 |
| James Chichester-Clark (Lord Moyola) | May 1969–March 1971 |
| Brian Faulkner (Lord Faulkner of Downpatrick) | March 1971–March 1972 (suspension of the Northern Ireland Parliament and Government). |

*(Brian Faulkner was also the Chief Executive member in the power-sharing Executive of 1974.)*

## APPENDIX 7

## SECRETARIES OF STATE FOR NORTHERN IRELAND

| | |
|---|---|
| William Whitelaw (Con) | March 1972–December 1973 |
| Francis Pym (Con) | December 1973–March 1974 |
| Merlyn Rees (Lab) | March 1974–September 1976 |
| Roy Mason (Lab) | September 1976–May 1979 |
| Humphrey Atkins (Con) | May 1979–September 1981 |
| James Prior (Con) | September 1981–September 1984 |
| Douglas Hurd (Con) | September 1984–September 1985 |
| Tom King (Con) | September 1985–July 1989 |
| Peter Brooke (Con) | July 1989– |

# APPENDIX 8

# THE ANGLO-IRISH AGREEMENT 1985

## AGREEMENT
## BETWEEN THE GOVERNMENT OF THE UNITED KINGDOM OF GREAT BRITAIN AND NORTHERN IRELAND AND THE GOVERNMENT OF THE REPUBLIC OF IRELAND

The Government of the United Kingdom of Great Britain and Northern Ireland and the Government of the Republic of Ireland;

Wishing further to develop the unique relationship between their peoples and the close co-operation between their countries as friendly neighbours and as partners in the European Community;

Recognising the major interest of both their countries and, above all, of the people of Northern Ireland in diminishing the divisions there and achieving lasting peace and stability;

Recognising the need for continuing efforts to reconcile and to acknowledge the rights of the two major traditions that exist in Ireland, represented on the one hand by those who wish for no change in the present status of Northern Ireland and on the other hand by those who aspire to a sovereign united Ireland achieved by peaceful means and through agreement;

Reaffirming their total rejection of any attempt to promote political objectives by violence or the threat of violence and their determination to work together to ensure that those who adopt or support such methods do not succeed;

Recognising that a condition of genuine reconciliation and dialogue between unionists and nationalists is mutual recognition and acceptance of each other's rights;

Recognising and respecting the identities of the two communities in Northern Ireland, and the right of each to pursue its aspirations by peaceful and constitutional means;

Reaffirming their commitment to a society in Northern Ireland in which all may live in peace, free from discrimination and intolerance, and with the opportunity for both communities to participate fully in the structures and processes of government;

Have accordingly agreed as follows:

## A

## STATUS OF NORTHERN IRELAND

### ARTICLE 1

The two Governments

(*a*) affirm that any change in the status of Northern Ireland would only come about with the consent of a majority of the people of Northern Ireland;

(*b*) recognise that the present wish of a majority of the people of Northern Ireland is for no change in the status of Northern Ireland;

(*c*) declare that, if in the future a majority of the people of Northern Ireland clearly wish for and formally consent to the establishment of a united Ireland, they will introduce and support in the respective Parliaments legislation to give effect to that wish.

## B

## THE INTERGOVERNMENTAL CONFERENCE

### ARTICLE 2

(*a*) There is hereby established, within the framework of the Anglo-Irish Intergovernmental Council set up after the meeting between the two heads of Government on 6th November 1981, an Intergovernmental Conference (hereinafter referred to as "the Conference"), concerned with Northern Ireland and with relations between the two parts of the island of Ireland, to deal, as set out in this Agreement, on a regular basis with:

(i) political matters;

(ii) security and related matters;

(iii) legal matters, including the administration of justice;

(iv) the promotion of cross-border co-operation.

(*b*) The United Kingdom Government accept that the Irish Government will put forward views and proposals on matters relating to Northern Ireland within the field of activity of the Conference in so far as those matters are not the responsibility of a devolved administration in Northern Ireland. In the interest of promoting peace and stability, determined efforts shall be made through the Conference to resolve any differences. The Conference will be mainly concerned with Northern Ireland; but some of the matters under consideration will involve co-operative action in both parts of the island of Ireland, and possibly also in Great Britain. Some of the proposals considered in respect of Northern Ireland may also be found to have application by the Irish Government. There is no derogation from the sovereignty of either the United Kingdom Government or the Irish Government, and each retains responsibility for the decisions and administration of government within its own jurisdiction.

ARTICLE 3

The Conference shall meet at Ministerial or official level, as required. The business of the Conference will thus receive attention at the highest level. Regular and frequent Ministerial meetings shall be held; and in particular special meetings shall be convened at the request of either side. Officials may meet in subordinate groups. Membership of the Conference and of sub-groups shall be small and flexible. When the Conference meets at Ministerial level the Secretary of State for Northern Ireland and an Irish Minister designated as the Permanent Irish Ministerial Representative shall be joint Chairmen. Within the framework of the Conference other British and Irish Ministers may hold or attend meetings as appropriate: when legal matters are under consideration the Attorneys General may attend. Ministers may be accompanied by their officials and their professional advisers: for example, when questions of security policy or security co-operation are being discussed, they may be accompanied by the Chief Constable of the Royal Ulster Constabulary and the Commissioner of the Garda Siochána; or when questions of economic or social policy or co-operation are being discussed, they may be accompanied by officials of the relevant Departments. A Secretariat shall be established by the two Governments to service the Conference on a continuing basis in the discharge of its functions as set out in this Agreement.

ARTICLE 4

(*a*) In relation to matters coming within its field of activity, the Conference shall be a framework within which the United Kingdom Government and the Irish Government work together

(i) for the accommodation of the rights and identities of the two traditions which exist in Northern Ireland; and

(ii) for peace, stability and prosperity throughout the island of Ireland by promoting reconciliation, respect for human rights, co-operation against terrorism and the development of economic, social and cultural co-operation.

(*b*) It is the declared policy of the United Kingdom Government that responsibility in respect of certain matters within the powers of the Secretary of State for Northern Ireland should be devolved within Northern Ireland on a basis which would secure widespread acceptance throughout the community. The Irish Government support that policy.

(*c*) Both Governments recognise that devolution can be achieved only with the co-operation of constitutional representatives within Northern Ireland of both traditions there. The Conference shall be a framework within which the Irish Government may put forward views and proposals on the modalities of bringing about devolution in Northern Ireland, in so far as they relate to the interests of the minority community.

## C

## POLITICAL MATTERS

### ARTICLE 5

(*a*) The Conference shall concern itself with measures to recognise and accommodate the rights and identities of the two traditions in Northern Ireland, to protect human rights and to prevent discrimination. Matters to be considered in this area include measures to foster the cultural heritage of both traditions, changes in electoral arrangements, the use of flags and emblems, the avoidance of economic and social discrimination and the advantages and disadvantages of a Bill of Rights in some form in Northern Ireland.

(*b*) The discussion of these matters shall be mainly concerned with Northern Ireland, but the possible application of any measures pursuant to this Article by the Irish Government in their jurisdiction shall not be excluded.

(*c*) If it should prove impossible to achieve and sustain devolution on a basis which secures widespread acceptance in Northern Ireland, the Conference shall be a framework within which the Irish Government may, where the interests of the minority community are significantly or especially affected, put forward views on proposals for major legislation and on major policy issues, which are within the purview of the Northern Ireland Departments and which remain the responsibility of the Secretary of State for Northern Ireland.

ARTICLE 6

The Conference shall be a framework within which the Irish Government may put forward views and proposals on the role and composition of bodies appointed by the Secretary of State for Northern Ireland or by departments subject to his direction and control including:

the Standing Advisory Commission on Human Rights;

the Fair Employment Agency;

the Equal Opportunities Commission;

the Police Authority for Northern Ireland;

the Police Complaints Board.

# D

## SECURITY AND RELATED MATTERS

ARTICLE 7

(*a*) The Conference shall consider:

(i) security policy;

(ii) relations between the security forces and the community;

(iii) prisons policy.

(*b*) The Conference shall consider the security situation at its regular meetings and thus provide an opportunity to address policy issues, serious incidents and forthcoming events.

(*c*) The two Governments agree that there is a need for a programme of special measures in Northern Ireland to improve relations between the security forces and the community, with the object in particular of making the security forces more readily accepted by the nationalist community. Such a programme shall be developed, for the Conference's consideration, and may include the establishment of local consultative machinery, training in community relations, crime prevention schemes involving the community, improvements in arrangements for handling complaints, and action to increase the proportion of members of the minority in the Royal Ulster Constabulary. Elements of the programme may be considered by the Irish Government suitable for application within their jurisdiction.

(*d*) The Conference may consider policy issues relating to prisons. Individual cases may be raised as appropriate, so that information can be provided or enquiries instituted.

## E

## LEGAL MATTERS, INCLUDING THE ADMINISTRATION OF JUSTICE

### ARTICLE 8

The Conference shall deal with issues of concern to both countries relating to the enforcement of the criminal law. In particular it shall consider whether there are areas of the criminal law applying in the North and in the South respectively which might with benefit be harmonised. The two Governments agree on the importance of public confidence in the administration of justice. The Conference shall seek, with the help of advice from experts as appropriate, measures which would give substantial expression to this aim, considering *inter alia* the possibility of mixed courts in both jurisdictions for the trial of certain offences. The Conference shall also be concerned with policy aspects of extradition and extra-territorial jurisdiction as between North and South.

## F

## CROSS-BORDER CO-OPERATION ON SECURITY, ECONOMIC, SOCIAL AND CULTURAL MATTERS

### ARTICLE 9

(*a*) With a view to enhancing cross-border co-operation on security matters, the Conference shall set in hand a programme of work to be undertaken by the Chief Constable of the Royal Ulster Constabulary and the Commissioner of the Garda Siochána and, where appropriate, groups of officials in such areas as threat assessments, exchange of information, liaison structures, technical co-operation, training of personnel, and operational resources.

(*b*) The Conference shall have no operational responsibilities; responsibility for police operations shall remain with the heads of the respective police forces, the Chief Constable of the Royal Ulster Constabulary maintaining his links with the Secretary of State for Northern Ireland

and the Commissioner of the Garda Siochána his links with the Minister for Justice.

ARTICLE 10

(*a*) The two Governments shall co-operate to promote the economic and social development of those areas of both parts of Ireland which have suffered most severely from the consequences of the instability of recent years, and shall consider the possibility of securing international support for this work.

(*b*) If it should prove impossible to achieve and sustain devolution on a basis which secures widespread acceptance in Northern Ireland, the Conference shall be a framework for the promotion of co-operation between the two parts of Ireland concerning cross-border aspects of economic, social and cultural matters in relation to which the Secretary of State for Northern Ireland continues to exercise authority.

(*c*) If responsibility is devolved in respect of certain matters in the economic, social or cultural areas currently within the responsibility of the Secretary of State for Northern Ireland, machinery will need to be established by the responsible authorities in the North and South for practical co-operation in respect of cross-border aspects of these issues.

## G

## ARRANGEMENTS FOR REVIEW

ARTICLE 11

At the end of three years from signature of this Agreement, or earlier if requested by either Government, the working of the Conference shall be reviewed by the two Governments to see whether any changes in the scope and nature of its activities are desirable.

## H

## INTERPARLIAMENTARY RELATIONS

ARTICLE 12

It will be for Parliamentary decision in Westminster and in Dublin whether to establish an Anglo-Irish Parliamentary body of the kind adumbrated in the

Anglo-Irish Studies Report of November 1981 (Cmnd 8414). The two Governments agree that they would give support as appropriate to such a body, if it were to be established.

# I

# FINAL CLAUSES

## ARTICLE 13

This Agreement shall enter into force on the date on which the two Governments exchange notifications of their acceptance of this Agreement.

In witness whereof the undersigned, being duly authorised thereto by their respective Governments, have signed this Agreement.

Done in two originals at Hillsborough on the 15th day of November 1985.

| For the Government of the United Kingdom of Great Britain and Northern Ireland: | For the Government of the Republic of Ireland: |
|---|---|
| MARGARET THATCHER | GARRETT FITZGERALD |

*(Note: The above version of the Anglo-Irish Agreement is that of the United Kingdom. The Republic of Ireland's version of the Agreement is largely but not completely identical; the main difference between the two versions is that the Republic's version records that the Agreement is made between and signed on behalf of the "Government of Ireland and the Government of the United Kingdom.")*

# BIBLIOGRAPHY

This is a select bibliography: the following is a list of publications pertinent to the matters covered in this book. For bibliographies covering wider aspects of what is now a very extensive range of material on Northern Ireland, see for example:


Rolston, Tomlinson *et al*: *A Social Science Bibliography of Northern Ireland, 1945-1983: material published since 1945 relating to Northern Ireland* (1983).

Rowthorn and Wayne: *Northern Ireland—The Political Economy of Conflict* (1988), pp 213-220.

Wilson: *Ulster—Conflict and Consent* (1989), pp 310-320.


For a full chronology of events, see:


Flackes (and Elliott): *Northern Ireland—A Political Directory 1968-1988* (1989), pp 1-57.

Hall: *20 Years—A Concise Chronology of Events in Northern Ireland from 1968-1988* (1988).


BOOKS


Barritt and Carter: *The Northern Ireland Problem* (1972).

Beckett: *The Making of Modern Ireland: 1603-1923* (1966, 1981).

Bew and Patterson: *The British State and the Ulster Crisis* (1985).

Birrell and Murie: *Policy and Government in Northern Ireland: Lessons of Devolution* (1980).

Bogdanor: *Devolution* (1979).

Boyle and Hadden: *Ireland—A Positive Proposal* (1985).

Buckland: *Irish Unionism 2: Ulster Unionism and the Origins of Northern Ireland 1886-1922* (1973).

Buckland: *The Factory of Grievances: Devolved Government in Northern Ireland* (1979).

Buckland: *A History of Northern Ireland* (1981).

Calvert: *Constitutional Law in Northern Ireland: a study in regional government* (1968).

Darby: *Conflict in Northern Ireland: The Development of a Polarised Community* (1976).

Dicey: *England's case against Home Rule* (1886) (ed Feuchtwanger, 1973).

Hand: *Report of the Irish Boundary Commission 1925* (1969).

Harkness: *Northern Ireland since 1920* (1983).

Kenny: *The Road to Hillsborough* (1986).

Lawrence: *The Government of Northern Ireland: Public Finance and Public Services* (1965).

Lijphart: *Democracy in Plural Societies: A Comparative Exploration* (1977).

Mansergh: *The Irish Question 1840-1921* (1965).

Mansergh: *The Government of Northern Ireland: A Study in Devolution* (1936).

Neill (ed): *Devolution of Government: The Experiment in Northern Ireland* (1953).

O'Leary, Elliott and Wilford: *The Northern Ireland Assembly: 1982-1986* (1988).

Quekett: *The Constitution of Northern Ireland. Part I: The Origin and Development of the Constitution* (1928). *Part II: The Government of Ireland Act 1920 and subsequent enactments* (1933). *Part III: A Review of Operations under the Government of Ireland Act 1920* (1946).

Rea (ed): *Political Co-operation in divided societies* (1982).

Rose: *Governing without consensus: An Irish perspective* (1971).

Stewart: *The Narrow Ground: Aspects of Ulster 1609-1969* (1977).

Townshend (ed): *Consensus in Ireland* (1988).

Wallace: *Northern Ireland: 50 years of Self-Government* (1971).

Watt (ed): *The Constitution of Northern Ireland : Problems and Prospects* (1981).

Wheare: *Federal Government* (4th ed, 1963).

Wilson (ed): *Ulster under Home Rule: A Study of the political and economic problems of Northern Ireland* (1955).

## ARTICLES

Anson: "The Government of Ireland Bill and the Sovereignty of Parliament" (1886) *Law Quarterly Review* (vol 2), p 427.

Boyce: "British conservative opinion, the Ulster question, and the partition of Ireland, 1912-1921" (1970-71) *Irish Historical Studies* (vol 17), p 89.

Calvert: "Gallagher v. Lynn re-examined—A Legislative Fraud?" (1972) *Public Law*, p 11.

Connolly and Loughlin: "Reflections on the Anglo-Irish Agreement" (1987) *Parliamentary Affairs* (vol 40), p 80.

Crick: "Northern Ireland and the concept of consent" in Harlow (ed): *Public Law and Politics* (1986), p 39.

Donaldson: "The Senate of Northern Ireland" (1958) *Public Law*, p 135.

Donaldson: "Fundamental Rights in the Constitution of Northern Ireland" (1959) *Canadian Bar Review* (vol 37), p 189.

Gearty: "The Northern Ireland Act 1982" (1982) *Public Law*, p 518.

Graham: "Religion and Education—The Constitutional Problem" (1982) *Northern Ireland Legal Quarterly* (vol 33), p 20.

Greer: "The Northern Ireland Assembly and Accountability of Government: The Statutory Committees, 1982-1986" (1987) *Parliamentary Affairs* (vol 40), p 98.

Hadfield: "Committees of the House of Commons and Northern Ireland Affairs" (1981) *Northern Ireland Legal Quarterly* (vol 32), p 199.

Hadfield: "The Northern Ireland Act 1982. Do-it-yourself devolution?" (1982) *Northern Ireland Legal Quarterly* (vol 33), p 301.

Hadfield: "Learning from the Indians? The Constitutional Guarantee re-visited" (1983) *Public Law*, p 351.

Hadfield: "More reports on Northern Ireland—Panaceas or Pandora's Box?" (1985) *Public Law*, p 240.

Hadfield: "The Anglo-Irish Agreement: Blue Print or Green Print?" (1986) *Northern Ireland Legal Quarterly* (vol 37), p 1.

Maguire: "Parliament and the Direct Rule of Northern Ireland" (1975) *Irish Jurist* (vol X n.s.), p 81.

Maguire: "The Reports of the Examiner of Statutory Rules for Northern Ireland 1974-1978" (1979) *Northern Ireland Legal Quarterly* (vol 30), p 306.

Maguire: "The Standing Advisory Commission on Human Rights 1973-1980" (1981) *Northern Ireland Legal Quarterly* (vol 32), p 31.

Palley: "Constitutional devices in multi-racial and multi-religious societies" (1968) *Northern Ireland Legal Quarterly* (vol 19), p 377.

Palley: "The Evolution, Disintegration and Possible Reconstruction of the Northern Ireland Constitution" (1972) *Anglo-American Law Review*, p 368.

Palley: "Constitutional Solutions to the Irish Problem" (1980) *Current Legal Problems* (vol 33), p 121.

Smyth: "The Northern Ireland Assembly 1982-1986: The Failure of an Experiment" (1987) *Parliamentary Affairs* (vol 40), p 482.

Symmons: "Who owns the territorial waters of Northern Ireland?" (1976) *Northern Ireland Legal Quarterly* (vol 27), p 48.

## GOVERNMENT PUBLICATIONS

Headings of a Settlement as to the Government of Ireland. Cd. 8310. (1916).

Report of the Review Body on Local Government in Northern Ireland. (The Macrory Report). (Government of Northern Ireland) Cmd. 546. (1970).

The Future of Northern Ireland. A paper for discussion. (HMSO NIO). (1972).

Northern Ireland Constitutional Proposals. Cmnd. 5259. (1973).

The Northern Ireland Constitution. Cmnd. 5675. (1974).

Northern Ireland: Discussion Paper 3. Government of Northern Ireland. (HMSO NIO). (1975).

The Northern Ireland Constitutional Convention: Reports and Proceedings. HC 1 (November 1975).

The Government of Northern Ireland: A Working Paper for a Conference. Cmnd. 7763. (1979).

The Government of Northern Ireland: Proposals for further discussion. Cmnd. 7950. (1980).

Anglo-Irish Joint Studies: Joint Report and Studies. Cmnd. 8414. (1981).

Northern Ireland: A Framework for Devolution. Cmnd 8541. (1982).

The Anglo-Irish Agreement: Review of the Working of the Conference. (1989).

## OTHER PUBLICATIONS

New Ireland Forum Report. (May 1984).

Northern Ireland: Report of an Independent Inquiry. (Established by the British Irish Association; Chairman Lord Kilbrandon). (November 1984).

# INDEX